Quality Assurance in Health Care: a Handbook

Roger Ellis

Professor of Psychology
and
Dean of the Faculty
of Social and Health Sciences
University of Ulster

and

Dorothy Whittington

Senior Lecturer in Psychology
and
Director of the Centre for
Health and Social Research
University of Ulster

Edward Arnold
A member of the Hodder Headline Group
LONDON   SYDNEY   AUCKLAND

Edward Arnold is a division of Hodder Headline PLC
338 Euston Road, London NW1 3BH

First published in the United Kingdom 1993

3 5 7 6 4
95 97 99 98 96

British Library Cataloguing in Publication Data
Ellis, Roger
Quality Assurance in Health Care: Handbook
I. Title   II. Whittington, Dorothy
362.1

0-340-55273-5

Typeset in Palatino by Saxon Graphics Ltd, Derby
Printed and bound in the United Kingdom by
Athenaeum Press Ltd, Gateshead, Tyne and Wear

Contents

Acknowledgements   vii

1 **Quality assurance in health care**   **1**
Introduction   1
Key concepts in quality assurance   2
The current emphasis on quality assurance in health care   6
Ways of using this book   8

2 **The development of quality assurance in health care**   **9**
Introduction   9
The historical development of quality assurance in health care   9
Themes in health care quality assurance   20
The essence of health care quality assurance   34
Conclusion   35

3 **The development of quality assurance in industry**   **36**
Introduction   36
The historical development of quality assurance in industrial
   and commercial settings   36
Themes in industrial quality assurance   57
Conclusion   64

4 **Techniques for quality assurance in health care.**
   Part One: Quality specific techniques   **66**
Introduction   66
Professional standards systems   69
Comprehensive review systems   80
Case selection techniques   99
Local problem solving techniques   104
Process measurement techniques   109
Quality control techniques   131
Outcome appraisal techniques   133
Consumer involvement techniques   150
Records techniques   153

5 Techniques for quality assurance in health care. Part Two: Generic techniques 155
Introduction 155
Consensus development techniques 156
Surveys 166
Psychometrics 176
Interpersonal skill analysis 183
Conclusion 188

6 The management of quality assurance in health care 189
Introduction 189
Organisational change 190
Innovation for quality in health care organisations 193
A framework for health care quality assurance management 196
Case studies of health care quality assurance management 204
Conclusion 213

7 Future developments in quality assurance in health care 215
Introduction 215
Future growth 215
Desirable developments 216
Conclusion 219

References 221

Glossary 246

Appendix 252

Index 261

Acknowledgements

Our thanks are due to: the University of Ulster for support and opportunity; Yolanda Bell for assistance in the early stages of the literature search; Patrick Teskey, Collette McKenna, Anne Cunningham, Janice McQuilkan, Anne-Marie Black, Eleanor Dickson and their colleagues in the library of the University of Ulster for their diligence and patience.

1

Quality assurance in health care

Introduction

Quality assurance is basically a simple idea. Standards are set for a product or service; production or delivery is organised so that these standards are met consistently; the customer therefore can be assured of quality. To apply the idea to health care, standards must be set for its delivery and everything must be managed to ensure that these standards are always met. Patients would therefore be assured that they would receive quality care.

The idea might be simple but its implementation is not. First, health care includes a vast array of services and interventions from the relatively simple and explicitly physical to the highly complex and psycho-social. Specifying standards for all these events is a demanding task. Second, there is the problem of agreement regarding appropriate standards. Much health care is highly technological and sophisticated. A high level of expertise is required to comprehend let alone specify standards. On the other hand patients, who are the consumers of health care, will have a view on the standards which must be met to satisfy them.

Once standards are agreed then there is the problem of ensuring that they are delivered consistently. Any aspect of health care has its obvious and visible causes but there is also a complex chain of supporting events. Reflect, for example, on the necessary preconditions for a nurse to be able to take a patient's temperature. This fairly rudimentary encounter is underpinned by the nurse's training, by the overall organisation and management of the ward, by the accuracy of the patient's records, by the availability of appropriate equipment, and by a myriad other services from car parking to purchasing and accounts. Specifying standards for a service is not enough. Standards also have to be set for the various activities necessary for its delivery.

Standards having been comprehensively specified, reality must then be checked regularly to make sure that they are indeed being met. If they are not then steps must be taken to put things right and to try to ensure that shortfalls do not occur in future.

A vast range of approaches and techniques have developed to assure quality for health care. This book aims to be in part a compendium of these methods. It is as comprehensive and up-to-date as possible, given the inevitable march of time from literature review to writing and publication. The central core of the handbook is to be found in Chapters 4 and 5. They provide a comprehensive listing, description and evaluation of techniques for health care quality assurance accounts of which have been published in the UK and US. Chapter 4 is concerned with techniques and approaches unique to health care; Chapter 5 covers methods which are used in health care but which have wider applicability and use.

There are two main traditions of quality assurance. One is quality assurance for health care the other quality assurance for manufacturing and service industry. Chapters 2 and 3 provide histories of these two traditions and identify the main issues and approaches from both. There is much potential for mutual exchange of ideas and experience between the two traditions.

Quality assurance for a service as complex as health care almost inevitably takes place in large organisations whether these be hospital or community based. Quality assurance therefore depends on the management of quality and its introduction and refinement involve organisational development. Chapter 6 covers these topics.

The remainder of this chapter provides an introduction to some key concepts in quality assurance; considers reasons for the current emphasis on quality assurance in health care; and sets out ways of using this book.

Key Concepts in Quality Assurance

The word *quality* can be used in two distinctly different ways. On the one hand, quality has connotations of excellence in the sense, for example, that a quality car is assumed to be an exceptionally luxurious, potent or durable product. On the other hand, quality can be a neutral term referring to the general character of some object or phenomenon. In that sense one can refer to good or bad quality. To pursue the example it is equally legitimate to talk of a car having poor quality or high quality. Common usage suggests that quality used alone would indicate excellence whereas the word may be modified by a further adjective to include both the best and the worst. This is no mere semantic hairsplitting. Part of the appeal of quality assurance may be its implication of excellence even though it would be quite consistent with common usage to assure quality at a low level.

What is unavoidably involved in the notion of quality is *standards* – whether these be good or bad. To be meaningful standards must be at least identifiable and recognisable if not actually measurable.

Assurance implies that one party is convincing another that certain standards will be maintained. If quality is assured for a particular petrol this is intended to give the customer confidence that certain standards with regard for example to octane rating, lead content and freedom from contamination will be maintained in every sample they buy.

While the convincing of a customer or other key person is one interpretation of *quality assurance* the term is also used more generally for all the steps which must be taken in order that the customer or other interested person will be consistently provided with quality. This broader meaning is used in the title of this book and widely in the literature even though a strict definition would limit its applicability to the process whereby customers, particularly, become convinced. This could be achieved through simple assertion, clever advertising or other potent persuasion and not necessarily through the kinds of processes described in this book.

One simple way of assuring quality for a product is to test each completed example against a set standard and reject any that fall short. Thus quality might be assured for one metre rulers by setting them against a standard and rejecting any that were too long or short. This is the simplest interpretation of *quality control*. However there is usually a complex set of processes which precede the emergence of a final product. Quality control can be used at any stage of this process starting with the acceptance of raw materials. Thus the production line for a car would have a large number of quality control points which might extend back into the factories supplying components and forwards into the showrooms of franchised dealers.

Rejecting the non-conforming element is a straightforward but wasteful procedure. Often quality control involves recycling of elements in order that they might conform next time. Thus a more complex definition of quality control might be 'measuring an entity against a standard and taking appropriate follow-up action'. This might include passing on to the next stage for conforming products or rejecting or recycling for the non-conforming examples.

Any production line that involves frequent rejection or recycling is obviously going to prove expensive and probably uneconomic. Action should therefore be taken to identify the reasons for the number of substandard products and to put matters right. This use of *analysis, feedback and rectification* as opposed to mere quality control is where quality assurance is often viewed as starting. There is a variety of available definitions for quality assurance, however, and it is certainly used in a number of different ways in the literature as, unfortunately, is quality control. Logically, it is worth confining quality control to the straightforward checking of entities against standards and quality assurance to the total process of assuring quality and hence standards. Quality assurance will, in this sense, have to include quality control.

There are aspects of health care which can be treated as physical products. For these it is relatively straightforward to specify standards. However, most of health care is better conceived as a *service* and here the process of quality assurance and quality control become far more difficult. To begin with quality control is not possible for service to an individual patient since once provided a service cannot be rejected or recycled. The best that a patient can hope for is a repeat of the service to a better standard.

More fundamentally, services are immeasurably complicated by their interpersonal, human and hence psycho-social nature. When behavioural and social variables are involved it is usually difficult to specify let alone agree standards. The contrast with physical events should be clear. To take an example from dentistry it is far easier to specify standards for the materials used in fillings than to do the same for the interpersonal behaviour of the dentist to the patient. What is an acceptable joke to one patient might be a frivolous insult to another. One might appreciate a detailed explanation of what is being done while another might find this boring or worrying. Standards would have to be set in terms of acceptability and effect with consequent difficulties of specification and measurement.

Given that standards are to be set in some identifiable form, who should be involved in their determination?

One view of quality is that it is *that which satisfies the customer*. A more sophisticated view is that it is that which satisfies *stated or implied needs*. Thus needs may be implied and met through certain standards which the consumer may not comprehend. This is particularly true of health care where technical and professional sophistication may be involved in a service which, while it is intended to meet the stated or implied needs of patients, may be wholly inscrutable to them, in process if not in effect. Thus standard setting might be primarily the province of the professional.

Mention of customers raises the issue of the most appropriate term for the *consumers* of health care. 'Customer' usually implies one who buys a service. Given this purchasing power and the dependence of the provider on it, the satisfaction of customers becomes an economic necessity. However most of the health care system in the UK (and some part of the system in almost all countries) is insulated from a direct market relationship between patients and professionals. The word *client* may then be used to imply the provision of a professional service carrying with it obligations on the professional to satisfy patients' needs whether they are paying or not. There is no reason why 'patient' should not carry the same implications and no doubt it frequently does. However, the more radical aspects of quality assurance tend to be signalled by other words such as 'consumer', 'customer' or 'client'. All carry with them a central concern for the recipient of services and their satisfaction and at least the implication that this emphasis will modify the more producer oriented nature of much professional practice.

The concept of a *feedback loop* or *cycle* is important in quality assurance. In brief, standards are set, performance or outcomes are checked against these standards and, if there is a shortfall this is used as feedback to critical parts of the system so that performance may be modified to meet standards. Alternatively, the standard may be modified to one that is achievable. In both cases knowledge of results is a critical element in the cycle.

The idea of *audit* is another common element in quality assurance. The term has two main interpretations. A quality audit is an audit of an organisation's quality assurance procedures to ascertain whether they are operating as stated and meeting their objectives. Such an audit is analogous to a financial audit which takes a similar approach with regard to financial systems.

Audit is sometimes used in a broader sense to cover any checking of reality against stated or predicted standards. Thus hospitals may be asked to specify waiting list times and the progress of patients might be audited, or, synonymously, *monitored*, to ascertain whether waiting times are being met, exceeded or reduced.

If an organisation sets out in detail the procedures which it will follow to maintain and hence assure quality then this constitutes its *quality system*. The establishment and implementation of this system constitutes *quality management*.

If the production of a quality product or service is to be managed so that standards are met consistently then this can readily be shown to depend on all elements in the organisation – human and material. In particular the commitment and competence of all staff are required since all have a part to play. This perhaps obvious fact is captured in the notion of *total quality management* (TQM) where the word 'total' indicates the involvement of everyone.

The management of quality is so important that standards have been set for systems of proven effectiveness. One such is *British Standard (BS) 5750* and its European equivalent, International Organisation for Standardisation *(ISO) 9000*. Drawing on the experience of a number of successful organisations a set of procedures have been set out by the British Standards Institution. An organisation is required to work out for its business the critical functions which must be followed if standards are to be set and met and customers satisfied. The organisation is audited (see above) to check that its procedures are in place and operating. If they are, then the organisation is awarded the standard *'kitemark'* subject to an annual review. The kitemark signals to customers or other interested parties that they can be confident that standards will be maintained for the product or service concerned. Quality is, thus, assured.

Another approach to assuring quality for the customer is assured is through the various *charters* which are being developed. The idea of, for example, a patient's charter is that the patient has certain rights to guaranteed standards of service. In the event of these standards not being met then there must be a right of complaint and redress. This is not a total quality management system but at least it allows the customer a voice and the right to action and it is likely to affect the standards of service providers by encouraging greater consistency. This will be more readily achieved through some system of quality management.

To summarise, quality assurance involves the following. Quality must be specified in terms of standards. If patients, employers and indeed providers themselves are to be assured that these standards will be met some kind of system will be necessary and it will have to be managed whatever its level or scope. The system will include feedback loops. It may be audited to see if it is performing as predicted. Successful systems may be awarded some formal recognition such as a kitemark.

Underlying this whole approach is a *commitment to the explicit and the rational*. It is thus required that standards, procedures and processes should be made explicit and that there should be a sustained and rational *measurement* of performance and attention to improvement. Central to all this will be the *commitment and competence of staff* whose development to meet the requirements of the system will be a necessary component.

The Current Emphasis on Quality Assurance in Health Care

Over the last ten years there has been a dramatic increase in references to and interest in quality assurance as it applies to health care. How is this to be explained?

A World Health Organisation working group on quality assurance discerned four sets of reasons: economic, social, political and professional (WHO, 1985).

Demand for health care is increasing. Not only are people living longer and requiring care over a longer period and into an extended old age but also expectations are rising through education and general interest. Resources cannot keep pace with this demand. There is therefore an increasing emphasis on value for money and cost-effective solutions. As resources become more straitened there is a commensurate need to ensure that standards, i.e. quality, are upheld. So quality assurance is advanced as a way of ensuring that standards are maintained and that resources are used as effectively as possible.

The so-called economic arguments do, obviously, overlap with social factors. The demand for health – for cure or alleviation of undesirable conditions and for longer life – is a social variable and reflects the values and preoccupations of the western world in the late twentieth century. Another important social pressure is the consumer movement. Patients expect to be told what is being provided for them and to have redress if the service falls below standard. In its sharpest form this leads to the litigious patient who is ready to sue if there are deficiencies in or inappropriate consequences of treatment. Thus, in the US particularly, one reason for quality assurance is the need for medical practitioners to ensure quality to avoid litigation. So the laity is less gullible to the professional conspiracy. Patients expect explication and reject appeals to authority, special and hence inscrutable expertise, or professional mystique. The explicit and rational procedures of quality assurance meet the demands of the consumer for knowledge, understanding and control.

Driven by these economic and social factors there is, as all readers of this book will know, sustained political pressure to bring health care into a market, or simulated market, where quality must be assured for the patient who is conceived as a customer. In order to achieve this customer orientation and to improve cost effectiveness, approaches are imported from business and commerce. It is suggested that while health care may not be a business it should be run in a business-like way. But it is important that this drive for efficiency should not be seen as just cost-cutting or a move to shift costs from the public purse to the private consumer. Quality assurance with its immediately attractive connotations of high standards and its proven record in manufacturing and service industry is the ideal slogan for this political approach. This is not intended as a cynical view since this book should show the genuine contribution which quality assurance can make to the improvement of patient care; but it is to recognise the immediately appealing features of an emphasis on quality assurance and the danger that it might be dismissed as a smokescreen to hide a fall in standards and resourcing.

Last but not least is the appeal which quality assurance can have for the professional who wants to do the best possible job for the patient. There is considerable evidence that health professionals, who are by definition and nature altruistic and committed to improvement, find quality assurance appealing. Professions are also inherently self- perpetuating, however, and intensely protective of their role and status. Quality assurance systems which do not recognise the importance of professional competence and judgement are likely to be regarded as intrusive and to be rejected or obstructed. Many professions, however, have seen quality assurance as a route to clarify their unique and indispensable contribution and have recognised that power through knowledge can be more durable than power through mystique. This is particularly apparent in the newer health professions where a commitment to reason, explication, research and quality assurance is seen as a basis for professional advancement.

So, for all these reasons, quality assurance has become an all-pervasive feature of health care systems. Managers, health care practitioners, trainees, educators, researchers, all need to understand and become involved in quality assurance procedures for their work. This handbook has been devised to give an up-to-date and comprehensive coverage of the approaches, methods, techniques and instruments which have been used to assure quality in health care. In presenting the various initiatives which have been described in the large literature which has developed over the last ten years we have tried to provide a framework which should make selection easier.

Ways of Using This Book

This book is designed for health professionals in practice and in training, for health service managers, for health researchers and for interested consumer and patient representative groups. It is particularly aimed at the growing number of people who have suddenly discovered that they are involved in (or even specifically responsible for) the establishment and implementation of quality assurance procedures and systems but who recognise a need for more or better organised guidance through the labyrinth of competing approaches and techniques.

Some readers will seek an overview only. They might best begin with Chapters 2 and 3 and might dip into subsequent sections in the light of that preparation. Others may have specific needs and might proceed directly to the compendium Chapters 4 and 5. They should find reference to the Appendix (p. 252) which provides an annotated listing of the compendium contents helpful. Readers with managerial responsibilities might find it most useful to begin by working through Chapters 2 and 3, to proceed directly to Chapter 6 and then to dip into relevant sections of the compendium. Finally, some readers may find the book's own logic compelling and may wish to work their way straight through.

2

The development of quality assurance in health care

Introduction

Chapter 1 introduced some basic ideas behind quality assurance in industry and health care. This chapter will trace the historical development of health care quality assurance and will briefly contrast US and UK patterns. It will also identify and discuss a number of themes in the debate on appropriate frameworks for its continuing development. It will conclude by identifying four essential characteristics of health care quality assurance.

The Historical Development of Quality Assurance in Health Care

Quality assurance for health care is often taken to be an innovation of the late twentieth century. In the UK literature at least it is difficult to find explicit reference to it before about 1980. In fact, however, its gestation has a much longer history. Three stages can be discerned. First, is the *embryonic* stage when such mechanisms as existed were implicit and not specifically referred to as quality assurance. This is followed by the *emergent* stage during which the term 'quality assurance' gains currency, concepts are explicitly discussed and procedures are self-consciously implemented and evaluated. The pattern of development remains haphazard however; depending on the enthusiasm and commitment of individual professionals and managers and (towards the end of the period) the professional associations. Finally, health care quality assurance arrives at what can be described as the *mandatory* stage. Now government, professionals and patients are in broad agreement that quality assurance for health care is essential: the health care system should be managed so that the quality of care is guaranteed and the best possible care is provided for the greatest possible number in the most economical way. There is debate about systems of quality assurance and about the degree of participation and control to be afforded to government, professionals and patients, but it is debate over ways of tackling quality assurance rather than over its importance.

Embryonic Health Care Quality Assurance

Concern for the quality of health care is as old as care itself. There were systematic schools of medicine and thus traditions of good practice in ancient Egypt, Assyria, China, Japan and Mexico. In pre-literate cultures too, novice practitioners spent substantial periods in the company of experienced shamans or medicine men acquiring the 'mystery' of the craft. Written codes of professional conduct for physicians were current in Greek and Roman times and some (like the Hippocratic oath) remain points of reference for practitioners. Thus from the earliest times providers of health care have articulated guidelines for both education and practice. Such guidelines reflect concern for the quality of care and, in embryo at least, for its assurance.

It can be hypothesised, too, that the early recipients of care had some interest in its quality. As long ago as 1700 BC the Mesopotamian king Hammurabi promulgated a legal code which included specific (and drastic) penalties for surgical incompetence. In sixteenth-century Spain Juan Cuidad Duarte responded to his own experience of treatment by flogging by setting out standards for the humane treatment of the mentally disordered. After his death he was canonised as Saint John of God and the Order of Charity for the Treatment of the Sick was established to implement his principles throughout Europe. The Church was thus endorsing the importance of quality of care. In 1518 the Charter of the Royal College of Physicians in London was drawn up stating that one of the functions of the College was to 'uphold the standards' of medicine 'both for their own honour and for public benefit'. Both providers and consumers of care were thus taken to have a legitimate interest in its quality.

Emergent Health Care Quality Assurance

Concern for health care quality and recognition that practitioners have a duty to uphold standards are thus far from novel. Quality assurance in health care is innovative only insofar as it involves explication and systematisation of *methods* of setting, appraising and maintaining standards.

Such methods typically involve the regular observation, review and improvement of care. In the nineteenth century Florence Nightingale's reputation was built upon just that cycle of standard setting, observation, review and improvement. The improvements she effected in the hospital at Scutari were only possible because her observations allowed her to demonstrate that hospitalisation of wounded soldiers led to an increase rather than a decrease in mortality. Her *Notes on Nursing* (1859) were in fact standards for nursing care and remained benchmarks for high but achievable quality for many years.

The first advocate of regular review of medical practice, however, was Ernest Avery Codman, a surgeon practising in a Boston hospital in the early years of this century. Codman recalled each of his patients one year after discharge and checked on accuracy of diagnosis, success of surgery, overall benefit derived from treatment, and existence of side effects. He also recognised that practitioner competence was not the sole determinant of quality and published (Codman, 1916) a far-sighted, if dogmatic, volume on economic and organisational as well as clinical aspects of hospital efficiency. Sadly, his colleagues were so unimpressed by his activities that they asked him to leave their hospital. He set up his own hospital and called it 'The End Results Hospital' – thus becoming the first physician to market assured quality.

Despite Codman's perspicacity most early ventures in systematic quality assurance seem to have been only indirectly concerned with end results and to have concentrated instead on the education and licensing of practitioners. In the early years of this century the American Medical Association and the Carnegie Foundation sponsored an evaluation of medical schools. This became the Flexner Report (1910) which suggested uniform standards for theoretical and practical education. In the UK and elsewhere in Europe the gradual formalisation of the health care professions saw similar standards set for education and training. The Royal Colleges began their inspections of relevant departments, units and wards to satisfy themselves that facilities and procedures were appropriate for medical students. Likewise the professional bodies for nursing and other health professions set up procedures for the inspection of practical training facilities, offered guidelines on curriculum content, set rules for the balance between classroom learning and practical placement, and began to involve themselves in course evaluation and examination. In recent years the rate of change in health care practice and technology has led the Colleges and professional bodies to take similar interest in standards for continuing education. There has even been discussion (HMSO, 1975; Duncan, 1980) of systems of regular relicensing.

All of these activities reflect considerable confidence in the effectiveness of professional education as a guarantee of quality and are some way away from Codman's focus on the effects of care. From the 1930s onwards, however, there has emerged a stream of studies of health care outcomes. Notable among these are both British and American investigations of preventable maternal death. These began in the 1930s and continue in modified form to the present day (Hooker, 1933; Maxwell, 1984; HMSO, 1986). Other regular UK enquiries include reviews of anaesthetic deaths (Lunn and Mushin, 1982), deaths in people under 50 (Royal College of Physicians, 1978) and perioperative deaths (Buck et al., 1987). There have also been studies of the outcomes of cardiac surgery (Society of Cardiac and Thoracic Surgeons of Great Britain and Ireland, 1985); of the use of diagnostic testing (Young, 1980; Fowkes et al., 1986); and of the use of Caesarean section (Rosenburg et al., 1982). The Office of Population Censuses and Statistics also publishes regular data on preventive services (targeting congenital malformation, infections, cancer, accidents and suicide), on treatment services (adverse effects, case fatalities and survival data from cancer registries) and overall measures of expectation of life, mortality, and morbidity. Similar statistics are collected and disseminated in the US and indeed in many other countries. At a much less formal level many hospitals and clinical units have a long-standing tradition of holding clinical meetings at which unusual or problematic cases are considered, thus constituting a kind of peer group review of quality. The starting point for almost all of these reviews and enquiries is scrutiny of medical records. They have thus established a methodological bias towards the retrospective analysis of professional accounts of care.

From the 1980s onwards quality assurance has been an explicit topic in national and international discussion and debate among health care professionals. In 1983 the European Member States of the World Health Organisation set up a working group charged with the responsibility of developing a strategy for the introduction of quality assurance to national health authorities, health professionals, the scientific community and health consumers. Their conclusions (WHO, 1985) led to the adoption of a commitment among the European Member States 'to have built effective mechanisms for ensuring quality of patient care within their health care systems' by 1990. The working group also recommended the development of strategies for the collection and dissemination of information on quality assurance and for encouraging professionals and others to involve themselves. Partly in response to this recommendation the King's Fund set up a quality initiative in 1984 which has given support to a range of projects and publications.

In UK community medicine the Royal College of General Practitioners launched a quality initiative in 1983 (RCGP, 1983; 1985a, b) and by 1990 Hughes and Humphrey were able to refer to an 'extremely large collection of examples' of local quality activities (p. 9). These are more diverse than the records based scrutiny of outcomes discussed above. They range from large-scale patient and practitioner surveys (Health Care Research Unit, Newcastle upon Tyne University, 1990) to informal practice meetings reviewing both the process and outcomes of care in individual cases (Irvine, 1990a).

A similar efflorescence of quality assurance initiatives has taken place in UK hospital medicine. These are often referred to as 'medical audit' (HMSO, 1990a, b; Shaw, 1990) but the activities themselves are essentially those of observation, review and improvement which are the defining characteristics of quality assurance. Despite this rapid development there has been great variation in the enthusiasm and commitment evinced by hospital consultants and physicians (Shaw, 1990; Pollitt, 1991). Active opposition has been tempered, however, by the perception that failure to participate may result in systems imposed by less well-informed managerial or government forces.

The professional bodies for non-physician health care groups have been particularly active in encouraging a range of quality assurance initiatives. In the UK the Royal College of Nursing set up a 'Standards of Care' project as early as 1965. This has now developed into a major programme of research, development and education (Kitson, 1986; RCN, 1990). The Chartered Society of Physiotherapy, the College of Occupational Therapists, and the College of Speech and Language Therapists, have all published guidelines and standards (COT, 1989; CSP, 1990; CSLT, 1991) and several other groups are considering the matter. In the US, too, there has been particularly substantial activity in the development of quality assurance systems by and for non-physician groups. Indeed major surveys of quality assurance activities in the UK (Dalley et al., 1991) and in the US (Casanova, 1990) have both demonstrated that the profession most heavily involved in quality assurance is nursing and that it is followed in degree of involvement by the rehabilitation professions such as occupational therapy and physiotherapy.

Explicit reviews of the quality of care have thus developed as a result of professional concern for standards of practice as well as for standards of education. Almost by definition, however, these reviews have tended to be confined to the work of single professions. Significant exceptions to this are the systems of hospital accreditation which take as their subject of review the entire operation of specified health care organisations. As early as 1915 the American College of Surgeons responded to the inadequacy of hospital records systems by developing the Hospital Standardisation Programme. This obliged hospitals seeking accreditation as training hospitals to submit their records systems to the College for scrutiny. It soon became evident that accredited hospitals tended to develop a positive reputation, to attract more patients and to be financially profitable. Accreditation thus grew in popularity and in scope and in 1952 the College of Surgeons joined with a number of other professional associations to form the Joint Commission on the Accreditation of Hospitals. This body has now become the Joint Commission on the Accreditation of Healthcare Organisations – JCAHO. The JCAHO is a voluntary, non-profit-making body, funded by fee income and charitable donation. It inspects and accredits hospitals and other facilities, encourages and engages in research and education, and sets and publishes standards for a wide range of hospital functions. It still focuses much of its work on records of care but has moved far beyond its original concern for simple accuracy (JCAH, 1988; McAninch, 1988; Wilkinson, 1990). Application for accreditation is voluntary and while possession of a sound accreditation record is obviously good publicity, non-accredited organisations may still practise. Similar accreditation systems exist in Canada, Australia, New Zealand and elsewhere (Sketris, 1988) and pilot accreditation exercises are in hand in the UK (Brooks and Pitt, 1990).

Mandatory Health Care Quality Assurance

In the United States as elsewhere the 1960s saw both increase in demand for expensive health care and gradual decrease in national prosperity. This naturally led to public and governmental concern over the costs of care and to widespread discussion of relationships between costs and quality.

The US government Medicare/Medicaid systems of public health insurance were heavily criticised for encouraging the provision of unnecessary care. This led to the establishment of systems of cost containment and 'utilisation review' for all health care organisations taking publicly supported patients. The systems adopted were largely based on retrospective scrutiny of hospital records and billing systems. They were unpopular, and were regarded by practitioners as both intrusive and ineffective (Greenblatt, 1975). They also did little to contain costs (Wells and Brook, 1988). Despite these manifest deficiencies other groups of 'third party payers' operating private or semi-private health insurance schemes (e.g. Blue Cross, the various military veterans' associations, employer groups) imposed similar procedures. The government system was further elaborated in 1972 with the establishment of the Professional Standards Review Organisation (PSRO) programme. PSRO was funded by Congress but was run through regional groups consisting primarily of physicians. Concurrent and retrospective reviews of care were undertaken but again they were largely based on records. Professional reactions to the PSRO systems were strong. They were thought to represent an attempt at external control of medical practice, to breach medical confidentiality (Wells and Brook, 1988) and to be 'a disguise for government efforts to control costs rather than to improve quality' (Webber, 1988, p. 111). In 1982 they were replaced by a modified system called the Peer Review Organisation programme. This programme is more obviously in professional hands and has encouraged more diverse methods of quality review (Webber, 1988). Specific sanctions are employed if facilities or physicians have failed to meet standards but it has been widely suggested (US General Accounting Office, 1990; US Committee on Government Operations, 1989) that the programme's impact on actual quality of delivered care remains both limited and haphazard.

Despite its substantial history and despite these recent excursions into government control the formal US system of health care quality review is diverse and in some respects fragmentary. Balfe et al. (1987), Spath (1989), Black (1990), and O'Leary (1991), for example, all observe that the various systems which have evolved do little to examine the impact of provision on the health of communities or regions. They have thus made overview of national quality exceedingly difficult and have tended to mask the inequities of access which the extension of review activities into aspects of primary (or ambulatory) care (Mushlin and Appel, 1980; Miller, 1989) and into 'small area studies' (Wennberg and Gittelsohn, 1973; Keller, 1988; Spitzer and Caper, 1989) has begun to highlight.

Health promotion and education activities also seem almost universally ignored although the development of accreditation procedures for the recently popular 'managed care' organisations (Wilkinson, 1990) may redress this imbalance. In these organisations employers contract with providers to purchase a system which will not only pay for care for sick employees but will do all that can be done to maintain a healthy work force. Almost for the first time in the American system something is being done to provide 'a personal physician who would be the primary care giver as well as the coordinator and counsellor when care is provided by others' (Donabedian, 1989, p. 419).

A recent briefing report to the chairman of the US Bipartisan Commission on Comprehensive Health Care (US General Accounting Office, 1990) notes the extent to which both quality of care and its review remains related to its source of funding. It recommends a comprehensive national strategy including (p. 23) 'national practice guidelines and standards of care; enhanced data support to quality assurance activities; improved approaches to quality assurance at the local level; and a national focus for developing, implementing and monitoring a national system'. The report also notes that despite the range of existing quality assurance systems the number of expensive malpractice suits brought by consumers of health care in the United States shows little sign of diminishing.

Maxwell (1984) identifies the paradox that medical practitioners operating in the notionally more bureaucratic UK National Health Service are actually less subject to scrutiny of their clinical practice than are their American counterparts. This is all the more surprising since concern for quality of care was a primary factor in the genesis of the NHS. Aneurin Bevan, introducing his Bill to the House of Commons in July 1948, said that the proposed service was designed to 'universalise the best' and 'to provide the people of Britain, no matter where they may be, with the same level of service'. Each of these statements of intent implies a system for specifying, checking and maintaining quality.

In fact the development of quality assurance in the NHS has been far from systematic although there have been many worthwhile initiatives. Both individual practitioners and professional bodies have been active in the promotion of a range of activities. Many of these have been encouraged and even financially assisted by both local health authorities and central government. Particular encouragement has been given to the development of explicit standards and quality assurance procedures in areas concerning safety in the manipulation of potentially hazardous materials. The relevant professional groupings in clinical chemistry, pathology, radiology, and nuclear medicine have all produced guidelines and other publications on issues of quality control, laboratory practice and patient and practitioner safety. In pathology specifically the National External Quality Assessment Scheme (NEQAS) was set up in 1969. This makes inspection of facilities and regular statistically based quality control of test procedures and results mandatory in all NHS laboratories.

As in the US, UK governmental interest in systems of quality assurance has grown in formality and insistence since the early 1960s. Here too this has no doubt been a response both to the increasing costs of provision and to the decreasingly secure national resource from which it must be financed. As early as 1956 the Guillebaud Committee (HMSO, 1956) when given the remit of examining costs in the NHS commented 'it is one of the problems of management to find the right indices for efficiency'. They went on to propose comparisons between health authorities in respect of such indicators as the average occupancy of beds, the length of stay of patients, bed turnover intervals, and waiting times.

In 1969 a series of scandalous revelations about poor quality care in psychiatric and mental handicap hospitals led to the establishment of the Health Advisory Service which is an advisory body on care of the elderly and mentally ill and of the Development Team for the Mentally Handicapped. These bodies were intended to gather evidence on standards of care on a regular basis, to note instances of poor quality care and to make recommendations for improvement as appropriate. They still report but a recent review of the impact of HAS has found that 'remarkably little appears to have changed since 1969'

(Day et al., 1988, p. 10). Routine response to instances of poor quality elsewhere in the NHS has been handled through the Community Health Councils and through various formally and informally managed complaints procedures. The incidence of malpractice and damages litigation in the UK is much lower than in the USA but it has been argued that this is as much to do with interprofessional solidarity between the legal and medical professions and the general docility of the British consumer as it has to do with either the quality of care or the adequacy of complaints procedures (Pollitt, 1988).

Both the Merrison Committee (HMSO, 1975) and the Alment Committee (HMSO, 1976) were set up to enquire into the nature of medical training and competence but took it upon themselves to comment on the importance of assessment of quality of practice. The 1979 Report of the Royal Commission on the Health Service contains substantial sections on quality of care in both hospital and community settings. Its recommendation 63 is that there should be 'a planned programme of peer review of standards of care and treatment ... set up for the health professions by their professional bodies and progress monitored by the health departments'. By the 1980s governmental allusions to quality assurance for health care were edging towards prescription. The Griffiths Report (HMSO, 1983) suggested quality assurance as one of several industrially derived methods of management which could be adopted in the health service and the Financial Management Initiative (HMSO, 1982a) led to the production of a long series of 'performance indicators' which regional and district health authorities were expected to use for internal and external comparisons. These indicators were restricted to resource efficiency measures such as staff, beds, number of patients and length of stay, and were not developed by clinicians. Hardly surprisingly they were widely regarded as confusing, irrelevant and intrusive by both practition-ers and local managers (Pollitt, 1987; Klein and Carter, 1988; Whittington, 1989; Black, 1990). Despite this their use and develop-ment continues to be recommended (HMSO, 1990b) and the recent extension of the work of the Audit Commission to the health service is likely to consolidate their place in the evaluation of service provision (Boyce, 1992).

Finally, the 1989 'Working for Patients' white paper (HMSO, 1989) and the subsequent Health Service Reform Bill confronted the issue of quality assurance directly. One of the central proposals was that all doctors and other health professionals in hospital, primary care and community settings should be involved in some form of 'medical audit'. Working papers associated with the reforms and the recent Report of the Standing Medical Advisory Committee (HMSO, 1990b) have subsequently filled in details of the roles of local health authorities and medical audit committees and of the extended remit of postgraduate medical education committees.

Quality assurance in the National Health Service has thus become not just a matter of professional concern or enthusiasm but a mandatory part of service provision. There is now considerable activity at all levels in the service (and indeed in private UK health care) in discussing, piloting and establishing procedures. Dalley and colleagues (Dalley and Carr-Hill, 1991; Dalley et al., 1991) surveyed quality activities in all 199 District Health Authorities in England and Wales in 1989. They found evidence of some form of quality activity in 148 districts and were sent details of 1478 specific initiatives. They comment, however, that there was a problem in 'capturing an accurate and comprehensive picture of these activities ... the range is very broad and diverse' (Dalley et al., 1991, p. 48). They also suggest that communication about quality both within and between authorities is often very poor with resulting confusion and alienation of individuals who perceive quality initiatives as intrusive or even threatening.

In both the UK and US then, the 1980s have seen the proliferation of diverse systems of quality assurance. Different approaches have been advocated and established by professional groups, by government, and by (in the UK) financial managers and (in the USA) third party payment agencies. Consumers have been increasingly vocal in their criticism of provision at both service and individual case level and politicians in both countries have appreciated the electoral benefits of responding to their concern. Despite these similarities a number of substantial differences can be discerned between the patterns of US and UK development. These contrasts highlight several of the focal points in the debate as to the most appropriate means of establishing what is now almost universally regarded as the essential framework for health care quality assurance.

Health Care Quality Assurance in the US and the UK

The most obvious difference between health care quality assurance in the US and the UK is its date of formalisation. Loose professional control and wide variations between States in procedures for licensing US practitioners led to early concern for consumer protection against quackery and fraud. This led to the establishment of accreditation systems as early as 1915. These and related procedures have worked as a quality check in the otherwise market oriented system of provision and are in principle widely approved by consumers, government, third party payers, and professionals. Criticism is at the level of refinement not rejection. In the UK on the other hand, systematic organisation-wide quality assurance in specified hospitals, units or practices is a relative novelty. Maxwell (1984) suggests that this is in part the result of more careful control of education and admission at the points of initial qualification and subsequent specialism, and in part the result of the medical profession's 'collective allergy' to rational examination of the case for such audit. Pollitt (1991) examining the politics of medical audit in the US and UK makes much the same point and comments 'thus we observe the spectacle of a thoroughly public system (the NHS) that has minimal public accountability and a mixed public/private, largely profit-oriented system (Medicare) which has (at least on paper) quite sophisticated arrangements for the protection of publicly financed patients and the publication of detailed quality data' (p. 14). Whatever the reason for the disparity in the patterns of development in the two countries, most of the approaches and techniques now available for quality assurance in health care were first developed in the US and are only now being tentatively adapted for the UK.

Other distinctions between quality assurance in the two countries derive from differences in the funding and control of the services provided. Health care in the US is essentially a private market over which the state casts a loose regulatory network. Conversely, health care in the UK is substantially a state provided service with limited pockets of private provision and recent initiatives to establish 'internal' markets. It is not surprising that the techniques of quality assurance have gained currency at different nodes in the two systems or that the inevitable interplay between the concerns of professionals, patients and paymasters has thrown up different patterns of quality checks. In the US the financial pressures of recent years have been expressed in tension between third party payers and professional providers over the detail of payment for individual patients' care. Quality assurance procedures have thus focused on the care provided in individual cases and professionals have cited these procedures in defending themselves against the accusation that they provide unnecessary or unnecessarily expensive care. In the UK much of the wrangling has been about perceived underprovision and about the effects of cutbacks on particular regions, professions or specialisms. Black (1990) terms this UK preoccupation a population as opposed to an individual perspective. He suggests that it generates a wider view of quality assurance giving higher priority to issues of equity and access than has been the case in the US. Quality assurance at this population level naturally draws attention to gaps in provision and to average standards of care whereas monitoring of individual episodes of care and of facility based delivery is more likely to highlight outstanding individual instances of both high and low quality. It is debatable which of the two approaches is most likely to lead to actual improvement in quality but no doubt both are necessary and perhaps the two health care systems can learn from each other. In the US this would lead to more emphasis on access, equity and quality of overall lifespan service. In the UK it would lead to greater responsiveness to the needs of individual consumers and more open review of the care provided by individual practitioners.

Themes in Health Care Quality Assurance

Alongside the proliferation of practical initiatives in quality assurance there has developed a large and potentially confusing literature. This offers everything from micro-economic analysis and mathematical modelling to blow by blow accounts of service encounters with agitated consumers. Common themes can be discerned however. They include the following.

- Definitions of quality and quality assurance.
- Measurement and methodology in quality assurance.
- Participation in quality assurance.
- The organisational contexts of quality assurance.
- The relationship between costs and quality.

Definitions of Quality and Quality Assurance

Several authors have suggested that health care quality is in the eye of the beholder. Anderson (1986, p. 24) suggests that 'employers define health care quality in terms of value obtained for their health care dollars .... For the patients quality means feeling better ... and for the hospitals quality means care that they can get paid for'. Less cynical perhaps is Roberts and Prévost's (1987) categorisation of high priority elements of quality for patients, providers and (third party) purchasers. In this categorisation patients prioritise 'responsiveness to perceived care needs; level of communication, concern and courtesy; degree of symptom relief; and level of functional improvement'. Providers on the other hand prioritise 'the degree to which care meets the current technical state of the art; and freedom to act in the full interest of the patient' while purchasers are most interested in 'efficient use of funds available for health care; appropriate use of resources; and maximum possible contribution of health care to reduction in lost productivity'. Conscious of such differences in perspective Rodriguez (1988a, p. 4) emphasises that quality is socially constructed and that it may depend 'on who is assessing it – and what values and consensus are used in evaluation – and by what implicit or explicit standards or gauges it is being objectively or subjectively evaluated'.

Faced with such a moving target for definition several authors have recourse to anatomisation or naming of parts. Avedis Donabedian (1966; 1980; 1985) distinguishes between technical and interpersonal aspects of quality health care and between quality of structure, process and outcome with respect to each aspect. The technical aspects of quality care concern the physical manipulation of material things. The orthopaedic surgeon replacing a hip joint remains in the technical arena just as long as the patient remains unconscious. When giving preoperational reassurance or postoperative instructions for self-care the surgeon has ventured into the interpersonal. Interpersonal interventions are just as important as technical ones but are much less predictable in their impact. In recent publications Donabedian (1987; 1989; 1991) refers to a third aspect of quality health care which he terms the moral aspect. This includes choices which must be made between types of provision and judgements about levels of access within attainable resources. These as he rightly notes are issues of social justice and political philosophy.

Donabedian's other categorisation of quality dimensions – structure, process, outcome – are more frequently quoted and, unfortunately, misquoted. Structure for example is frequently taken to mean the resources in the care system including the number, type and training of health professionals, the buildings and equipment available, the materials supplied, and, ultimately, the cash devoted to care. It is more properly defined, however, as including what Donabedian (1987, p. 76) describes as 'the more subtle features of organisation: differentiation, coordination, power, specification of work procedures, visibility of consequences, and so on'. He notes too that 'more detailed study is necessary so we can tell by what mechanisms the more obvious features of organisational structure exert their influence' (ibid.). Standards for the structural aspects of care are at least implicitly set and modified with each round of budgeting and allocation at each organisational level in each health service but the grounds on which judgements are made are often obscure. Both health economics and health related organisational studies have much to do in explication and illumination.

Process is more readily defined. It refers to the actual delivery of care from the point of patients' first signalling a desire to be considered for potential treatment (or indeed to be kept well) to the point at which they can be declared either fit or beyond further care. It thus includes access, diagnosis, treatment interventions and their administrative and technical support, discharge and community after-care arrangements, and health promotion and education activities. Finally, outcomes can be defined as the end results of care. They include health status, improvement of function, longevity, comfort and, more broadly, quality of life.

Despite the popularity of Donabedian's categorisations it can be argued that they are in fact categories of care rather than of the quality of care. Donabedian himself consistently refers to professionals, patients and others making judgements in respect of technical or interpersonal structure, process or outcome quality. The making of such judgements implies criteria on which to base them. Somewhat closer to such quality criteria are Maxwell's (1984) dimensions of health care quality and the JCAHO's (Wilkinson, 1990) seven major characteristics of health care quality. Maxwell gives the following dimensions.

- Access to services.
- Relevance to need (for the whole community).
- Effectiveness (for individual patients).
- Equity (fairness).
- Social acceptability.
- Efficiency and economy.

The JCAHO list is accompanied by explanatory questions and is as follows.

- Efficacy: Is the care/procedure useful?
- Appropriateness: Is it right for this patient?
- Accessibility: If right can this patient get it?
- Acceptability: If right and available does this patient want it?
- Effectiveness: Is it carried out well?
- Efficiency: Is it carried out in a cost-effective way?
- Continuity: Did it progress without interruption, with appropriate follow up, exchange of information and referral?

An obvious problem with all such reductionist exercises is the fact that quality is an integrated whole. Important questions concern for example the relationships between structure, process and outcome. Donabedian himself (1980) comments that measurements of the quality of structure and process are only an adequate indicator of outcome quality *if* we know the relationships between one and the other. Yet as Berwick and Knapp (1987) remark we know so little about the actual relationships between care and changes in health status and well-being that 'making an understanding of effectiveness a prerequisite for measuring quality is probably a formula for paralysis' (p. 51).

Ellis (1988) distinguishes between input, process, output and outcome as significant elements in health care. Input, that is the resources applied, and output, the number of patients treated, are relatively easy to measure; process, that is the application of resources, and outcome, the long-term effect on patients, are significantly more elusive. The temptation is to relate input to output with a relative neglect of process and outcome.

Lohr and Harris-Wehling (1991) report a recent study on quality review and assurance carried out by the American Institute of Medicine on behalf of Medicare. Undaunted by the difficulty of the task the IOM Committee undertook an exercise in one sentence definition of quality health care. During their study many definitions of quality and accounts of the parameters of care were assembled and analysed. In total some 100 definitions were reviewed and arranged along 18 dimensions from which eight were selected for retention. This led finally to the definition: 'Health care quality is the degree to which health services for individuals and populations increase the likelihood of desired health outcomes and are consistent with current professional knowledge.'

Among the advantages claimed for this definition by Lohr and Harris-Wehling are its implication that patients and populations should be consulted about the desirability of outcomes; its recognition of both the importance and the limitations of medical and scientific knowledge; and its suggestion of continuing improvement.

Being able to define, or at least recognise health care quality is not at all the same as being able to assure it. In Chapter 1 it was suggested that the simplest definition of quality assurance was that it was the sum of procedures established for making sure and being able to guarantee that high levels of quality are maintained. These procedures include specification of standards, observation of practice, comparison of practice with standards, and instigation of action for improvement as necessary. The basic model thus comprises specification and appraisal of quality followed by action for quality improvement. Examining the credentials of staff, inspecting hospital records for instances of poor quality care, setting up clinical meetings to review unusual cases and all the other activities commonly described as quality assurance are thus variations on the main theme of specification, appraisal and improvement. Such a sequence of procedures is a necessary condition for quality assurance.

Several authors have elaborated the sequence and have presented it as an iterative cycle. The American Nurses' Association model set out in Figure 2.1 is one such cycle (ANA, 1982). The implication of representing the process cyclically is that the cycle (or sections of it) must be repeated in an ongoing, dynamic 'quest for quality'.

The World Health Organisation's working group on quality assurance (WHO, 1985) noted that difficulties in achieving consensus on 'appropriate operational definition' of quality had handicapped the development of effective quality assurance since the design of such programmes depends to some extent on the definition of quality adopted. Their own report avoids precise definition of quality assurance but gives a very full statement of its aim. It is as follows:

> to assure that each patient receives such a mix of diagnostic and therapeutic services as is most likely to produce the optimal achievable health care outcome for that patient, consistent with the state of the art of medical science, and with biological factors such as the patient's age, illness, concomitant secondary diagnoses, compliance with the treat-

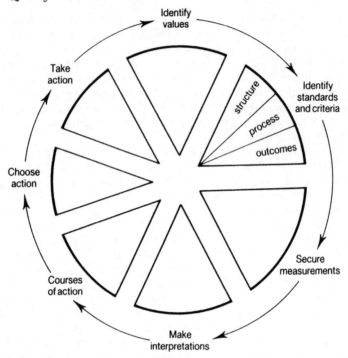

Fig. 2.1 The American Nurses' Association model for quality assurance

ment regimen, and other related factors; with the minimal expenditure of resources necessary to accomplish this result; at the lowest level of risk of additional injury or disability as a consequence of treatment; and with maximal patient satisfaction with the process of care, his/her interaction with the health care system, and the results obtained' (WHO, 1985, p. 5).

This aim is to be achieved through monitoring, assessment and improvement activities throughout the system of primary, secondary and tertiary care, and health promotion. The WHO group also stress three positive aspects of effective quality assurance programmes. First, they should provide a mechanism for public accountability by providing 'objective evidence that (public) funds are being spent efficiently and effectively'. Second, they should provide a 'managerial tool for problem solving in health care organisations' and should be an 'integral management component at each level of organisational function'. Finally, they should 'facilitate the process of innovation in health care delivery' including technological, organisational and interdisciplinary advance.

Measurement and Methodology in Quality Assurance

Health care is essentially a service – a collection of things that people do to, for and with other people. The evaluation of health care quality is thus subject to the many problems associated with measurement of intangible psycho-social phenomena. Biological change associated with technical care of clearly identified disease or injury is relatively easy to observe and measure. Monitoring change in health related knowledge, perceptions, attitudes, and values is more difficult since none of these variables is directly observable. Most difficult of all yet central to the evaluation of health care are teasing out the relationships between the mix of technical and interpersonal processes which make up care and assessing their combined impact on patient health, well-being and quality of life. Fortunately, some of these problems are familiar methodological issues in the social and behavioural sciences and many of the techniques adopted for health care evaluation and quality assurance are standard tools in psychology, sociology and economics. Other parts of the methodological debate, however, seem to be more specific.

Particular intractability attaches itself to the measurement of treatment outcomes. As many authors have observed these are difficult to disentangle from the confounding influences of broader societal variables such as diet, housing, poverty, and health related knowledge, attitudes and expectations (Klein, 1980; Donabedian, 1986; Whittington, 1989). It is thus difficult to know whether patient improvement or deterioration is genuinely the result of care provided or a response to concurrent but unrelated change in circumstances.

A second specific problem concerns the evidential basis for quality appraisal. All observation involves selection of information and the selection made can have considerable impact on the conclusions which seem to follow. In health care quality appraisal quite different conclusions might be reached depending on the focus of assessment and the measurement techniques employed. In the US for example there is a strong tradition of record based retrospective case review. Its advantages include relative ease of execution, minimal interference with the episodes of care being reviewed, and the possibility of maintaining high levels of confidentiality. Its substantial disadvantages, however, hinge on the possible inaccuracy of the records made or even of the recall of participants. Concurrent review gives greater accuracy and flexibility but it too has disadvantages including intrusion in the process of care, and lack of confidentiality for patients and practitioners. Choice of concurrent or retrospective method might thus affect the appraisal made.

A related problem concerns the choice of areas of care which are to be the subject of scrutiny. As Roberts (1987) points out 'it is impractical and unnecessary to monitor all aspects of all care all of the time' (p. 70). Again a selection is required and again it may influence the validity of the appraisal made.

It has become traditional in American record based quality assurance to screen records for areas of care which are high in volume, cost or risks (Williamson, 1978). Thresholds and definitions need to be established but once this is done screening identifies areas of care for which relevant review groups can be set up. It is assumed that quality in these areas is somehow more important than in low volume, low cost or low risk areas.

Kessner et al.'s (1973) 'tracer' methodology adopts a different approach to identifying areas for appraisal. The aim is to obtain a representative or illustrative view of a health care system by tracing the quality of care for selected conditions. It is assumed that the way health care professionals routinely care for common ailments is an indicator of the general quality of care and of the overall effectiveness of the system delivering it. Kessner et al. suggest that useful tracer conditions have the following characteristics:

- They are easy to define.
- Medical care is likely to improve them.
- Good and less good care are relatively easy to discriminate.
- The effects of non-medical factors on the condition are adequately understood.
- There is a reasonably high incidence of the condition.

Their original list of tracer conditions was developed for a primary care audit. The conditions were otitis media, visual disorders, iron deficiency anaemia, hypertension, urinary tract infections and cervical cancer. A more recent evaluation of general practice in the north east of England (Health Care Research Unit, University of Newcastle upon Tyne, 1990) also adopted the tracer methodology but added two further criteria namely that the tracer conditions should cover the range of morbidity encountered by the practice concerned; and that they should be susceptible to treatment given the competence and experience of the staff and the availability of relevant resources.

Tracer methodology identifies conditions for which variation in treatment outcomes should be discernible and which are dealt with in relatively high volume by the practitioners concerned. It relies, however, on the extent to which such treatments are in fact representative of the general quality of care and makes no allowance for differences in practitioner response to relatively infrequent conditions.

Roberts (1987) describes a third approach to identification of areas for review. This he terms the sentinel approach. Categories of 'red flag' incidents are identified which merit in-depth enquiry into the circumstances which gave rise to them. Records are screened for these occurrences and cases are selected for full retrospective scrutiny.

Sentinel occurrences are almost always instances of bad rather than good practice and the technique is thus open to the criticisms that it seems punitive to the groups being reviewed and that it fails to identify and encourage good quality.

Roberts (1987) also highlights the significance of human judgement in appraising quality. However cases are selected and however carefully observation and measurement are carried out and evidence assembled, a judgement must then be made appraising quality as high or low, acceptable or requiring improvement. Roberts (1987) identifies two main approaches to such judgement. The *implicit* approach requires judges to use a high degree of inference in making their appraisal while the *explicit* approach deliberately minimises the inference required.

Implicit review systems make use of consensus among groups of peers or acknowledged 'experts'. These groups may be used to scrutinise actual care episodes – as in the clinical meetings on which medical audit procedures are often based; or to examine records, systems or whole hospitals. They may attach numbers and values to the judgements they make but the criteria on which they base them remain implicit and unarticulated. In the absence of explication they necessarily employ a high degree of inference in moving from observation to evaluation.

Explicit review involves careful specification of criteria for judgement (essentially standards of care) *prior* to the review. It thus falls more obviously within the common definitions of quality assurance. Again criteria may be set by groups of peers or groups of acknowledged experts. Simple lists of criteria may be developed or they may be grouped algorithmically to reflect clinical decision making in what has come to be known as a 'criteria map' (Greenfield et al., 1975; Greenfield, et al., 1981). There is considerable debate (Roberts, 1987) about the relative merits and optimal combinations of explicit and implicit methods.

Participation in Quality Assurance

Enumerating the various groups who might wish to be involved in health care quality assurance would produce a very long list. It would include all the health professions from consultants and other physicians to nurses, therapists, laboratory staff, social workers and many more. It would also include the various support groups such as clerical and administrative staff, buildings and estates staff and manufacturers of equipment and supplies. Consumers and their various statutory or voluntary representative groups would feature, as would political parties and pressure groups. Various third party purchasers such as the private health insurance organisations and employer groups, and the owners of profit or non-profit private care facilities would appear. Groups of external consultants, educators and even academics specialising in health care quality assurance could also be said to have a place. Finally, all of the civil servants in the various sectors of government responsible for health provision and all of the service managers would have to be included.

In fact quality assurance in health care is carried out by groups which vary widely in size, composition and complexity. Accreditation agencies like JCAHO are large organisations, dedicated to quality assurance, employing people of diverse backgrounds and fostering, executing and monitoring quality assurance activities throughout health care. On the other hand, many perfectly successful local initiatives are carried out by two or three individuals of much the same background who are meanwhile continuing to perform routine tasks and duties.

Accreditation agencies draw on relevant professional and managerial groups when setting out guidelines and standards but surveys and visits are always carried out by personnel from outside the relevant facility or organisation. At a more local level most of the American systems for auditing medical records use quality assurance staff (most often nurses) specially employed to screen records for suitable cases for review. The review itself, however, generally involves both quality assurance staff and staff chosen for their particular knowledge of the area of care. Neither exercise is external to the health care organisation but both are at some distance from the individuals actually responsible for the care. Many such systems end by submitting reports to external organisations whether for accreditation or for confirmation of funding. Legal difficulties have sometimes arisen in these cases (Bersoff and Kinports, 1988; London and Harris, 1988) where physicians whose careers have suffered as a result of negative review reports have sued the individuals involved in the peer review group.

Professional groups at local, national and sometimes international levels have developed guidelines, standards and procedures for education, certification and practice and these are long-standing. These same groups have seen the newer quality assurance initiatives as something to be involved in and to use to protect and enhance their status. This has had the rather unfortunate effect of ensuring that very many quality assurance initiatives are monoprofessional. Thus while the nursing profession has produced by far the greatest number of quality assurance systems and techniques they are almost exclusively for and about nursing. Even in hospital-wide quality assurance systems (Wilson, 1987) the structure is typically one of separate committees for physicians, for nursing, for occupational therapy, for dietetics and so on through the various professions. There may be a hospital quality committee to which they all report but the bottom layer is fragmented. Some progress towards interprofessionality is being made in the contexts of community and ambulatory care (Kind, 1989; Miller, 1989) and the rehabilitation professions are actively involved in developing interprofessional systems (England et al., 1989; Normand et al., 1991; Whittington and Finlay, 1991). Some small initiatives in hospital locations have taken patient groups or wards as the starting point and have deliberately tried to involve everyone associated with their care – although even so the groupings have tended to be restricted to health professionals and not to include auxiliaries, or cleaning, kitchen or clerical staff.

Not only are health care quality assurance groups largely monoprofessional they are also notably free from consumer participation. There is a substantial literature on patient satisfaction (Hall and Dornan, 1989; McIver and Carr-Hill, 1989; Evason and Whittington, 1991) and on the relationship between aspects of practitioner behaviour and patients' compliance with instructions (Hall et al., 1988; Ley, 1988). In very few cases, however, is any indication given of what was done with the results of the study, i.e. of its impact on quality of care.

Despite the relative lack of consumer participation in health care quality assurance, consultation by means of small-scale consumer survey is widespread. Thus many of the newer initiatives in quality assurance for primary care or for the growing number of US health maintenance organisations include an element of consumer survey (Smith and Mukerjee, 1978; Zimney et al., 1980; Freeborn and Pope, 1981; Eppel et al., 1991). Carr-Hill and Dalley (1991) report from their investigation of NHS quality management initiatives in England and Wales that about 12% of quality activities consisted of consumer surveys but give no indication of how these were followed up or of whether they were carried out as part of some more systematic assessment and assurance of quality. A further 8% of quality activities also fell into the category of 'customer relations' activities including distribution of leaflets, and complaints and suggestions schemes.

The Organisational Contexts of Quality Assurance

The crux of all quality assurance activities is the extent to which they have an impact on the improvement of care. It has been suggested, however, that many systems pay insufficient attention to the 'action for improvement' phase and that they have become mechanistic 'inspection' exercises in which professionals and organisations submit to periodic appraisal without any real commitment to change (Sisman, 1990; O'Leary, 1991). The briefing report to the US Bipartisan Commission (US General Accounting Office, 1990, p. 8) states categorically 'Quality assurance systems typically concentrate on quality assessment and on the identification of the relatively small number of providers whose care is obviously unacceptable. They do comparatively little to directly improve the overall levels of quality provided by the majority of health professionals'. In similar vein, Barter (1988, p. 707) comments 'there is no proof that (accreditation) surveys improve the quality of care in the surveyed institution or for the individual patient by one iota' and 'When surveyors leave, the facility concentrates not on improving patient care but on cleaning up the deficiencies so that it will look better for the next survey. The charts may look better and the length of stay may be shortened, but the quality of patient care is much the same.'

This unease about the outcomes of quality assurance has led to increasing emphasis on the notion that quality action must be seen as a kind of organisational development and that it must be explicitly planned and managed. As early as 1981 Jessee commented 'coming to grips with concepts of individual and organisational change is critical to the success of any quality assurance ... programme' (p. 13). More recently a number of authors recommend adoption of organisational development models current in industrial quality assurance (WHO, 1985; Fine, 1986; Roberts, 1987; Buckland, 1989; Keyser, 1989; Williams, 1989; Wong, 1989; Dagher and Lloyd, 1991).

O'Leary (1991) in an editorial in the house journal of the JCAHO documents the increasing emphasis in JCAHO publications on 'Continuous Quality Improvement' (CQI) rather than quality assurance. The distinction he suggests resides in the acknowledgment of the 'humanity and complexity of health care organisations'. This acknowledgment leads in turn to more proactive efforts at prevention rather than remediation and to greater inter-professionality and organisation-wide involvement in quality activities.

Whether in professional (Duncan, 1980) or government (HMSO, 1966; 1983) circles, first thoughts on quality assurance in UK health care appealed directly to industrial experience of quality control, assurance and management for models and concepts. This was not so in the US where industrial and health care quality assurance developed over similar time-spans and almost entirely separately. It may be, therefore, that the relatively late emergence of UK health care quality assurance will allow for fuller consideration and exploitation of industrial theories and techniques of quality action and improvement than was possible in the US.

The Relationship between Costs and Quality

Changes in the economic and demographic contexts of health care are significant generators of increased interest in the identification, measurement and assurance of quality. In its simplest form the argument is that as increasing numbers of people make demands on static or diminishing resources efforts must be increased to ensure that the best possible care is made available to the greatest possible number of patients. This involves expunging waste from the system, using available resources as efficiently as possible, addressing issues of distribution and allocation of resources and, finally, ensuring that care delivered through the application of these resources is effective in achieving appropriate outcomes.

Relationships between cost and quality are not simple. The fundamental problem in health economics is definition of the product – essentially the same problem as was addressed in the discussion of definitions of quality in health care. Its significance in the economic context is that without such a definition it becomes next to impossible to understand, predict or control supply and demand. Veatch (1989), for example discusses the obvious efficiency of devoting resources to preventive medicine thereby avoiding the higher costs of subsequent curative or palliative care. He puzzles over the consistent public resistance to such expenditure and 'preference for very inefficient interventions to protect the identifiable lives of the very ill'. This preference he suggests resides in part in personal identification with current suffering. Cure of this is more attractive than the vague, futuristic and probabilistic outcomes of prevention programmes. Local fund-raising for the purchase of expensive equipment or travel to distant centres of excellence for individual highly publicised sick infants exploits the same sympathy for and understanding of the specific and immediate instance. In essence the issue is one of demand for resource allocation being linked with different perceptions of quality. In a similar way demand is distorted by confusion of price with quality. As medicine has become more technologically sophisticated it has become easier for enthusiasts to persuade the less well informed that the glossily expensive and very up-to-date machine is the best buy.

A further difficulty in understanding demand in health economics is its relative independence from the effects of increased supply. Increasing the supply of more tangible products will eventually lead to a satiated market in which no more can be sold unless prices fall or products are diversified. In health care, however, demand seems virtually insatiable – the ultimate goal being happy, healthy immortality for all! The check on the price of health care is not the amount of it in the market but the competing demands of other desirable products for a share of the national resource.

A common economic technique in other more tractable areas is cost-benefit analysis or, as it has come to be known, utility analysis (Drummond et al., 1988). Such analysis requires that all costs and benefits be measured on a common scale. In financial cost benefit analyses the common scale is simply money. In health care value must be placed on human life and specifically on the trade-off between longevity and quality of life over any specific span. A number of techniques have been developed for quantification of that trade off the most popular of which is the quality adjusted life year, or QALY (Williams, 1985; Cairns et al., 1991; McCulloch, 1991), in which a value is placed upon a year of life in a particular health state in relation to a year of perfectly healthy life. The costs of care are then measured against its QALY value and optimum quality of care is that which achieves the highest possible QALY rating for minimum possible expenditure. These techniques begin to address questions of efficiency in provision of health care but are less immediately relevant to the resolution of the problems surrounding distribution and allocation, or indeed of the total amount of care that can or should be made available.

Nations vary in the proportion of the gross national product that they devote to health care. The US spends some 10%, the UK spends about 5% and some Scandinavian countries spend as much as 20%. It has been commonly observed (Rodriguez, 1988b; Donabedian, 1989) that whatever the relationship between expenditure and quality, whenever gross expenditure begins to exceed about 10% of GNP there is public protest about increasing costs. In the UK concern may in fact be about costs of health care as a major subset of public expenditure which is itself the target for government cost-cutting on grounds of more general political/economic ideology. Alternatively, public concern may genuinely be concern for quality of service within what are perceived to be diminishing resources. Whatever the logic, all are agreed that resources must be stewarded and there is increasing discussion of techniques for capping costs while maintaining quality.

Rodriguez (1988b) examines causes of rising health care costs in the US and alongside the usual comments on increasingly expensive drugs and technology identifies excessive market exploitation by the medical industrial complex (the second largest such complex in the US economy); excessive numbers of physicians only surviving by stimulating demand for unnecessary care; the spread of 'defensive' medicine where marginally desirable care is provided more to prevent possible malpractice litigation than for the good of the patient; and administrative waste. Not all of these would apply in other systems but it is interesting to note that he cites comparative figures for administrative waste at 22% of overall health care expenditure in the US as against 10% in the UK and 8.2% in Canada.

Woolhandler and Himmelstein (1988) in establishing a quantitative case for the creation of a 'free' national health programme in the US present a devastating analysis of the effects of the various cost containment exercises which have been undertaken since the 1970s. They point for example to sharp increases in the numbers of the uninsured and underinsured; to health indices for minorities and the poor which have stagnated or even declined; to increasing costs of bureaucracy; and to increasing administrative intervention in clinical practice. Significantly, they also identify a concurrent growth in surplus health resources including unoccupied beds and increasing numbers of physicians chasing a shrinking number of paying patients. Despite the elaborate exercises undertaken costs do not seem to have been held back and quality may even have declined.

The issue then becomes one of developing methods and techniques for containment of cost alongside maintenance of quality at both population and individual practitioner/patient levels. The two are inextricably linked. In the UK the recent NHS reforms are conceived as an exercise in introducing market forces as a stimulus to such developments. Thus each provider/purchaser contract should specify both costs and quality of care process and outcome. It remains to be seen how far professionals and managers will achieve the difficult balance between their role as provider of the best possible care for individual patients (a precept enshrined in the Hippocratic oath) and their more novel role as publicly accountable steward of scarce national resources. However that balance is achieved the techniques of quality assurance will have a part to play.

It is often pointed out that quality assurance itself has associated costs and that it is susceptible to the same kind of cost benefit analysis as has been advocated for health care. Thus Williamson (1978, 1988) and Wong (1989) use Deming's (1982) analysis of industrial quality control costs in their discussion of health care quality assurance. For Deming quality control or assurance is only successful when the costs of monitoring quality are substantially less than the costs of poor quality. Stebbing (1990) also uses the Deming model when he suggests that one way of prioritising between possible quality initiatives is through an analysis of quality costs. The analysis identifies areas where (a) failure costs are high and (b) quality assurance and improvement costs would be relatively low. These are the areas where quality procedures should have the highest priority.

In health care Williamson (1978) proposes a similar method of 'health accounting' to determine quality assurance priorities. The basic concept here is the 'achievable benefit not presently achieved' (ABNA). Thus only problems which have some reasonable prospect of improvement under present general conditions of care are eligible for inclusion. Prioritisation considerations should then include both costs of likely action for improvement and benefits likely to accrue both to individual patients and to the total number of patients the quality of whose care is likely to be affected. These benefits are the inverse of the 'failure costs' in the area and cost-effective quality assurance must ensure that the costs of assurance and improvement (e.g. in staff time devoted to quality activities instead of to actual patient care) do not match or exceed the costs to patients of the original poor quality care. Accounting of this kind is more difficult when dealing with health outcomes than when dealing with physical products but judgements can still be made according to the general principle.

The relationship between quality and cost effectiveness in health care is thus fundamental, complex and insufficiently explored.

The Essence of Health Care Quality Assurance

Having examined the historical development of health care quality assurance and having identified a number of themes in the debate as to its ideal form and application it should now be possible to identify what appear to be the essential parameters of health care quality assurance. They are as follows.

Concern for Excellence and Standards

All quality assurance initiatives whether implicit or explicit, focusing on individual care or population service, undertaken by professionals, managers or consumers, must reflect an abiding interest in the provision of the highest possible quality care. If such concern is not given primacy quality assurance cannot take place. It should extend to all aspects of care including the technical, the interpersonal and the moral.

Specificity and Explicitness

Despite the many difficulties health care quality assurance is, in aspiration at least, a rational, explicit and practically based exercise. Standards are specified and operationalised and measurement tools are developed for their appraisal. Respect for professional judgement and careful analysis of social and ethical dilemmas provide essential context but the operation itself remains an attempt at developing empirically rigorous procedures for the observation, analysis and review of care and indeed, reflexively, for the observation, analysis and review of techniques for appraising and improving quality.

Adoption of a Cyclical Model

All quality assurance systems involve appraisal of quality standards followed by action for quality improvement. The American Nurses' Association cycle of quality assurance detailed in Fig. 2.1 is an elaboration of the sequence. At each stage in the cycle the observations and events of the previous stage influence the decisions to be made and action to be undertaken in the next. If any one stage is missed or inadequately carried out the others will suffer and the ultimate aim of quality maintenance or improvement will not be achieved. The cycle is what is known as an 'open' system, that is one in which direction is determined but actual destination may not be. This openness is necessary to allow for the idea of continual quality improvement. Today's highest possible standards may not satisfy the consumers and professionals of tomorrow.

Commitment

Finally, both individuals and organisations must be positively motivated to implement quality assurance. Concern for quality and even compliance in the implementation of quality assurance procedures are necessary but not sufficient. At the individual level time and energy must be devoted to the exercise and persistence displayed in the face of opposition. At the organisational level there must be recognition that quality assurance does not just happen. It must be managed. That implies commitment of time, energy and resources not just to the quality assurance system itself but to designing and modifying it to match and complement the organisational climate in which it operates.

Conclusion

This chapter has examined the historical development of health care quality assurance, particularly in the US and the UK. It has also identified a number of issues of concern to health care practitioners and quality assurance specialists world wide. It concluded by identifying four essential characteristics of health care quality assurance.

A particular theme which has emerged is the extent to which health care quality assurance might profitably look to industrial models and techniques for solutions to problems in its own context. The next chapter will examine the nature and development of industrial quality assurance.

3

The development of quality assurance in industry

Introduction

The previous chapter explored the development of quality assurance in health care. In this chapter the historical development of industrial quality assurance will be outlined and broad themes will be highlighted. The significance of each of these themes for health care quality assurance will be explored.

The Historical Development of Quality Assurance in Industrial and Commercial Settings

The idea of guaranteeing quality is anything but new. The earliest records reveal concern for the quality of medical care and as might be expected they also reveal concern for the quality of manufactured products. Thus the tomb paintings in the ancient Egyptian city of Thebes show not only the manufacture of bricks by slaves but the presence of a man inspecting completed bricks and discarding rejects.

Despite such early instances of inspection most preindustrial manufacture was carried out by individual craftsmen working in direct relationship with their customers. In such contexts each individual customer's wishes could be designed into the product from the very beginning and the customer could be consulted again at various stages in production. The process remains familiar from the (rapidly disappearing) trade of bespoke tailoring. Minute modifications are made to seams and cut as the customer comes to each fitting, and if he has changed his mind on some issue of lapel size or trouser bottom width then that too can be accommodated. Customers also expect to be seen by the same craftsman tailor on each visit to the company and expect the company to employ the best such craftsmen. The guarantee of quality thus resides in the traditional skills and dedication of individual workers and the company controls that quality through the twin processes of selection and training. Training is usually through a lengthy system of apprenticeship in which the trainee is expected not only to master the skills of an individual craftsman but also to imbibe and replicate his pride, dedication and commitment to work of the highest possible quality. As was noted in the last chapter some of the earliest procedures for quality assurance in health care were also to do with education, training and licensure. The assumption in early medicine as in early manufacture was that once novices with the right general aptitude had been exposed to the right procedures for education and socialisation they could be expected to provide a lifetime of high quality work. The implicit additional assumption was that the work environment and customer demand would remain fairly stable throughout that lifetime so that initial education would remain relevant.

The European craft guilds of the middle ages provided a guaranteed framework within which quality skills and attitudes could be transmitted from generation to generation and consumers of their products could thus be assured of continuing quality. As the guilds grew in influence and as their goods were marketed over increasing distances they found it useful to mark them with symbols indicating their provenance and by implication their quality. Thus woollen cloth from Colchester which was exported to most of Europe was marked with a special stamp and could be sold at a higher price than other cloth without incurring the wrath of the monks who scrutinised and controlled merchants' prices (Aquinas, ed. Gilbey, 1963).

Throughout the middle ages, however, most goods were produced in low volumes for local markets. The craftsman would be personally known to his customer and would tailor his product to his customer's wishes. Where products involved the assembly of separate parts he would match them by hand and eye and would normally be involved in the entire process of production from design through manufacture and possibly sale as well (Chandler, 1977). This basic pattern was sustained right into the eighteenth and early nineteenth century.

Woodward (1972, p. 7) writing on the history of the British Standards Institution (BSI) comments that formal industrial standards 'could well be said to owe their origin to the coming of the railways ... with hitherto undreamed of facilities for transporting goods the world had entered a new era'. In the course of the Industrial Revolution the entire process of manufacture and of training and deployment of labour changed and new ways of assuring the quality of products were needed. There was a vast increase in the number of points of manufacture and the diversity in size and quality produced by each manufacturer made it difficult for the buyer to know what he was getting or to reorder with any degree of confidence. The problem was particularly marked in the manufacture of what was then the new technology where large numbers of appropriately engineered parts were needed for the assembly of looms, steam engines, iron ships and agricultural machinery. Purchasers found that materials and components bought from different sources simply did not fit together and so parts had to be either manufactured on the spot – which was expensive if only small quantities were needed – or modified after purchase.

The American Civil War brought the new technology to warfare for the first time and when the war resulted in large-scale slaughter unaccompanied by significant progress toward victory for either side pressure grew for the development of higher quality weaponry. Thus the United States Ordnance Department and the various arms manufacturing plants became involved in what was known as the 'American' system of manufacturing (Hounshell, 1984). In this system special machinery was used to produce interchangeable parts by following a carefully controlled and uniform sequence of operations. Inspection based on a system of gauges matched to an agreed standard product was introduced. This is thought to be the first instance of manufacturing inspection based on objectively verifiable measurement rather than judgement by eye alone. The same techniques were subsequently to be adopted by the hugely successful Singer sewing machine and McCormick harvester companies. By the early years of the twentieth century Frederick W. Taylor (the father of the 'scientific management' school) was singling out inspection as one of eight separate functions required for efficient shop floor management. In his view the inspector was 'responsible for the quality of the work and both the workmen and the speed bosses must see that the work is finished to suit him' (Taylor, 1919, p. 101). The inspector's task was both separate from manufacture itself and crucial to it in ensuring that defective pieces were either returned for modification or rejected altogether. Taylor also noted that the inspector alone needed to be experienced in each aspect of the production process. He thus highlighted the fact that in conditions of mass production most workers were responsible for only a limited part of the work and often had only a hazy idea of the overall process.

In the United Kingdom and elsewhere in Europe similar pressures were resulting in the development of manufacturing standards throughout the engineering industry. As early as 1840 Sir Joseph Whitworth developed a standard screw thread and by 1901 the Institution of Civil Engineers was setting up a committee to consider the advisability of standardising production of iron and steel sections (Woodward, 1972). Up until then each manufacturer in iron and steel had been forced to carry large and expensive stocks of sections to his own idiosyncratic specifications. The committee gradually extended its activities to standards for cast iron pipes, cement, locomotives, electrical cables and many other goods. Its work became particularly important in the manufacture of munitions and aircraft during the First World War and by the 1920s it was selling standards on a wide scale for use throughout the engineering and allied industries. In 1929 it was awarded a Royal Charter and in 1930 it finally became the British Standards Institution with a general council and three divisional councils to organise standard setting and promulgation in engineering, building and industrial chemistry respectively.

In these early years inspection was the key component in ensuring that goods produced matched standards set. Quality was largely defined as conformance with standards and there was general agreement that the purchaser's 'principal interest in quality [is] that evenness or uniformity which results when the manufacturer adheres to his established requirements' (Radford, 1922, p. 5). Standards were sometimes set by manufacturers themselves but in the engineering and electrotechnical industries in particular there was widespread adoption of the standards set by the BSI, by the American National Standards Institute, or by the various analogous bodies which were established in Germany, France, and many other countries. In the munitions industries in particular responsibility for inspection gradually passed from the manufacturer to the purchaser – in this case usually a government. Thus an early version was established of the system of purchaser quality specification now widespread among large retailers such as Marks and Spencer, who will only buy from manufacturers if specified quality is maintained.

Inspection was generally carried out at the end of the entire process of manufacture or at least at the end of significant parts of the process. Poor quality or shoddy goods were either rejected out of hand or were returned to an earlier stage in the process for modification or recycling as raw material. Costs thus accrued from the employment and training of inspectors and from the labour and materials which had gone into the goods they rejected but it was expected that these costs would be offset by the increased sales which would result if quality could be guaranteed. Little attention was paid to the causes of defective production and the inspector's duties were more those of a guard preventing the escape of shoddy goods than of a trouble-shooter preventing their creation.

By the 1930s the costs of quality control, as it had come to be called, were escalating and attention began to be paid to restricting inspection to carefully selected samples of goods. Thus the BSI published standards for the sampling of wagon loads of coal and coke (Woodward, 1972). Checking the weight and contents of 10 wagons in 100 was no doubt better than checking one in 100 but it was realised that checking the other 90 was probably unnecessary. More influentially for the development of statistical quality control, the American

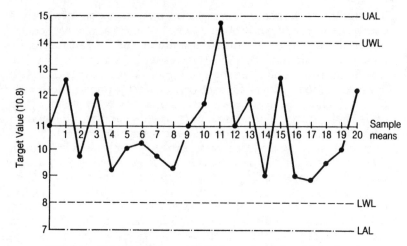

In this instance the product has been sampled 20 times and mean values of size or other relevant characteristic have been calculated and plotted against the target value

The process is 'in control' if:

1. No values are beyond the upper and lower action limits (UAL/LAL).
2. No more than one in 40 values are beyond the upper and lower warning limits (UWL/LWL).
3. No two consecutive values are in the same warning zones.
4. No runs of more than six values are consecutively above or below the target value.
5. No trends of more than six values are continuously either rising or falling.

Fig. 3.1 A process control chart

Bell Telephone Company set up an 'inspection engineering' department whose responsibilities were to extract the *maximum information* about the quality of units being produced at the new Hawthorne Electrical plant on the basis of the *minimum inspection*. The most significant member of the group was W. A. Shewhart whose 1931 book *Economic Control of Quality of Manufactured Product* remains a seminal text in the design of quality control systems.

Shewhart recognised that variability in production was inevitable and that the task of the quality control engineer was not the pursuit of invariability but the pursuit of acceptable levels of variation or variation within agreed limits of tolerance. Variation could come from many sources including raw materials, machine performance and human operator behaviour. Control of such variation according to Shewhart was a matter of statistical prediction as 'when, through the use of past experience we can predict, at least within limits, how the phenomenon may be expected to vary in the future ... prediction means that we can state, at least approximately, the probability that the observed phenomenon will fall within the given limits' (Shewhart, 1931, p. 6). Quality control and the science of statistical description and inference were thus linked inextricably.

Shewhart and his colleagues advocated the use of graphical representations of the processes of production – often referred to as 'process control charts' – which allowed quality personnel to see at a glance when manufacturing processes were producing goods or components which were faulty. Thus, as in Fig. 3.1, it could be made clear that the bulk of the production was or was not falling within the pre-set limits. The occurrence of 'outliers' beyond these limits suggested that something needed to be investigated and corrections made. Modifications were being made not just to defective products but to the *processes* of production.

In the UK, too, the idea of statistical control was spreading and in 1935 the BSI commissioned the distinguished statistician, E. S. Pearson to assist in the production of BS 600, a standard which dealt with the application of statistical methods to quality control. A wide range of statistical techniques are now available from the relatively simple construction of production histograms and process control charts to much more complex applications of analysis of variance, regression analysis and multi-factorial experimental design. Ingle (1982) provides a simple introduction to basic techniques while Ross (1988) and Oakland (1986) give guidance on more complex methods. In health care contexts the major applications of quality control methods are in areas of care involving the manipulation or production of physical materials. Thus the UK National External Quality Assessment Scheme (NEQAS) for radiology, clinical chemistry, pathology and nuclear medicine uses inspection, sampling and standard setting techniques which would be entirely familiar to quality control engineers in other settings (De Verdier et al., 1986; Shaw, 1990).

The main distinctions between quality inspection and quality control as it developed in the 1930s were thus the development of statistical analysis and the emphasis on the process of production. Costs could be reduced if workers, supervisors and managers were given feedback on the effectiveness of their work and encouraged to produce fewer and fewer substandard products or components. Inspection itself was thus minimised both by the use of sampling techniques and by the fact that the number of substandard products which had to be spotted for rejection or recycling should have diminished. Similar broadening of the focus from simple product standards was evident in the various standards organisations beginning to produce codes of practice alongside their various standards. This reflected recognition that the quality of a product – its fitness for purpose – also depended on its installation, maintenance and use. Thus in 1932 the BSI produced a standard (BS 449) for structural steel for use in the building industry which incorporated guidelines for storage, installation and maintenance alongside the product specification information. Such guidance is now commonplace.

By the end of the Second World War product standardisation and quality control had become internationally established and accepted. Their influence, however, was largely confined to the factory floor. Management had a role in setting up procedures but saw the quality department as separate from management and substantially additional to the rest of the workforce. It can even be argued that the very elaboration of techniques and development of specialist expertise which led to the success of control activities also led to their isolation. Quality initiatives were also more or less restricted to manufacturing industry. In the service and retail sectors they remained small scale and largely a matter of dealing with customer complaints. As was detailed in Chapter 2 health care quality assurance proceeded along its own lines with little or no reference to the development of ideas and techniques in industry.

The next important development in industrial quality assurance took place not in the UK or USA but in Japan. Almost immediately after the Japanese surrender in 1945 the allies determined to rebuild and recast both Japanese industry and Japanese society. As part of this grand plan they established the Civil Communications Section within the General Headquarters Allied Command. The Industrial Division of the CCS was charged to work with Japanese producers of communications equipment to improve production methods. They in turn recognised the importance of quality control and drafted in a team of engineers most of whom had worked previously at the Bell Telephone or Western Electric Companies where Shewhart had also worked.

From 1950 onwards the CCS ran a series of seminars for top Japanese business men from all sectors of industry. The main theme was 'scientific management' but the emphasis was quality. Several quality control specialists were imported to help run the seminars including the American W. Edwards Deming. His contribution so impressed the Japanese that they not only awarded him the 'Second Order of the Sacred Treasure' which was a high Imperial honour but also created the Deming prize for quality which remains one of the most sought after industrial honours in Japan. Deming taught statistical control techniques and encouraged his students (and their management and production colleagues) to adopt a systematic approach to problem solving which became known as the Deming Cycle of planning, doing, checking and taking action (for remediation or improvement) (Deming, 1982; 1986; Gitlow and Gitlow, 1987). The Deming cycle is a recognisable version of quality assurance as opposed to the narrower quality control. Deming also pushed his top managers into becoming closely involved with all aspects of quality, introduced consumer research and survey techniques, and stressed the need to monitor the balance between the costs of organising the assurance of quality and the benefits of increased sales and reduced waste of labour and materials associated with such assurance.

The seminars were attended by the most influential of Japan's new generation of entrepreneurs and managers and were exceptionally popular. The Japanese Union of Scientists and Engineers (JUSE) and the Japanese Federation of Economic Organisations both of which remain powerful business organisations took particular interest and publicised and popularised the new approaches throughout Japanese industry and commerce. Among other American experts who were drafted in to give advice were Joseph Juran and Armand Feigenbaum. Juran was particularly interested in the management of quality activities and fostered the notion that both commitment and actual practical involvement from top management were prerequisites of success (Juran, 1979; 1988). Feigenbaum had been head of quality at General Electric where he had had close contacts with the rapidly evolving Japanese electronics industry. He argued for the involvement of the entire workforce in quality – not just the isolated or grafted on quality department (Feigenbaum, 1983). Quality was thus to be designed in through a system of total quality management committed to the idea of a quality process leading to quality products. Participation, non-directive leadership and 'bottom-up' responsibility were also emphasised since as Feigenbaum put it 'quality is everyone's job' (Feigenbaum, 1956).

The new methods took strong root in Japanese managerial culture and spread and were consolidated throughout the 1960s and 1970s. There is considerable debate (see Garvin, 1988, ch. 10 for a fuller discussion) as to the extent to which the success of the ideas was the result of their congruence with existing Japanese traditions or the result of the economic and industrial vacuum created by Japan's military defeat. Some authors have even suggested that the success with which the quality movement took hold can be attributed not just to organisational values but to the characteristic values of the national culture. Thus Japanese workers are thought to be particularly fastidious, to refer and adhere more readily to group values than their more individualistic Western counterparts and to regard defective products as reflecting badly on individual and company honour (Benedict, 1946; Moritani, 1982; Johnson, 1983). Other commentators, however, (De Vos, 1985) are less convinced of the homogeneity of Japanese culture. Garvin (1988) for example notes that the analysis does not take account of Japan's reputation in the 1930s and 1940s for production of particularly shoddy goods. He also makes the point that Japanese subsidiaries in the US, Europe, Asia and Latin America seem able to attain high levels of quality production without the presence of a Japanese workforce.

Whatever the reason the adoption of the new management techniques went hand in hand with the manifest post-war success of

Japanese industry. By 1960 Japanese awareness of quality issues and their importance in the burgeoning 'economic miracle' had reached such proportions that the government designated November of each year a 'quality month'. During each November there would be widespread quality publicity, conventions and seminars would be organised and various competitions and other events would be given maximum media coverage.

Japanese quality assurance thus incorporated the American models of quality control and went beyond them. It was distinct from them in emphasising the importance of involving the entire workforce (including the most senior levels of management) in proactive planning for a quality process leading to quality products. Ideally poor quality would not occur at any stage in the organisation's operations and all employees would be involved in a constant search for improved quality. One particular technique which exemplifies all of these characteristics and which can more obviously be attributed to the Japanese themselves is the quality circle.

Despite the rapid growth of quality initiatives and despite Juran and Feigenbaum's emphasis on the participation of all employees in the activities, the 1957 report of the Japanese Ministry of International Trade and Industry was able to comment on lack of contact between management and shopfloor workers; lack of formal quality and other training for foremen and first line supervisors; and lack of managerial receptiveness to ideas generated at foreman level or below. Partly in response to these problems and partly in response to increasingly confrontational industrial relations Kaoru Ishikawa, a chemical engineer and management scientist at Tokyo University, began in 1960 to publish his ideas for quality circles (Ishikawa, 1982; 1985). These ideas were further developed in the magazine *Genba-To-QC* or *Quality Control for Foremen* and included proposals for shopfloor meetings of foremen and their subordinates. The main purpose of the proposed quality circles was at that stage the encouragement of study and discussion of quality control problems and techniques. The first quality circle was established in the Nippon Telephone and Telegraph Company in 1963 and growth thereafter was phenomenal. Not all circles are nationally registered so estimates vary but consultation of several sources suggests that by 1963 there were 200 circles; by 1967, 10,000; by 1969 20,000; by 1973 500,000; and by 1978 there were a million circles involving 10 million workers. The function and operation of the circles changed considerably during this period of remarkable development. Their main objective altered from simple study and discussion to the practical identification and solution of local quality problems. This involved the use of the traditional statistical techniques for data collection, presentation and analysis but also involved much more emphasis on interpersonal skills and techniques for group problem solving and decision making. Thus there was heavy emphasis on training for group leadership and facilitation for the foremen and supervisors who were to be the group leaders. The discussion technique known as brainstorming (Osborn, 1957) in which as many ideas as possible are collected before any attempt is made to agree on one was particularly popular. Graphic display of data and use of diagrammatic techniques such as Ishikawa's 'fishbone' cause and effect analyses (Ishikawa, 1982, ch. 9) were used extensively to ensure maximum involvement of sometimes relatively unskilled personnel. Circles usually met once weekly, had five to 10 members and were supposed to be based on so-called natural work groups. Stress was laid on voluntary attendance although the popularity of the groups and factory-wide publicity regarding their activities must have made non-attendance difficult.

At an early stage in the development of quality circles it was realised that communication between the shopfloor groups and middle and upper management was vital and groups were offered training in presenting ideas at management meetings and seminars. As Feigenbaum's ideas on the involvement of the entire organisation in quality activities took hold circles and groups began to be developed at other organisational levels. Along with these developments there came closer attention to the co-ordination of quality systems within companies and the use of quality coordinators or facilitators to ensure smooth and effective communication networks between the various parts of the systems. Thus the Japanese concept of quality assurance broadened until today the Japanese Industrial Standard Z8101–1981 refers to 'means to produce goods or services economically which satisfy customers' requirements...[involving] the co-operation of all people in the company'. The approach is known as company-wide quality control (CWQC) (Kogure and Akao, 1983). Garvin (1988, p. 191) notes that CWQC involves four principal elements as follows:

- The involvement of functions other than manufacturing in quality activities.
- The participation of employees at all levels.
- The goal of continuous improvement.
- Careful attention to customers' definitions of quality.

Garvin also suggests that once quality assurance has broadened in this way it is more appropriate to refer to the quality assurance system as a system of 'strategic quality management'.

Outside of Japan the first indications of the usefulness of quality assurance as a company-wide system of management were to be found in the work of James Halpin and Philip Crosby (Halpin, 1966; Crosby, 1979; 1984; 1986). In the early 1960s Halpin and Crosby were associated with several missile projects at the American Martin Company. There they conceived the idea that quality could best be defined as conformance to requirements and, contrary to Shewhart's notion that error was inevitable, developed what they called the 'zero defects' approach. In this approach Crosby suggested that with the right approach to management, perfect, error-free production was not only economically desirable but also technically possible. He stressed the importance of management commitment and involvement and pointed out that quality improvement was a continuous process which should suffuse the entire organisation.

Throughout the 1960s and 1970s quality assurance in the UK was substantially limited to industrial quality control and loosely defined quality assurance for products available for purchase by the general public. The BSI had been involved during and after the Second World War in the production of government approved utility goods and subsequently extended the notion of approved consumer products into the British Standard 'kitemark' scheme. Kitemark certification for consumer products had begun with a 1930s scheme compelling car manufacturers to fit windscreens with safety glass conforming to a published British Standard. Approved manufacturers were allowed to stamp their glass with the kitemark. After the war kitemarking was extended into a range of consumer durables including furniture, carpets, washing machines and so on. The emphasis on safety was maintained in the kitemarking of toys, motor cycle helmets, lifejackets and eventually car safety belts. BSI had thus become at once a guardian of industrial standards, a channel for government views on international competitiveness and a consumer watchdog. Recognising the need for reconciliation of these interests in 1971 BSI set up a 'quality assurance council' which was representative of industrial, government and consumer interests. Its remit was 'to promote the adoption of reliable certification schemes acceptable to manufacturers, Weights and Measures departments, and the purchaser' (Woodward, 1972, p. 91).

In the USA too consumer protection became an issue of public concern in the 1960s and 1970s. Between 1973 and 1978 the number of product recalls demanded by government protection agencies such as the National Highway Traffic Safety Commission rose from 7 million to 29 million and between 1974 and 1981 the number of product liability suits filed in federal district courts grew by an annual average rate of 28% (Garvin, 1988). Several of these cases received international publicity and faced the companies involved with the costs of litigation, of replacing the defective goods and of a massive downturn in demand for their other products.

At much the same time it was becoming increasingly evident to Western industrialists that Japanese manufacturers were rapidly outstripping them in sales of electronic goods and components, of a range of consumer durables and even of automobiles. A major factor in this apparently uneven contest was the consistently high quality of the Japanese products. In 1980 the Hewlett-Packard company carried out an exercise in comparative testing of microchips from three major US manufacturers and three Japanese manufacturers. At the point of delivery the chips from each of the Japanese companies had a defect rate of 0% while the three US manufacturers' chips had defect rates from 11% to 19%. After 1000 hours of use the discrepancy between the failure rates of the Japanese and American chips was even greater (Robinson, 1980).

Top managers throughout the Western world were thus increasingly sensitised to the importance of quality assurance as practised in Japan. Garvin (1988, p. 23) comments as follows:

> With their companies' reputations, market shares and profitability at risk the topic could no longer be ignored. Nor could it be relegated to lower levels of the organisation, where functional loyalties might interfere with the broader strategic vision. What emerged from the environment was a new approach to quality, one strongly shaped by the concerns of upper management.

The development of systems for the management of quality assurance began to seem important to UK industry and to government too. Specifically, the White Paper on Standards, Quality and International Competitiveness (HMSO, 1982b) and the Act which followed in 1983 strengthened various quality-oriented organisations including the BSI and empowered the Department of Trade to run a 'National Quality Year'. In the UK and the US Japanese models of quality management were increasingly appealed to and the 1980s saw the establishment of quality circles and other Japanese influenced quality management initiatives in a wide range of companies and organisations.

As might be anticipated not all of these initiatives were successful. Price (1990, p. 2) reflecting on the impact of what he terms the 'quality revolution' suggests that it has been 'patchy to say the least ... ranging from the cataclysmic to the inconsequential'. The strongest vein of criticism has been that the ideas are no more than gimmickry or just another bandwagon from the business schools which may work in Japan but is likely to be rejected in the different milieu of Western traditions and approaches. A particular theme in the current literature (both critical and promotional) is the importance of conceptualising the establishment and management of quality assurance systems as organisational development. As such its success or failure is likely to be subject to the same determinants as any other such development. Its introduction may need to be tailored to existing levels of education and skill, to predominant managerial styles, to local histories of industrial dispute and relationships, to current product and financial viability, to the balance of power between particular influential individuals, and to what has come to be called organisational 'culture'. Once introduced the quality system itself may need to be monitored, modified and subjected to its own quality assurance. In other words quality assurance needs to be just as positively managed as any other organisational function.

This approach to quality assurance is often referred to as 'total quality management' or TQM. Oakland (1989, p. 14) defines TQM as 'an approach to improving the effectiveness and flexibility of businesses as a whole. It is essentially a way of organising and involving the whole organisation; every department, every activity, every single person at every level'. He goes on to identify 10 central features of successful TQM as follows:

- Development of understanding through education and awareness programmes.
- Commitment and policy development.
- Organisation for quality.
- Measurement of quality costs.
- Planning of quality.
- Design for quality.
- Statistical process control.
- Quality systems documentation and control.
- Training, education and communications.
- Teamwork, involvement and problem solving.

Each of these will now be dealt with briefly.

Understanding through Education and Awareness Programmes

Oakland follows Deming, Juran and others in emphasising the vital importance of senior management in getting quality assurance started. Their commitment must be more than mere sloganising and must be firmly based in understanding and knowledge of the origins and operation of quality assurance. Senior managers who try to impose quality management without involvement or whose lack of knowledge exposes them to a credibility gap can doom the enterprise from the outset. Oakland therefore suggests that education programmes for senior management are the necessary starting point for any TQM initiative.

Commitment and Policy Development

The next step is the articulation – and presentation in written form – of a clear and explicit company policy for quality. This should involve commitment to the establishment of organisation for quality; to the identification and recognition of the primacy of customer's needs; to budgeting for quality; to assurance of quality in bought in services and materials; to prevention of error rather than detection; to education and training for quality at all levels; and to periodic review of the entire quality system.

Organisation for Quality

Once policy has been articulated and disseminated the next step is the development of an appropriate system of delegated responsibilities and channels of communication. This will vary according to the nature and needs of the organisation. General principles include maintaining a balance between the creation of elite or specialist groups who take responsibility for quality away from the general workforce and creating a system in which there is no-one who feels particularly accountable or who has the technical expertise to carry out the relevant quality tasks. In large or multifaceted organisations it may be important to ensure adequate representation of special interest groups or of different geographical or functional locations. Despite the general emphasis on worker participation and facilitation of local problem solving it is important to create a structure within which ideas can be aired and rapidly approved at the highest necessary levels. Many quality management schemes have been derided as 'talking shops' because initiatives were never seriously discussed beyond the factory floor.

Measurement of Quality Costs

This step involves identification of aspects of the company's activities where quality seems to be a particular issue. This may be because errors in this area are particularly costly or have widespread implications; or may be because errors are particularly frequent. A company-wide audit of quality 'failure costs' alongside costs of quality monitoring and quality improvement is an invaluable tool in planning the overall system of quality assurance priorities.

Planning for Quality

The quality plan depends on the nature of the company's activities but it is likely to include clear guidelines for the following:

- Specifications for raw materials, equipment and services to be brought in.
- Quality control for such goods and services at the point of purchase.
- Flow charts and systems for stock control and purchase scheduling.

- Process control systems.
- Sampling and inspection procedures.
- Equipment maintenance schedules.
- Packaging specifications and controls.
- Procedures for delivery control and customer service.

Design for Quality

Quality can be defined as that which meets customer requirements. This implies designing products which reflect customers' needs rather than the convenience or prejudices of the producers. The design function must therefore be based in sound market research; must involve actual or potential customers at the prototype or pilot stages; must allow for modifications after piloting or 'preoperational' testing; and must be subject to periodic review after product launch.

Statistical Process Control

Statistical process control was included in the quality plan as set out above but it is such an important and technically sophisticated aspect of quality assurance that it merits separate consideration. All of the techniques of quality engineering and statistical analysis focusing on the reduction of variation in production are relevant at this stage. They may be relatively simple descriptive displays and checklists or may use advanced inferential methodology. Information derived from such analyses is made available to other levels and functions in the organisation.

Quality Systems Documentation and Control

Each aspect of the quality plan requires detailed development in explicit procedures for specified personnel. In a truly organisation-wide quality system there will be such a set of procedures and standards for each department and arguably each employee. In many organisations all this requires is writing down what is already done – but many organisations have discovered that until such explicit documentation of activities was initiated no-one really knew who did what and unnecessary overlaps and gaps in responsibilities and poor scheduling had resulted. Such quality documentation is often collected in a quality manual which not only allows employees to check their own patterns but provides an overall view of company policy and mission.

The quality system itself must be subject to periodic review and modification. This may be undertaken internally but increasingly TQM firms commission external auditors to undertake the scrutiny. For many this leads to involvement in the accreditation procedures of the BSI and its European analogue the International Organisation for Standardisation (ISO). They have published a standard for quality systems known in the UK as BS 5750 and in the European context as ISO 9000. Firms who subject themselves to quality audit by BSI or ISO are expected to provide documented and operational evidence for the following:

1. A defined and documented quality *policy* which commands the commitment and support of senior management.
2. A clear *organisation* for quality with designated individual and group responsibilities.
3. A quality *system and manual* which is subject to *review.*
4. Quality *document control* ensuring that all quality documents are up to date and modified as appropriate.
5. A system for *contract dialogue and review* between company and major customers which ensures that customers' preferences remain paramount.
6. Control of *design* activities again with an emphasis on customer involvement and market research.
7. Control of *purchased* material, equipment and services and of *purchasing procedures.* This may include periodic appraisal of vendors or sub-contractors.
8. Control and maintenance of traceability of *customer supplied goods or materials* (as in goods returned for service or raw materials supplied for processing and return).
9. *Process Control* including descriptions of plant and equipment, clear instructions for use, procedural standards, instrumentation and calibration, and any special set-up or start-up procedures.
10. Use of statistical techniques and systems for *statistical process control.*
11. *Checking, measuring, inspecting and testing* of incoming materials and equipment, of goods in process and of finished products.
12. *Identification and traceability* of goods and equipment at all stages in process, stock, or dispatch storage.
13. Control, calibration and maintenance of *inspection and test equipment.*
14. Clear indication of *test and inspection status,* i.e. waiting for test, passed test or failed test.
15. Clear identification and segregation of *non-conforming or defective goods or services* whether purchased, during the production process, or at finished product stage.
16. Clear procedures for *corrective action* when failures occur in the system, when complaints come in from customers, or when purchased goods or services are defective.
17. *Preservation of product quality* until it reaches the customer, e.g. during packaging, storage and transit.

18. Adequate arrangements for post-sales *servicing and maintenance* including clear instructions for customer use.
19. *Record systems* which provide appropriate, concise and up-to-date information.
20. Arrangements for regular staff *training* based on sound task analysis.
21. Quality system *audits and reviews*. Audits determine whether the system is meeting its objectives. Reviews assess the effectiveness of the system and its objectives.

Companies who are awarded BS 5750 status are allowed to publicise themselves as 'quality' firms and can expect to increase sales accordingly.

Training, Education and Communications

Education and training for senior management was the first step in Oakland's account of the implementation of TQM but once the system is in place there is a constant need for quality oriented education and training at all levels. Similarly, the success and co-ordination of the search for total quality is heavily dependent on regular publication and feedback of results, on rapid and effective communication about proposed changes and developments, and on company-wide publicity for particularly successful efforts. It may also be useful to involve customers in such communication. In large or segmented organisations it is often useful to think of internal colleagues as customers and to design quality activities and communications accordingly. Thus the executive may be the secretary's customer and the secretary may be the reprographic section's customer.

Teamwork, Involvement and Problem Solving

Oakland places teamwork, involvement and problem solving at the end of his list of important features of successful TQM but it is clear that he concurs with other authors about their centrality. Thus he comments (Oakland, 1989, p. 237) that 'employees will not be motivated towards continual improvement in the absence of: commitment to quality from top management; the organisational "quality" climate; a team approach to quality problems'. Such teamwork and involvement implies genuine participative decision making; bottom-up communication channels; effective interpersonal skills at all levels in the organisation; and possibly recourse to specific team building and group problem solving techniques such as those commonly used in quality circles.

TQM is thus a comprehensive approach to the management of

quality throughout organisations. Just as Japanese quality assurance went beyond and included the original American and European techniques of product standardisation and quality control, TQM has gone beyond quality assurance to strategic planning, goal setting and mobilisation of the entire organisation in a constant search for the improvement of quality. It includes but is not limited to the production function and it is eclectic in its use of techniques such as statistical process control or quality circles first developed in narrower quality contexts. System accreditation through BS 5750 or ISO 9000 is similarly useful but not essential to TQM firms – and conversely many firms are accredited whose managers would not describe their approach as TQM.

Of particular recent interest (Townsend and Gebhardt, 1986; Price, 1990) has been the concept of quality as an epiphenomenon of so-called organisational culture. In this view no amount of detailed planning for quality systems and procedures and indeed no amount of reference to externally agreed standards for such systems will be successful unless each employee has internalised the values characteristic of the quality ethos. The idea of quality culture has had particular impact in the development of quality systems for the service industries such as tourism, catering and banking. Services are essentially things that people do to, with, and for other people and their products are often difficult to isolate and operationalise for measurement. Special techniques are therefore required for quality appraisal and improvement. Similar difficulties are evident in health care quality assurance and it may be therefore that service industry quality assurance is a particularly rich source of relevant ideas and techniques.

Di Primio (1987) identifies the 'irreconcilable differences' between product producing companies and service organisations as follows.

- Services are intangible and outcomes are, therefore, difficult to measure.
- No inventory control can be established over services – they cannot be stored for future use and requests for them cannot be backlogged. They are thus extremely 'perishable'.
- Service organisations have a strong client presence and hence interaction with clients is often face-to-face.
- The process of delivering services requires a delivery system that is user friendly and time sensitive.
- Client satisfaction measures are even more important features of performance evaluation than they are in production industries.

Several other authors (Clark, 1989; Gummeson, 1989) also focus on the centrality of relatively intangible 'process' quality in the service industries and suggest that service industries have lagged behind production industry in developing quality initiatives partly because of the strong product orientation of early quality inspection and control. Gummeson suggests that recent attention to quality in the service sector is a function first, of widespread consumer articulation of dissatisfaction; second, of the recognition even in production industry of the importance of the service elements of their activities; and finally, of increasing restriction, cost control and development of internal competition in the public services.

Gummeson (1989) and Stebbing (1990) both emphasise the importance of designing service systems so that they fit consumer requirements rather than producer convenience and point out that timeliness is of even greater importance in the service context than elsewhere. Both Stebbing and Oakland (1989) recommend the use of flow charting as a technique for slimming down the number of operations needed in providing services and thus increasing speed of service delivery. Stebbing also points out that documentation and record control are prime targets for quality improvement in the service industries where they are often the only means of tracing the consumer's progress through the system but where they can readily become over-bureaucratised and unnecessarily repetitive. Clark (1989) points out, however, that good computer software can not only assist this traceability of consumer progress but can allow consumers themselves to be given instant feedback on the progress of their particular delivery. The dissatisfied airline customer whose luggage has got lost can be made considerably less dissatisfied if given regular and accurate feedback on the efforts which are being made to find and retrieve it.

This need for regular consumer information and feedback is one aspect of the obvious importance of employee/consumer interaction in service industries. Carlzon (1987) refers to such service 'encounters' as 'moments of truth' and points out that even exemplary service can be poorly perceived by a customer whose access to it is via brusque or socially unskilled 'front of house' employees. Ellis and Whittington (1981) and Rackham and Morgan (1977) discuss the importance of social skill training for such personnel in a wide range of service settings, including health care.

Recognising the need for quality initiatives in the service sector the BSI and ISO have recently produced a discussion document which is a prototype version of BS 5750/ISO 9000 specially modified for the service industries (BSI Draft Document 90/97100 or ISO DIS 9004–2). They suggest that quality assurance in the service sector will lead to the following.

- Improved productivity and cost reduction.
- Improved market opportunities.
- Improved service performance.

The quality system should respond to the human aspects of service provision by the following.

- Managing the social processes involved in the service.
- Regarding human interactions as a crucial part of service quality.
- Recognising the importance of customers' perceptions of the organisation's image, culture and performance.
- Motivating personnel and developing their skill to meet customer expectations.

The preamble to the standard points out that all industries have some element of service provision. Its writers propose a continuum from the 'high product orientation' industries such as vehicle manufacture (service elements relating to sales, maintenance, etc.) to 'low product orientation' such as provision of banking or legal services. They also comment that service customers can be internal to an organisation as well as external. Control of quality in service provision is recognised as being more difficult than in product oriented industries for the following reasons:

> In most cases the control of service and service delivery characteristics can only be achieved by controlling the process that delivers the service. ... It is usually not possible to use final inspection to influence service quality at the customer interface, although remedial action is sometimes possible during service delivery (p. 7).

The standard adds, however, that 'the more definable the process, whether by mechanisation or by detailed procedures, the greater the opportunity to apply structured and disciplined quality system principles' (p. 7).

Management responsibilities for quality assurance are set out including development of explicit and available statements of quality policy and objectives; creation of a co-ordinated system of delegation and organisation for quality; and provision for periodic formal reviews of the quality system. The system itself should be based on appropriate staff motivation, development and training and should be allocated adequate material resources.

The structure of the proposed standard quality system is based on a model of the service organisation in which service needs are established through a process of interaction with the customer involving market research, preparation of a service brief and service design. This then leads to service and service delivery specification which in turn leads to actual delivery. Feedback and quality evaluation is built into the system at various stages and is undertaken by customers and suppliers (i.e. by employees providing the various aspects of the service).

A quality manual is required, as are a quality plan, detailed quality procedures, specified quality documentation, and provision for periodic audit and review. In these respects the standard is very similar to the original BS 5750. A significant difference, however, is the inclusion of a separate section on 'interface with customers'. Communication with customers is said to mean 'listening to them and keeping them informed in a readily comprehensible way' (p. 16) and involves the following:

- Describing the service, its scope and availability.
- Stating how much the service will cost.
- Explaining the interrelationships between service, delivery and cost.
- Explaining to customers the effects of any problems and how they will be dealt with should they arise.
- Ensuring that customers are aware of the contribution they can make to service quality.
- Providing adequate, readily accessible facilities for effective communication to and from the service organisation.
- Determining the relationship between the service on offer and the real needs of the customer.

Operational elements of the quality system are then spelt out for marketing (including research and advertising), design, delivery, and performance analysis and improvement. The design team are given particular responsibility for the development of techniques for quality control which includes three main steps namely identification of key elements in the delivery of the service; analysis of these elements to identify measurable indicators of quality of performance; and definition of actions which can be taken to ensure that service quality remains within acceptable limits. Much more attention is paid than in BS 5750 to the involvement of customers in the process of design and to the validation of service design at the points of piloting and launch.

Specification of the operational elements of the quality system for service delivery again places particular emphasis on assessment by customers. Reliance on customer complaints for feedback is discouraged and measures of satisfaction should be ongoing and actively sought. They should cover all aspects of the service and should ask the customer to compare perceptions of the service with perceptions of personal need. Employee assessment should also be ongoing, should refer to perceived customer satisfaction and should involve assessment of both the entire service delivered and the employee's personal contribution to it. There should be clearly specified and timely procedures for dealing with instances where service delivery is outside specified limits of acceptable quality.

The draft standard concludes by setting out a specification for performance analysis and improvement based on methodologically sound systems for assessment and evaluation of both the actual process of service delivery and customer and supplier perceptions of and attitudes to it. These procedures include behaviour analysis, surveys and questionnaires and should themselves be periodically reviewed for reliability, validity and other safeguards against lack of precision or irrelevance.

BS 90/97100 (ISO DIS 9004–2) follows the same broad pattern of emphasis on clear specification of standards for management of quality, organisation for quality, and documented procedures for assessment of quality throughout the production/service delivery process, as BS 5750. It also recognises the distinctive characteristics of service provision and the centrality of employee/customer interaction and proposes relatively standard techniques from the behavioural and social sciences as sensible approaches to performance evaluation. As will be clear from subsequent chapters its basic approach could have considerable applicability in health care.

Themes in Industrial Quality Assurance

The history of industrial quality assurance outlined above can be characterised as a persistent attempt to replicate the mediaeval craftsman's pride in his capacity to please his customer while at the same time exploiting each new technique for the production and distribution of goods and services. Thus the development of mass production and assembly line construction necessitated the development of product standardisation and inspection; the development of larger scale production runs and processes led to statistical quality control; the increasing complexity and cost of inspection and control led to the principle of 'getting it right first time' and to the prevention philosophy of quality assurance; and finally the increasing size and complexity of modern organisations led to emphasis on the management of quality and in particular on the importance of people in ensuring the production and delivery of quality goods and services. Within this overall pattern of response to increasing complexity a number of themes can be detected. They are similar to those identified with respect to health care in Chapter 2. They concern the definition of quality and quality assurance; the scope of quality assurance; measurement and methodology in quality assurance; the contexts of quality assurance; and costs and quality assurance.

Definitions of Quality and Quality Assurance

Quality is notoriously difficult to define. In health care in particular there is tension between definitions which reflect different stakeholding perspectives. Patients, professionals and paymasters may all have differing views and difficult ethical and political dilemmas underlie decisions about care priorities and resource distribution for quality care.

Definition of quality in the industrial context may at first seem easier. Typical definitions include those which stress consumer perspectives such as 'that which most consistently meets customer needs' or which is 'fit for its purpose'. These, however, are difficult to use in practical quality assurance since they assume that manufacturers either know or are able to determine what consumers' needs are, that their needs are relatively stable and that there is some reasonable correspondence between their needs and their likely purchasing behaviour. The large sums spent on market research and analysis bear witness to the fallibility of each of these assumptions. Other definitions place the emphasis on conformity and reduction of variability. Thus Gilmore (1974, p. 16) gives 'quality is the degree to which a specific product conforms to a design or specification'. Just as consumer oriented definitions avoid the issue of how the supplier is to determine consumer requirements these definitions avoid issues of the quality of the design or specification itself. Yet other definitions introduce the issue of value for money or price but ignore the complex relationships which economists recognise between price, satisfaction and demand. People may buy products which are unsuited to their purpose and are even downright unreliable but be perfectly satisfied because they are expensive and thus perceived as giving their owner status – on the other hand they may be emotionally attached to the 'cheap and cheerful', again paying little attention to the product's suitability or durability.

Even in the industrial context then, quality is difficult to define and may in Garvin's (1988) term be 'transcendent' – that is recognisable when met but ultimately indefinable. Despite the difficulties, pragmatism has overcome disputation and working definitions have emerged. They reflect four main emphases as follows:

- Achievement of a predetermined target or standard.
- Involvement of customer requirements in the determination of such a target or standard.
- Consideration of available financial and other resources in the determination of such a target or standard.
- Recognition that there is always room for improvement and that targets and standards are subject to review.

Identification and definition of the optimum procedures for ensuring that targets are achieved has also presented difficulty. The title of this book refers to 'quality assurance' but that reflects the expression's particular currency in health care in the 1990s as much as its precision. As has been made clear above there would be some merit in referring to quality management instead. In both health care and industrial settings there has been increasing recognition of the importance of setting individual quality initiatives in a wider context of organisation or service-wide participation and management. There is also agreement that the process is cyclical and ongoing involving something like Deming's original cycle of Plan, Do, Check, Act iterated for as long as production or service delivery continues.

The Scope of Quality Assurance

Industrial quality assurance was initially limited to production engineering and to the production function within that industry. Its history has been one of expansion. It is now applied throughout the organisation from marketing and design through finance, personnel, and purchasing, to the various processes of production or service delivery, and to dispatch, sales, service and customer after care, not forgetting the vitally important involvement of management itself. Its scope has similarly extended from engineering to the whole range of industrial and commercial enterprise and to companies of multi-national or small business dimensions. Application in the public services seems on first consideration to be something of a novelty but as was demonstrated in Chapter 2 something very like it has in fact operated in many areas of public service. There are differences in the particular techniques and approaches which are relevant to different industries and services and as will be established in subsequent chapters health care may well be a very special instance indeed. That will not, however, imply that techniques first evolved in the industrial setting will be by definition impossible to adapt for health care.

Measurement and Methodology in Quality Assurance

Measurement is absolutely central to quality assurance in the industrial context. Indeed one of the things the mediaeval Colchester guildsmen guaranteed about their cloth was the length of each bolt and no doubt the inspector of ancient Egyptian bricks was concerned that each brick should be the same size as his standard brick. The statistical techniques for process control developed by Shewhart in the 1930s and considerably advanced by engineers in more recent years (Ross, 1988) are as sophisticated as any and rather more so than those used in typical health care evaluations. Statistics, however, are only as good as they are relevant and their excessive use can have the effect of isolating their expert users and creating an elitist approach to quality assurance. As quality assurance expanded into a company-wide activity measurement remained central but tended to be more economically applied and wherever possible to be presented as simple user friendly graphical representations. Thus it is possible to use a cause and effect diagram as a simple aid to discussion and consensus development or to go beyond it to the collection of correlational data which in turn form the basis for the derivation of a numerically weighted version of the diagram.

The extension of quality assurance to the entire company also led to its application in areas where the main activity was either paper based or service based. The techniques of flow charting, traceability maintenance, and documentation updating and control which developed in these contexts are relatively simple but clearly relevant in public service and health care contexts. Similarly, the issues of product or service sampling which arise in this wider application of quality assurance are common to both private and public sector organisations.

As might be expected the problems of measurement of intangible outcomes encountered in quality assurance in the service industries are particularly salient in health care and in each context appeal must be made to the traditional methods of the social and behavioural sciences. Likewise the centrality of customer or patient satisfaction as an indicator of quality of provision is emphasised in both service industries and health care. It should be noted, however, that whereas in the service industries there is ready recognition that the customer really does know best the tension between the arcane professional mystery of modern high technology medicine and patients' perceptions of 'feeling better' make determination of need and establishment of standards more difficult in health care.

Finally, in both health care and industry there is recognition of the value of both external and internal quality review. Industrial standards are of long standing as are external reviews of at least the structural components of care. In both contexts also there has been more recent recognition of the possibility of involving external reviewers not so much in the assessment of quality of the actual product or service but as reviewers of the internal process of quality assurance. Thus BS 5750/ISO 9000 and its draft service industry modification sets out standards for the quality system and its management and American health care organisational accreditation systems lay down similar guidelines.

The Organisational Contexts of Quality Assurance

As industrial quality assurance has extended beyond clearly product oriented industries and as company-wide participation has become the norm so the organisational contexts of quality assurance have become more and more important. Increasingly, the development of measurable standards and clearly documented procedures is seen to be a necessary but by no means sufficient part of assuring quality. Of greater importance in maintaining and indeed exceeding predetermined standards of excellence are the attitudes and perceptions of everyone associated with the organisation. The intangibles of organisational 'climate' and 'culture' are increasingly appealed to as essential features of successful quality assurance. Hutchins (1990) for example suggests that management for total quality involves establishing small local cells of 'craftsmanship' in which workers identify, resolve and set standards for their own local quality problems in their own way. Their activities are then loosely coordinated through a 'quality council' which has a direct line of communication to senior management in much the same way that the original Japanese quality circles made periodic reports to management but were themselves entirely shop floor groups. According to Hutchins such localisation of quality encourages a feeling of ownership and greater likelihood of pride in personal and group achievement akin to the internalised values of the mediaeval craft groups. Without such internalisation a climate of quality cannot be said to exist. Similarly, many authors from Deming and Juran onwards emphasise that senior management must not merely exhort but must be seen to be actively committed and involved in quality activities throughout their organisation. Of particular importance is management's ability not just to promulgate standards or to set up systems but to facilitate genuine rather than lip serving changes leading to increased product or service quality. This may hinge on the way power is distributed and used in the organisation (Price, 1990), on managers' leadership styles (Garvin, 1988) or on the existence of effective individual champions of the quality cause (Peters and Waterman, 1982).

In an even wider context there is a marked increase in recognition of the centrality of consumers' perceptions in design and standard setting for both products and services. Higher standards of education and awareness and rapid communications have led consumers in all sectors to be more vocal and more articulate in the expression of preference. The fraudulent salesman or the producer of particularly shoddy or unsafe goods can no longer move to the next town – people there will have read the same newspapers and watched the same televised exposé. A further incentive for the greater involvement of consumers in the specification of standards is increased competitiveness in a period of economic recession and shrinking demand. The only edge a company may have over its competitors is the extent to which it can precisely predict and produce to meet the changing needs and preferences of consumers.

Interestingly, many of the suggestions that health care quality assurance could profitably adopt models from industrial quality assurance refer to contextual issues such as these. Jessee (1981, p. 18) comments as follows:

Knowledge of theories and techniques to encourage change in both individuals and organisations is as critical to quality assurance as is an understanding of more clinically related concepts. The most accurate diagnosis of a health care problem and the most valid assessment of the factors contributing to it will not produce the desired improvement unless effective techniques for changing individual and organisational behaviour can be applied when necessary.

In similar vein, Williams (1989, p. 101) advocates the adoption of TQM in health care on the grounds that traditional health care quality assurance programmes 'have not been well integrated with other management systems, nor have they provided real incentives to managers to improve work processes and service outcomes'.

Berwick and Knapp (1987) suggest that health care quality assurance has three lessons to learn from other industries namely the importance of organisational climate, the multi-dimensionality of quality and the importance of design. By emphasising the importance of design they stress the fact that just as the service industries in particular have recognised that it is vitally important to consult in depth with customers regarding appropriate design parameters so also the health care industry must learn to involve patients in the design and control of the service. Only such involvement will ensure the prevention of poor service. At present Berwick and Knapp argue, measures of satisfaction or dissatisfaction are generally used subsequent to the delivery of care which may therefore still include substandard instances – the equivalent of shoddy goods which in product oriented industries could have been returned for rejection or recycling but which in service industries and in particular in health care cannot be so retrieved.

Youll and Perring (1991) lay similar emphasis on the need for fuller involvement of health care consumers but stress the significance of the power differential between service providers and consumers (patients) in health care. Patients may be unaware of the possibility of involvement and even if aware of it may not know how to identify and communicate what needs to change. They suggest that the concept of the service 'culture' is valuable and argue that only by asking how such cultures can shift from 'seeing change as turmoil to seeing it as interesting and potentially positive' (ibid., p.14) can genuine dialogue between consumers and providers be established. Without such a dialogue quality care will remain elusive.

Costs and Quality Assurance

The moves from quality inspection to quality control and from there to quality assurance were in both cases partly based on considerations of cost. Quality costs are traditionally categorised into costs associated with failure including the various costs associated with the production and delivery of poor quality goods and services and costs associated with prevention including the various costs associated with quality control, assurance or management. A cost-effective quality system is one in which the costs of prevention are less than the costs of failure. Thus quality control was cheaper than quality inspection because not every item was inspected and fewer inspection-hours were required and quality assurance and management are more cost effective than quality control because they aim (ideally) to prevent failure altogether.

More recent considerations of quality management, organisational change and consumer involvement have also been partially cost driven. Thus it can be argued that the relationships between organisational culture and the establishment of sound quality management are symbiotic. While the initial establishment of quality management cannot take place without some degree of cultural orientation towards change, once such management has been shown to be successful the orientation towards change and creative development will itself be more marked. This in turn should ensure that the organisation will respond more flexibly to the next set of changes in the business environment and it will thus have a greater chance of continuing financial buoyancy. Similarly, the closer the relationship with consumers and the more thorough the marketing and design exercises the more likely it is that the organisation will be ready to respond to changes in market size and share and to exploit the latest shift in consumer preference. This again should lead to increased and continuing profitability.

A final cost advantage of establishing organisation-wide quality assurance resides in the change it should make to the company's public image. Gunn (1988) argues that many large and well-established companies are as much concerned with their image and reputation for social responsibility as they are with naked profitability. Marks and Spencer are a good example of an organisation which is a national institution as much as a business organisation. Their image is closely associated both with high product quality and with compassionate treatment of employees and any departure from either characteristic would be likely to lead to damaged image and possibly to decreased market share. Their recent decision to declare several hundred of their staff redundant was no doubt sensible in terms of immediate profitability but it may have had repercussions on consumers' perception of the store. If they were disappointed in the organisation they would be less likely to patronise it. For organisations of that kind the maintenance of high quality standards has long-term and indirect implications for profitability as well as more direct and short term advantages.

As was noted in Chapter 2 health economics is in several significant respects different from the economics of other marketplaces and the relationships between costs and quality in health care are complex. Nonetheless, as Wong (1989) points out the broad relationships between failure costs and prevention costs obtain in health care as elsewhere. Prevention costs are relatively easy to quantify and like those in industrial quality assurance are substantially the costs of the human and material resources involved in setting up, maintaining and monitoring quality systems. The difficulties reside in quantifying the costs of failure. To establish the degree of quality failure in health care it is first necessary to establish what health care quality is. Only then can performance be measured against it and the degree of failure established. As repeatedly noted health care quality is difficult to define and measure.

Despite these essential difficulties the basic relationships between failure and prevention costs do obtain in health care quality assurance. Similarly, the indirect advantages of improved employee morale, increased organisational flexibility, closer relationships with consumers and improved public image which accrue in industrial quality assurance must also operate in health care – even if they have to be measured in social or even ethical units rather than dollars or pounds.

Conclusion

So what can health care learn from industrial quality assurance? Health care quality assurance and industrial quality assurance are slowly becoming more similar. It can be argued, however, that the traffic seems to be largely one way. There is little or no reference to the health care literature in the industrial context but very substantial reference in the other direction. There are differences too in the extent and nature of that reference in the UK and US health care literature. Thus in the US the preexisting traditions of quality monitoring and accreditation have created an orthodoxy within which it may be difficult to engender change in the direction of industrial models. In the UK on the other hand there is much more substantial reference to industry as *the* source of quality assurance techniques. As a result there is both a more ready acceptance of current approaches to organisation-wide quality management and a more ready recourse to defensive postures based on the notion that no industrial technique could possibly work in the public service, professionally owned, health care context. Dalley and Carr-Hill's recent (1991) survey of quality assurance initiatives in health authorities in England and Wales suggested that while all authorities were evolving strategies for quality management the implementation of those strategies in detailed local tactics and systems was patchy in the extreme. It can be argued that that is because quality management strategies are superficially easy to adapt from industry – policy can be articulated and top managers can make initial commitments. The difficulties arise when issues of ownership and tension between government, management, professional and consumer interests have to be worked through in the context of detailed local tactics, techniques and systems. These difficulties are compounded by the fact that at that level neither the UK industrial context nor the US health care context can offer models which can be immediately applied in the UK National Health Service. A process of adaptation and translation is required before the models will fit.

However that adaptation modifies the industrial template some basic characteristics are likely to remain. They include the following:

- Specification of standards.
- Development of techniques for the appraisal of standards.
- Adoption of a cyclical model of review and improvement.
- Involvement of consumers.
- Consideration of relationships between quality and costs.
- Recognition of the value of positive organisation wide quality management.

In each of these areas health care quality innovators should find it worthwhile to consider the industrial experience.

4

Techniques for Quality Assurance in Health Care

Part One: *Quality Specific Techniques*

Introduction

Previous chapters outlined the development of quality assurance in industry and in health care and considered issues of definition, scope, methodology, organisational context, and cost. In each chapter thinking of quality assurance as a cyclical process was shown to be useful. Thus it was suggested that all quality assurance begins with standard setting, progresses to appraisal of the achievement of those standards and concludes with identification and implementation of action for improvement. Standards are subject to periodic reappraisal and, on a longer time scale, to review for continuing appropriateness. The process is represented diagrammatically in the health care 'quality wheel' introduced in Chapter 2 (p. 24) and elaborated here.

Choices must be made at each stage in the cycle. These include choice of quality topic or problem, choice of organisational setting or patient group, choice of aspect of care (e.g. structure, process or outcome), choice of measuring technique(s), and finally choices regarding interpretation of the results of measurements and the determination of appropriate action(s) for improvement. This and the following chapter are designed to provide guidance on each of these choices.

The cycle in Fig. 4.1 below is a representation of an individual quality initiative and thus does not fully reflect the importance of organisational context and quality management. Models and systems for quality management will be dealt with separately in Chapter 6.

The present chapter and Chapter 5 are organised as a compendium of techniques for use at various stages in the quality cycle and in various settings. This chapter deals with techniques which are specific to quality assurance while the next one deals with techniques which have had extensive use in quality assurance but originate in

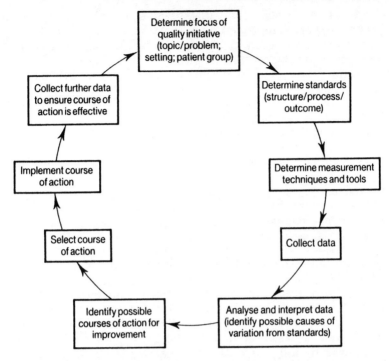

Fig. 4.1 The quality cycle

more broadly based research or management activities. Thus quality circles and systems for the observation and appraisal of the process of care are dealt with in this chapter while surveys and consensus development techniques are discussed in the next. While several of the techniques included were first developed in industrial quality assurance all have been applied in health care settings.

For ease of reference the techniques in this chapter have been grouped in broad categories. Each category is briefly introduced and related to the quality cycle. Its significance for quality management is also discussed. For each technique an indication is given of its background and scope including the profession(s) and care setting(s) for which it is intended. This is followed by a detailed description and a brief evaluative commentary. Commentaries are based on the critical literature where possible but also indicate advantages and disadvantages as perceived by the authors of this book. Each commentary considers the practicality of the technique, its take up in the settings for which it is designed and its potential generalisability to other settings. Where the technique specifies standards their derivation, validity and practicality as indicators of quality are considered. Where it includes measurement reliability, (consistency of measurement) and validity (the extent to which it measures what is intended) are commented upon (see Chapter 5, p. 180 for fuller discussion of reliability and validity). Sources are indicated as appropriate and suggestions are given for further reading.

The categories of quality specific technique covered in this chapter are as follows:

- Professional standards systems.
- Comprehensive review systems.
- Case selection techniques.
- Local problem identification techniques.
- Process appraisal techniques.
- Outcome appraisal techniques.
- Consumer involvement techniques.
- Records techniques.

The *professional standards systems* category contains the various guidelines and standards documents which health care professionals have published as a basis for quality assurance.

The *comprehensive review systems* category contains systems designed to be complete systems for quality assurance in a given area of care. The category is subdivided into systems which include specified standards as well as procedures for quality appraisal and improvement; systems designed to facilitate local standard setting as well as quality appraisal and improvement; and systems facilitating local appraisal and improvement without preliminary standard setting.

The *case selection techniques* category contains techniques for selecting cases for particular focus in appraising the quality of care.

The *local problem identification techniques* category contains techniques in which local groups are encouraged to identify problem areas which are then the subject of quality appraisal and improvement.

The *process appraisal techniques* category contains techniques which focus particularly on appraisal of the quality of the process of care.

The *outcome appraisal techniques* category contains techniques which focus particularly on appraisal of the quality of the outcomes of care.

The *consumer involvement techniques* category outlines ways of involving patients/consumers in quality assurance and improvement.

The *records techniques* section outlines approaches to record keeping for quality assurance.

The Appendix (p. 252) lists each individual technique (with its source) and indicates its category, the profession(s) for which it should be appropriate and the page on which it can be found. An alphabetical list is also provided.

Professional Standards Systems

Standard setting is a central focus in all forms of quality assurance. Innovators can choose, however, whether to develop standards of their own, to adopt or modify standards which have been articulated elsewhere, or to develop a system with elements of both. Thus in manufacturing industry companies could adopt product standards from the British Standards Institution, set local process standards through quality circles, and finally refer their entire quality system to BSI for accreditation under BS 5750. In health care the professional bodies have involved themselves either in setting high level guideline standards or in encouraging the development of local standards. They are thus both a source of standards and a source of advice on how to set them. The accreditation organisations on the other hand have tended to move away from specification of standards for practice to specification of standards for quality assurance systems and quality management. In other words they now provide health care equivalents of BS 5750.

Professional bodies have always been involved in setting standards. Each set of guidelines for education and practical training has been a kind of standards document. Similarly, codes of conduct and disciplinary ordinances have established thresholds below which quality should not go. In that sense they have set standards. Setting explicit positive standards for the quality of routine care is a more recent development. It is these standards which are considered here. UK standards systems are dealt with in detail. Standards systems from the US and elsewhere are discussed more generally.

Since the recent NHS reforms all UK health professions have recognised that they are about to be involved in formal quality assurance. Most resulting activities have been monoprofesional although some professions have recognised the virtue of multi-professional quality assurance.

Several professions have responded to the reforms by setting up working parties or research groups to develop standards. These groups have varied in the extent to which they have integrated the results of their activities with proposed or existing procedures for the assurance of quality. All, however, have conceived their work as providing a framework within which more local standards and quality assurance procedures might be developed. The documents they have produced are thus of assistance chiefly at the 'set standards' step in the quality cycle.

Standards published by the College of Occupational Therapists, the Chartered Society of Physiotherapy, the College of Speech and Language Therapists, and the Regional Pharmaceutical Officers' Committee will be considered here.

College of Occupational Therapists Standards

Background and Scope

In 1989 the College of Occupational Therapists began publication of a series of documents entitled 'Standards, Policies and Proceedings' which were the results of quality assurance workshops initiated in 1986. Eleven such documents have now been produced four of which give standards for practice with different types of occupational therapy patient/consumer. The other seven documents state policy on a range of issues from private practice in occupational therapy to use of animals in therapy and professional negligence and litigation. They will not be dealt with here.

The standards documents are prefaced by comment that they are 'intended for occupational therapists as guidelines to assist them in the practice of their profession. They are intended to facilitate uniformity of treatment given, and not as standards of care for any particular location'. The standards are thus prescriptive but flexible and allow that the circumstances of provision of care may make a substantial difference to the standards which any individual therapist can attain.

Description

The four sets of standards refer to practice with consumers with physical disabilities; with consumers who are developmentally disabled or mentally handicapped; with consumers in their own homes; and in mental health. Each document has six sections which refer in turn to standards for referral, assessment, treatment planning, treatment implementation, discharge, and reassessment. They are thus standards for the process of care in each of the main settings of occupational therapy practice. The standards are mostly expressed at a high level of generality, e.g. under discharge planning it is suggested that 'consideration should be given to community resources and other environmental standards'; or on reassessment 'the occupational therapist should reassess the consumer at an appropriate time interval following discharge'. One or two, however, are more specific – thus under referral for consumers in their own homes the therapist is recommended to record the referral 'preferably no longer than five working days after receipt'.

These six sections are followed by two sections which are identical in each of the four documents. In the first of these the therapist is recommended to review quality including the outcomes of the services provided. If care is not satisfactory a number of possible procedures are indicated but not described. They include peer review, multidisciplinary discussion and quality circles. It is then suggested that remedial action should be undertaken and that care should be subsequently reappraised. The final section recommends staff performance reviews and concomitant continuing education and updating.

Commentary

College of Occupational Therapists (COT) standards are relatively recent and there is little published evidence of their local application and use. They seem to have been generally well received, however. They are at a high level of generality and specification of standards for particular situations would require further detailed work.

The standards were the result of consultative processes but the extent to which they reflect actual practice or relate to positive patient outcomes cannot be determined. The seventh section which comes closest to actual assurance of quality and action for improvement does very little to assist the initiator of local quality action.

COT standards are clearly designed for that profession only but other groups might find the general approach to setting and disseminating standards a useful first step in quality assurance.

Chartered Society of Physiotherapy Standards

Background and Scope

Like other professional bodies the Chartered Society of Physiotherapy (CSP) has always taken an interest in the establishment of standards for education and practice. A number of relevant documents have been published since the society was first awarded its charter in 1942. In 1989 it recognised the growing demand for a statement of good practice which encompassed all areas of professional activity and which provided a nationally relevant framework for quality assurance. A working party was set up with a membership drawn from practising physiotherapists and from physiotherapy educators and an extensive programme of consultation through workshops and conferences began. The work was subdivided into consultation on standards for assessment; for communication and teamwork; and for environment, health and safety. The resulting standards were finally produced in 1990. The chairman of the quality assurance working party comments in the foreword to the standards document that it is intended as a 'framework for standard setting' which 'can be used as a tool for local standard setting' (CSP, 1990). The standards document itself is published alongside a range of other brochures outlining guidelines for good practice in specific areas of physiotherapy practice. At present these include work with the elderly, acupuncture, paediatrics, obstetrics and gynaecology, neurology, and respiratory care. Other guideline documents may be added.

Description

The 'Standards of Physiotherapy Practice' document is divided into six main sections devoted to standards for communication and teamwork: documentation; assessment; informed consent; environment, health and safety; and quality assurance. It also includes an Appendix setting out the Society's Rules of Professional Conduct. Each section begins with a short statement of definition and is then subdivided into standards numbering from two to six in the various sections and 26 in total. Standards are short statements at a high level of generality. They are followed by a number of more specific criteria. Thus 'The patient is acknowledged and respected as an individual' is followed by a list of criteria including 'The patient is addressed by the name of his choice' and 'The patient is given the physiotherapist's undivided attention wherever possible'. In the Documentation section 'Clear, accurate, up-to-date records are maintained' is followed by such criteria as 'Writing is legible' and 'All attendances are dated and initialled'.

The quality assurance section of the document defines quality assurance as a 'systematic method of evaluating the quality and appropriateness of physiotherapy services' which 'offers a means of correcting identified weakness'. It thus lays equal stress on quality appraisal and quality improvement. Six standards and related criteria follow. They cover annual review of the appropriateness, applicability and equity of provision (including consumer satisfaction and complaints procedures); periodic audit and peer review of aspects of patient treatment; designated responsibility for quality assurance; documentation, reporting and feedback regarding implementation of quality action; use of quality assurance information in long-term service development; and occasional review of the quality assurance procedure itself.

Commentary

CSP standards are designed to be nationally relevant and to be a stimulus to the development of more specific local standards. While there is little published evidence of local applications the document seems to have been well received. Its more specific criteria would be easy to use as a basis of quality appraisal.

The standards were developed through consultation and it is thus not possible to determine the extent to which they actually reflect practice or relate to positive patient outcomes.

The document is designed for physiotherapists only but the general approach to specification of both general standards and more specific criteria through consultation could be adopted by other groups.

College of Speech and Language Therapists Standards

Background and Scope

In 1989 the College of Speech Therapists (as it was then called) embarked on an extensive process of consultation with members aimed at producing a description of good practice in speech therapy. The resulting document was designed to fulfil a dual role as a guidebook for practitioners and 'an encouragement to those responsible for both providing and commissioning services to work to achieve the quality standards described' (CSLT, 1991, p. 2). Almost uniquely in professional standard setting and quality assurance the document is specifically designed to be accessible not just to members of the profession but also to its 'customers'. Customers are taken to comprise three main groups, namely commissioning authorities (service 'purchasers' in the contexts of the NHS reforms and of private practice); consumers (individual clients and their representatives, colleagues in other professions); and members of the profession (managers, clinicians, educators, students). The text aims to inform each group of readers as follows (CSLT, 1991, p. 9):

- To inform the decisions taken by the commissioners of services in relation to the identification of need, formulating service agreements and securing high quality services.
- To inform the users of ... services as to the range of speech and language therapy provision and the model of care as consumers they can expect to receive.
- To inform all strands of the speech and language therapy profession of the range of potential provisions and the profession's consensus on the appropriate model of care for an individual receiving therapy. To provide an indication of the skill mix and resources required to deliver a service. To inform clinical and managerial practice.

The book's aim is thus provision of information and guidance rather than establishment of quality assurance procedures. Standards are highlighted at various points in each chapter but quality assurance and professional audit are taken to be separate activities and are not dealt with per se.

Description

Communicating Quality (as the standards book is called) is designed to cover the entire span of professional activity. The first chapter provides information on the role of the College and sets out the code of ethics and professional conduct to which all of its members subscribe. It also provides 'core' guidelines and standards thought to pertain with all clients in all settings. These relate to access, admission to service, criteria for acceptance for treatment, programmes of care, outcomes, and administration and liaison. Some of these standards and guidelines are very specific, e.g. 'If the referral relates to an inpatient the client will be seen within two working days'. Many others, however, are at a high level of generality. In this chapter as throughout the book standards and guidelines are presented together with standards distinguished by being printed in colour. No clear definition is given of the difference between 'guidelines' and 'standards' but it can be deduced that a statement is only accorded the status of a standard if it represents a clear consensus within the profession and is thus a requirement. Guideline statements seem often to include the word 'may' while standards statements more frequently include the word 'should'. Interestingly, the statement 'there will be ongoing evaluation of the effectiveness of the pro-gramme [of care]' is only presented as a guideline.

The next three chapters categorise professional practice according to *location* (e.g. acute hospitals, domiciliary settings, day care, mainstream schools, special schools), to *client and service groups* (e.g. clients suffering from cardiovascular accident, clients receiving ENT services), and to *presenting disorders* (e.g. adult aphasia, developmen-tal language disorder, dysfluency). It is recognised that this triple categorisation leads to overlap and repetition of guidelines and standards but it is suggested that different readers may wish to access the material by different routes in order to develop a 'composite model of care'.

Each section of the three chapters presents a brief description of the relevant provision and a statement on aims and principles of delivery. These are followed by a series of guidelines and standards with respect to referral, assessment, intervention, discharge, interface/liai-son with other professionals, skill mix, and resource requirements. Thus in the 'traumatic brain injury' client group *aims* are set out under the following broad headings:

- To promote functional communication.
- To provide a service to clients with a swallowing disorder.
- To advise and support relatives/carers and employers on helping and coping with the client's communication deficits.
- To work within an interdisciplinary approach.
- To provide a consistent, intensive, persistent yet flexible approach.
- To support, advise and actively involve the client's family at all stages in the rehabilitation process.

Under *referral* a single standard is set for this group of clients.

- Open referral will exist except in the acute stage of management or in the case of a client with a swallowing disorder where a medical referral will be required.

Under *assessment* eight sets of detailed guidelines are set out covering aspects of continuity of assessment; appropriate areas of assessment (divided into those for which the therapist has either shared or sole responsibility); complementary assessments; importance of pre trauma levels of function; the therapist's particular interest in dysphagia in eating and swallowing disorders; the importance of social background assessment; and the appropriate environment for assessment activities. No standards are set.

The *intervention* and *discharge* sections give similarly comprehensive guidelines and set specific standards for reporting interventions to other members of the rehabilitation team, for discussing them with the client's family, and for the completion of a discharge report.

Under *interface/liaison with other professionals* there is a comprehensive list of the various professionals and individuals in the client's community with whom liaison may be required. The *skill mix* section sets out tasks in which the therapist may be expected to engage and discusses the possible use of assistants. Finally, the *resources* section sets out general accommodation and materials needs.

Subsequent chapters are more contextual and include information and guidelines on the legal framework of Speech and Language Therapy, on professional development and continuing education, on professional networks, on private practice, and on desirable skill mix (i.e. the balance of provision between qualified therapists, assistants and volunteers). There is also a very brief chapter on record keeping (with no reference to the function of records in quality assurance) and a chapter on service management. The latter includes the main statement on quality assurance and professional audit. Thus the manager's role is said to encompass 'quality and effectiveness of service' including promotion of leadership and direction, provision of local standards, development of quality assurance initiatives, production of annual service reviews, developing and maintaining audit, and critical interpretation and analysis of service data. The chapter also contains a separate section on audit which is defined as the 'evaluation of clinical outcomes'. It is suggested that 'a range of mechanisms may be implemented in order to audit the quality of a service' and a number of examples are given including collection of statistics, caseload review, peer review, and staff appraisal. Multi-disciplinary audit is commended.

Commentary
The CSLT standards book is a comprehensive source of information and guidance for practitioners, their consumers and their managers. It consistently commends interprofessional liaison in both practice and quality monitoring.

There is no published evidence on the local use of the document. It sets out clear (if sometimes rather unspecific) guidelines and standards for very many aspects of practice and where they cannot be specified it often outlines a range of acceptable options. It is both broad and variable in its coverage (including very general guidelines on service planning but quite precise recommendations on the avoidance of dangerous household pets encountered on domiciliary visits). Apart from the introductory account of the consultative processes through which the document was compiled there is no indication of the extent to which the stated standards and guidelines have been shown to relate to positive patient outcomes. Given these considerations the document may be difficult to use as a basis for local standard setting.

The document does not offer much advice on the way in which standards could provide a framework for systematic quality assurance. Indeed the brief sections on quality and audit included in the management chapter reveal a number of significant confusions. Thus it is assumed that audit can only be applied to outcomes despite the longstanding acceptance of Donabedian's definition of quality in terms of structure, process and outcomes and despite the fact that much the largest part of the book is devoted to guidelines for structure and process aspects of quality. There is no reference at all to the fact that quality appraisal should lead to action for quality improvement or to the establishment and management of quality systems.

The document is designed to have general relevance for speech and language therapists, the various professional groups with whom they work, their managers and their consumers. It should provide considerable insight into the aims and activities of speech and language therapy for each of the associated groups. Its general approach to setting out comprehensive information for such groups could well be adopted by other professions.

Regional Pharmaceutical Officers Committee Standards

Background and Scope
The Regional Pharmaceutical Officers Committee is a committee set up to encourage exchange of information and liaison between the English Regional Health Authorities regarding pharmaceutical practice and provision in hospitals and community units. It is not a professional body although its members are by definition senior members of the profession and thus in close contact with the Royal Pharmaceutical Society of Great Britain and other relevant bodies. On the other hand, it is not altogether a management group since it is to one side of the executive system of general management now in place in the NHS.

The 1989 edition of the Committee's standards document was conceived as a response to 'changes in the objectives of, and pressures on the NHS' which have 'intensified the rate of change within the pharmaceutical service' (RPOC, 1989, p. 1). Increased utilisation of acute beds, earlier discharge into community care, and demographic change are each identified as potential threats to the standards of the pharmaceutical service. The document is thus designed to counteract such threats. Its objective is 'to provide a guide to the non-pharmacist on the facilities required and service expected from the pharmaceutical service in England'. It is thus not a specific response to quality assurance or audit initiatives in the NHS but it would clearly have a central place in any such response from the pharmacy profession. Similar documents are in the latter stages of preparation in other parts of the UK and also exist in Canada. The Committee acknowledge a particular debt to the Canadian Society of Hospital Pharmacists upon whose standards document their own production is based.

Description

The document has two main sections. The first sets out brief general objectives for the pharmacy service as a whole, for patient care, for support services, and for education. The second specifies standards relevant to each general objective. Each set of detailed and specific standards is preceded by an introductory statement at a higher level of generality.

The objectives and standards are designed to reflect all relevant professional activity and cover a wide variety of functions, services and client groups. Thus the objectives and standards for the service as a whole cover management; premises; staffing; procurement, stock control and distribution of medicines; safety factors; and the establishment of a utilisation review service, a local formulary, and a pharmacy/drug and therapeutics committee. Patient care objectives and standards cover the various types of provision (e.g. ward and clinical services, parenteral nutrition services, radiopharmacy). They are also specified for prescription monitoring, drug information, adverse reaction reporting, patient counselling, medication history advice, health education, and clinical trials. Support services objectives and standards cover manufacturing and assembly of medicines; the role of the pharmaceutical service in surgical dressings; and quality control and assurance of medicines and other products. Finally, education objectives and standards deal with continuing education for pharmacists and the role played by pharmacists in the education of other professionals.

In each section the standards set out are detailed, explicit, and notionally comprehensive. As might be expected in an area where potentially hazardous substances are being handled and used there is considerable reference to relevant preexisting legislation and good practice guidelines regarding distribution and storage of medicines, hygiene and safety.

As previously noted the standards document does not set out to provide particular advice on methods of appraising or ensuring the achievement of standards. Nonetheless, a number of sections include material which could be interpreted as so doing. Thus the section on utilisation review specifies the responsibilities of the Medicines Utilisation Review/Clinical Economy Pharmacist as including 'monitoring expenditure on medicines for clinical teams and individuals and reporting any changes in trends' and 'negotiating changes in prescribing practice with clinical teams to promote economic and cost effective prescribing'.

Monitoring standards are also set for inpatient prescriptions (e.g. for legibility, potential efficacy, dosage, potential interaction effects); administration (e.g. for appropriate duration, errors and omissions); and patient response to therapy. It is recommended that a monitoring schedule should be set up so that intensive care services are monitored daily or as required, acute ward services once daily, long stay wards once weekly, and long stay psychiatric or mental handicap wards once monthly. An explicit system is described for the monitoring, reporting, investigation and relevant subsequent prevention of adverse reactions to medicines.

The section on quality control and assurance of pharmaceutical products makes specific reference to BS 5750 and specifies the existence of a nominated quality controller who is responsible to the pharmacy manager for (among other things) 'the approval or rejection of all starting materials, processes and environments used and finished products produced within the pharmaceutical service'. The controller is also to be responsible for aspects of laboratory safety, relevant staff training and supervision, and carrying out investigational and developmental work.

Commentary

The document provides a clear, detailed, and explicit set of standards for all aspects of practice. Where standards lack specificity suggestions are often made for increasing it at local level. Thus the standards for the establishment of a stock distribution system make repeated reference to the need for local procedures agreed by pharmacists, nurses and other relevant personnel. Guidance on monitoring procedures is often limited but again, the standards themselves are sufficiently detailed to provide a practicable framework for setting such procedures up.

No detailed information is presented on the development of the standards included in the document but there is consistent reference to other sources including several government and professional working parties and reports. It is likely that the standards thus represent a broad level of consensus on good practice.

While the standards are designed specifically for pharmacists their comprehensive and detailed coverage of all aspects of practice, education and management may provide a useful example for other groups.

Professional Standards Systems Outside of the UK

As might be expected the US systems of accreditation and mandatory quality assurance for third party funding have led to professional standard setting activity. Thus the American Medical Association (AMA) has met with the Academic Medical Center Consortium and the RAND corporation to develop 'practice parameters' and 'appropriateness criteria' (Burkholder, 1990).

The AMA parameters are said to be acceptable approaches to the diagnosis, treatment and management of specified conditions based on the best available evidence and practice. They are designed to assist practitioners in decision making. They include *standards* which Burkholder defines as 'irrefutable principles'; *guidelines* which identify a range of acceptable management schemes; and *practice options* which outline alternatives in areas where there is still controversy. A wide range of procedures from coronary angiography and coronary bypass surgery to cholecystectomy, hip surgery and abdominal ultrasound are currently the subject of parameter development. Burkholder suggests that the AMA parameters will not only assist practitioner decision making but will be a useful input into hospital-wide quality assurance and into the review procedures of the various third party funders.

The American Nurses' Association first disseminated generic standards in 1973 (ANA, 1973a) and followed this up with standards for each of maternal/child health nursing, psychiatric/mental health nursing, community nursing, medical/surgical nursing and gerontological nursing (ANA, 1973b; c; d; 1974; 1976).

Even earlier in the field than the nurses were the American Physical Therapy Association who first produced a document establishing norms for minimally acceptable practice in 1970 (APTA, 1977). Throughout the 1970s and 1980s there was considerable emphasis in US physical therapy on the improvement of record keeping as a basis for quality assurance and of the development of retrospective records based audit procedures. Of particular importance was the widespread adoption of Weed's (1968) problem oriented medical record keeping system (POMR) (see p. 000 below). Current APTA activities include establishment of treatment norms based on observation of practice, and the development of outcome indicators (Davis, 1989).

The American Society of Hospital Pharmacists were also early in giving central guidance and developed a model quality assurance system in 1978 (Oakley and Bradham, 1983). This offers guidelines and model standards in nine areas of hospital pharmacy from drug information and poison control to staff development and education.

In Australia and New Zealand treatment guidelines and standards have been produced for a number of specialties and professions including psychiatry (Andrews, 1984; 1985), physiotherapy, occupational therapy, and speech and language therapy (Glendinning, 1981; Australian Council on Health Care Standards, 1990; 1991).

Comprehensive Review Systems

The systems in this category are all designed to be relatively free-standing systems which provide a framework for each stage of the quality cycle.

Some of the systems are entirely local in development and use. They have been published by practitioners in the hope that what has worked for them may work elsewhere. Others have been centrally endorsed by professional bodies who have not themselves set standards. These bodies either hope that general standards will eventually emerge from the 'bottom up' or take the view that quality appraisal and review can take place without preliminary articulation of explicit standards. In each case local procedures are thought more likely to lead to actual improvement in quality than standards or procedures imposed from the 'top down'.

The review systems presented in this category have been subdivided into those which include specified standards alongside procedures for appraisal and improvement; those which provide guidance on local standard *setting* rather than specified standards; and those which suggest that appraisal and improvement can be effected without engaging in preliminary specification of standards.

Systems Including Specified Standards alongside Procedures for Appraisal and Improvement

Actual publication of locally set standards is relatively rare since such standards are by definition specific to the setting for which they were devised. Some examples do exist, however, and the systems included here have all been published not just as a case study in quality assurance but as a system of potentially transferable standards. They are Demby et al.'s (1985) Sunset Park/Lutheran Medical Centre quality assurance system for practising dentists; the East Berkshire Health Authority Heatherwood Hospital Physiotherapy Department quality assurance system (EBHA, 1990); Miller's (1989) AMBUQUAL system for the evaluation of ambulatory care developed at the Methodist Hospital of Indiana, Indianapolis, Indiana; and Bradford and Flynn's (1988) ambulatory care infection control quality assurance monitoring system developed at the University of California Davis Medical Centre.

Sunset Park/Lutheran Medical Centre Quality Assurance System for Practising Dentists

Background and Scope
Demby et al. (1985) note that while several systems exist for the evaluation of US dental practice few of them are applicable in private community dental practices where in fact the bulk of dental treatment is provided. The Sunset Park/Lutheran system they describe was devised to be used in such settings; to deal with multiple parameters of care; and to both appraise and improve the quality of care. It is outcomes oriented and provides specific standards for several aspects of care. It was developed in a research setting but was always intended for use in private dental practices. It was published to encourage wider use.

Description
The Sunset Park/Lutheran system is based on a comprehensive Reviewer Manual consisting of an account of the background to the system and of its objectives; a selection of audit protocols with instructions for use, written definitions of criteria (standards) and relevant photographs where appropriate; and an annotated bibliography for each of the 24 clinical assessment criteria used in the audit process. The material is designed to be used by a qualified dentist other than the practitioners in the clinic concerned. There is provision for training of reviewers although standards and criteria are set out as explicitly as possible so as to minimise unreliability of judgement.

The review process has four parts as follows:

- Oral health status indicators.
- Dental record and radiographic assessment criteria.
- Clinical assessment criteria.
- Assessment of treatment.

Criteria are most explicit in the first of these and progressively less so as the review proceeds through the four stages. The review centres on inspection of individual records and physical examination of a sample of 20 patients for each practice. No indication is given of the way in which the patients should be selected for inclusion in the sample.

The oral health status indicators are extremely specific and are based on those devised by Axelsson and Linde (1978). They include measures of plaque, pocket depth and gingival bleeding. A caries index is also obtained for each patient examined. The second part of the audit consists of inspection of records for completeness and accuracy (the reviewer judges records as acceptable/unacceptable on the basis of clearly specified criteria) and similar acceptable/unacceptable assessment of radiographic procedures with respect to number, frequency and quality of image. In the third part of the review the patient's mouth is again inspected and carefully guided judgements are made with respect to the quality of restorative dentistry, endodontics and prosthodontics. Finally, the reviewer makes a more implicit (checklist guided) overall review of treatment covering completeness of diagnosis; integration of non-dental considerations (e.g. other medical conditions, lifestyle, and occupation); appropriateness of treatment; logical sequence of treatment; and patient satisfaction with treatment (standard questions are put to the patients at the end of their examination and they also complete a standard anonymised questionnaire).

Information from the review is available to practitioners and the various possible review authorities and it is assumed (although Demby et al. do not give detail) that this will lead to action for improvement.

Commentary

The Sunset Park Lutheran system is a comprehensive set of specific standards for use in US dentistry. Demby et al. report that it has been used extensively in various practice settings including solo and group practices, hospital services, community health centres and residency training programmes. It covers the range of community dental treatment with the possible exception of patient education and health promotion activities.

Demby et al. are clearer on the derivation of the more specific standards for treatment outcomes (e.g. the caries index) than they are on the derivation of the rather less specific standards for logical sequence of treatment and patient satisfaction. They do not give any indication of statistical examination of their measuring instruments' reliabilities but do stress the importance of reviewer training. There is a lack of detail on patient group/case sampling, and action for quality improvement.

The system is designed for a specific profession in the US context. Nonetheless, it is a good example of a system which tries to review all aspects of care in a given setting and to integrate the various appraisals in an overall assessment of quality. The general principles underlying its development and use could apply in other professional contexts.

Heatherwood Hospital Physiotherapy Department Quality Assurance System

Background and Scope
The Heatherwood Hospital Physiotherapy Department system (East Berkshire Health Authority, 1990) was devised by a local group of physiotherapists working 'at all levels in the profession' (p. 2) in conjunction with a 'user's group' comprising an orthopaedic consultant, the secretary of the local Community Health Council, two Assistant General Managers and two members of the working group of physiotherapists. Quality assurance is defined as 'the process of identifying, achieving and maintaining standards acceptable to modern working practice' and it is suggested that standards should be set 'at the highest level commensurate with effective use of resources'. Standards should also 'be measurable' and should be 'monitored at appropriate intervals'. Action for quality improvement is stressed and it is pointed out that responsibility for quality extends beyond the physiotherapy department. The system was designed primarily for local use but is published for adoption and adaptation in similar departments.

Description
The Heatherwood standards cover the following areas of physiotherapy practice.

- Availability of service.
- Quality of environment: patient facilities.
- Quality of environment: staff facilities.
- Efficiency of service.
- Effectiveness of service.
- Effectiveness and efficiency of methods of communication.
- Effectiveness and efficiency of methods of recording (clinical and non-clinical).

The standards booklet also includes a users' guide and appendices containing samples of the instruments used in appraising some of the more complex aspects of quality.

Each standards area section sets out a number of relevant standards. Thus the standards for 'availability' specify who may refer inpatients and outpatients, describe categories of patients who may self-refer, and place precise limits on the length of time different groups should have to wait for an initial appointment. They also include rather less specific policy statements on giving patients convenient appointment times, on service outside normal working hours, on the accessibility of the department to patients with mobility problems, and on signposting.

The 'efficiency of service' section covers standards for waiting times and staff deployment, use of staff and other resources, and the logic and clarity of working systems. The 'effectiveness' section sets three standards referring to professional competence, user satisfaction and percentage of unexpected 'returnees'. In each of these sections there is a mix of very precise standards (e.g. 'patients should not be kept waiting for more than five minutes' and 'in normal circumstances a patient should always be treated by the same physiotherapist') and broad policy statements (e.g. 'normal working practice will include in service training').

The standards for quality of the patient environment include statements on cleanliness, tidiness, temperature control, hygiene, health and safety legislation, and privacy. They also include a general statement on professional helpfulness and politeness. Standards for the staff environment cover facilities in changing and relaxation areas, in office areas, and in working areas and cubicles. They also include a detailed description of the induction programme which each new member of staff should experience and brief but comprehensive statements on entitlements to in-service training and on the operation of staff appraisal procedures.

Communication standards deal with communication between professionals including communication with consultants and other non-physiotherapy groups. They are brief policy statements and are relatively unspecific.

Records standards are somewhat more precise. They recommend clarity, conciseness, legibility and comprehensiveness and specify the lengths of time for which records must be kept after patient discharge.

Each set of standards is followed by a detailed description of the 'working practices' at Heatherwood which seem to the authors of the standards to be significant in their achievement. Thus the 'availability' section describes the Heatherwood method for screening referrals and coding them for urgency, the method of contacting referred patients, the timing of appointments and a note to the effect that out of hours appointments can only be requested by specified individuals.

'Working practices' are then followed by suggested methods for monitoring standards. Thus evidence is collected on the achievement of availability standards by periodic review of referrals, patient contacts, inappropriate requests for out of hours appointments and physical access. Convenience of appointments and adequacy of signposting are assessed by means of a simple patient satisfaction survey details of which are given in the appendix. Achievement of other standards is monitored by a similar mixture of peer review and satisfaction surveys for patients, for medical and dental practitioners referring to the department and for non-physiotherapist members of the multi-professional team. An instrument is also included which is designed to assess the effectiveness of the service by examining the extent to which prognoses for individual patients are matched by treatment outcomes at the point of discharge. An example of each of these instruments is included in the appendices.

Commentary

The Heatherwood system is clearly set out and should be easy to use. It gives equal stress to each stage of the quality cycle.

The system reflects practice at Heatherwood but is published in the expectation that it will be acceptable to most (physiotherapy) departments, with any additions necessary to cover special circumstances. Each of the standards is accompanied by guidelines on 'working practices' and 'monitoring' and it is suggested that users outside of the Heatherwood setting may adjust these to suit their own circumstances. The Heatherwood standards have been generated in one setting only but as they are set at a fairly high level of generality they should transfer to other settings without undue difficulty. The areas covered are not dissimilar to those set out by the Chartered Society of Physiotherapy (see p. 71 above) and may therefore represent a generally acceptable analysis of physiotherapy practice. The additional detail on working practices and monitoring should be helpful to other groups setting standards within either framework.

No detail is given on the reliability or validity of the various measuring instruments but they are extremely simple and are designed to provide feedback on specified aspects of provision and to identify problems rather than to provide a quantitative basis for comparison with other departments. The method of assessing effectiveness by comparing prognoses with outcomes is ingenious although given that the reviews are all internal to the department it could possibly lead to trimming of prognoses to fit past outcomes rather than genuine estimation of what should be achievable with a given patient.

AMBUQUAL

Background and Scope

AMBUQUAL is a system developed at Methodist Hospital of Indiana (Benson and Miller, 1989) for quality assurance activities in ambulatory care (loosely equivalent to UK community care but often including outpatient services). It is based on a set of standards developed and weighted through consultation with ambulatory care reviewers from the JCAHO. It covers ten parameters of care.

While weighted predetermined standards are the nub of the AMBUQUAL system it provides assistance in the entire process of quality appraisal, incorporating instruments for data collection and measurement and a computer assisted methodology for scoring quality at various levels leading ultimately to a single number 'programme quality index' (PQI) score. Suggestions are also made for using its results in improving quality.

AMBUQUAL is multi-professional and can be used by different professional mixes or by single professions. All 10 parameters can be appraised at once but it is also possible to examine only one or two. The system can be used for external review or for quality assurance internal to a given health care organisation.

Description
The 10 parameters of care appraised in AMBUQUAL are as follows:

- Provider staff performance.
- Support staff performance.
- Continuity of care.
- Medical records system.
- Patient risk minimisation.
- Patient satisfaction.
- Patient compliance.
- Accessibility.
- Appropriateness of service.
- Cost of service.

Each of the ten parameters indicated above is divided into four 'aspects of care'. Thus patient compliance is subdivided into 'participation in health care plan development', 'understanding of health care plan', 'compliance with health care plan', and 'trust in health care providers'. Each of these four aspects of care have separate standards to be appraised by specified structure, process and outcome indicators and data sources. Thus 'compliance with health care plan' leads on to the standard 'patients state that they complied with their most recent treatment plan'. Its related data source is part of a patient satisfaction survey in which patients are asked to grade themselves for (a) doing what the doctor or nurse suggested, (b) taking their medicine as directed, (c) coming back when told. Data is collected for each of the various standards from a system of patient questionnaires, provider performance audits, procedure audits and other specified sources. Some data is objective (e.g. percentage compliance with a precise standard for medical recording such as presence of a particular kind of entry) and other data is based on reviewer judgement. Some standards and data sources are said to be site specific but others are thought to be transferable to other settings and are designated 'fundamental'.

Scores from the various data sources are entered on the computer which then generates scores (according to the predetermined weightings of importance) from zero to 100 at the standard, aspect, parameter, and PQI levels. It is suggested that methods of case selection and thresholds for taking action for quality improvement should be determined by each group or organisation deciding to use AMBUQUAL. The system thus identifies elements of quality care and weights them for relative importance but leaves precise determination of standards below which quality should not be allowed to fall to local groups. Recommendations are made as to the quality appraisal and action tasks for which various people in a typical ambulatory care organisation might take responsibility.

Commentary
AMBUQUAL is a local standards system relying on external expert judgement in the determination and weighting of its standards. The validity of these standards in the original or other settings has not been systematically established although the authors of the system refer to its successful use in a range of settings as 'supporting the validity of AMBUQUAL as an ambulatory QA system' (Miller, 1989). The system has been used in private group practices, in health maintenance organisations, in hospital based ambulatory centres, in community health centres, and in a regional cancer centre. It has also been used successfully by several centres going through review by the JCAHO (Miller, 1989).

While AMBUQUAL is designed for use in the context of US ambulatory care several aspects of the system could transfer to other professions and settings. Its multi-professionality is of particular importance in the community care context.

Davis Medical Centre Ambulatory Care Infection Control Quality Assurance Monitoring System

Background and Scope
The Davis Medical Centre Ambulatory Care Infection Control System (Bradford and Flynn, 1988) was developed as a system of quality assurance for use in the 143 outpatient clinics of the University of California Medical Centre in Sacramento, California. The clinics handle almost a quarter of a million patient visits per annum. The system is a preventive system designed to minimise the occurrence of nosocomial infections rather than to monitor their rate of occurrence as several other quality assurance systems do. It is based on review visits to each of the clinics where predetermined standards are appraised. Personnel participating in the reviews include the hospital epidemiologist, infection control practitioners, and the head nurse and physician directors of the clinics being reviewed.

Description

Pre-established monitoring standards are used in each clinic. Some are generic and are used in all reviews and some are specific to the clinics being reviewed. The standards are simple statements of conditions which must obtain (i.e. the goal is 100% compliance) for the prevention of infection. Standards were determined by expert judgement and reference to literature and according to Bradford and Flynn 'are basic concepts of infection control that are proved and have stood the test of time'.

Generic standards cover environmental surveillance, disposal of multidose vials, disposal of used needles, disinfection of flexible scopes, use of disposable equipment when indicated, hand washing routines, aseptic techniques, adherence to isolation categories, and reporting of communicable diseases. Each standard has a list of associated criteria. Thus the overall standard for environmental surveillance is 'procedure and treatment rooms are clean' and this leads on to seven associated criteria, e.g. 'disinfectant is available for use', 'tables are cleaned between each patient' and so on. Similar sets of standards and associated criteria are included in the clinic specific monitoring tools.

Appraisal of the achievement of criteria and standards is carried out by a mixture of interview with relevant staff, direct observation of practice, and chart review. Reviewers rate compliance with the criteria on a simple percentage basis for the episodes of care reviewed. Percentage scores for each standard are computed and an overall score is obtained by averaging across the number of relevant standards.

Clinic managers are responsible for remediation of identified problems and any that cannot be remedied within three months are referred to a Quality of Care Committee which operates as a problem solving resource and as a transmission channel for problems which can only be resolved elsewhere in the hospital system. The entire review process is repeated at three-monthly intervals and data from each review is accumulated.

Commentary

The Davis Medical Centre system is a clear simple system which could readily be adopted elsewhere.

Bradford and Flynn (1988) report its successful use in 20 of the Davis clinics during 1985 and 1986. No problems were identified in two of the clinics and a total of 11 were reported across the others. They included reuse of one time use items of equipment, reduced soaking times in cold sterilisation procedures, inadequate environmental cleaning, and an inadequate infectious waste disposal plan. Ten of the 11 problems had been resolved at a three-month follow up and the eleventh (which was likely to require structural alterations to the building) had been passed on to the Quality of Care Committee. The system was thus effectively spotting problems and engendering action for quality improvement.

The standards upon which the system is based are clearly derived from the literature on good infection control practice and Bradford and Flynn claim that they are generally acceptable. Their measurement relies on very simple observation, recording and counting and is thus likely to be reliable.

The system is clearly set out and should be easy to use in any setting where infection control is important.

Systems Giving Procedures for Local Standard Setting, Appraisal and Improvement

Many professional bodies have specified standards and guidelines for practice which are taken to apply in all of the settings where the relevant professionals work. These standards are at a high level of generality and several professional bodies suggest that their central standards should be used as a framework for more local exercises in specific standard setting. The local and specific should thus grow out of the central and more general.

Some professional bodies, however, adopt the opposite strategy. They provide guidelines for a process of local standard setting on the assumption that at some later date general standards may grow from the local and specific. The examples to be discussed here are the Royal College of Nursing's Dynamic Standard Setting System (DySSSy) (RCN, 1990); and the American Occupational Therapy Association's Quality Assurance Monitoring System (Joe and Ostrow, 1987).

DySSSy

Background and Scope

The Royal College of Nursing first established a 'Standards of Care' project in 1965. The project has now grown into a major programme of research, development and education (Kitson, 1986; 1990) culminating in the recent publication of DySSSy (RCN, 1990). DySSSy is a system for local standard setting and quality assurance which is typically carried out at ward level. It was developed from earlier work carried out by nurses in the West Berkshire Health Authority (Kitson and Kendall, 1986). DySSSy can be used in any area of nursing and lays particular emphasis on local relevance and specificity. It assumes communication of the results of appraisal of standards to quality assurance coordinating groups at higher organisational levels and possibly to other similar wards. The RCN have invested heavily in encouraging use of DySSSy and a UK wide network of users' groups and training activities has emerged known as the Quality Assurance Network (QUAN).

Description

DySSSy is explicitly based on a cyclical approach to quality assurance reminiscent of the American Nurses' Association's model of quality assurance (ANA 1982; Lang and Clinton, 1984). The DySSSy cycle is divided into three phases characterised as describing, measuring, and taking action. The phases are subdivided to give twelve steps in all. They are as follows:

- Describing
  - select topic for quality improvement;
  - identify care group;
  - identify criteria (structure, process, outcome);
  - agree standard.
- Measuring
  - refine criteria;
  - select or construct measurement tool;
  - collect data;
  - evaluate results.
- Taking action
  - consider course of action;
  - plan action;
  - take action;
  - reevaluate results.

Guidance is given on setting dates for reappraisal and for reviewing individual standards so the system assumes repeated progress through the three phases. While DySSSy is clearly a comprehensive review system giving guidance on each stage of the quality assurance cycle its main emphasis is on the setting of standards and criteria.

In many systems standards are broad statements subsuming a number of more specific criteria statements but in DySSSy criteria are statements of intent which lack quantification while standards are statements which include some notion of a quantitative threshold below which quality would be deemed unacceptable. It is suggested that once criteria and then standards have been set they should be rescrutinised to ensure that they are relevant, understandable, measurable, behavioural (where appropriate), and achievable in local circumstances.

Sample pro formas are given showing how each standard statement can lead to a listing of more specific standards for structure, process and outcome. The pro formas also suggest that standards should be ratified by some coordinating or senior person and that clear dates should be specified for reappraisal (i.e. comparing standards with practice on a further occasion) and review (i.e. reconsidering the appropriateness and value of the standard).

Rather less guidance is given on the selection or construction of appropriate measuring instruments. However, since many of the exemplified standards are very simple all that would be necessary would be direct observation and yes/no/not applicable judgement. Examples are also given of pro formas which permit calculation of compliance rates for the various standards. Some limited guidance is given on determining action for quality improvement.

DySSSy is very sensitive to the importance of group dynamics in ensuring the success of quality assurance activities. A number of suggestions are therefore made as to techniques for arriving at consensus. Specifically, both 'brainstorming' (Osborn, 1957) and 'nominal group' techniques (Delbecq and Van de Ven, 1971) are recommended (see Chapter 5, p. 159 and 162 for details of these techniques). Suggestions are also made regarding group membership. These are designed to ensure the smooth development of standards which are both appraisable and likely to lead to viable plans for quality improvement. The suggestions include the use of 'facilitators' who are people who have had previous experience with DySSSy and who are particularly skilled in group leadership.

Commentary

DySSSy is simple to use and has had very wide take up in the UK. It has been extensively used in the range of hospital nursing settings and variants have been derived for use in community nursing (Poulton, 1990). Its use of the terms 'criteria' and 'standards' has been criticised as confusing (Kemp and Richardson, 1990). While DySSSy places great emphasis on the measurability of standards it gives little guidance on how this might be effected. It is tempting to think that the complexities of health care outcomes and indeed processes have been avoided by always encouraging the setting of very simple standards. Kemp and Richardson (1990) also suggest that insistence on standard setting for every ward may be wasteful of time and labour. It can be countered, however, that this ground level involvement may be an effective way of creating a 'quality culture'.

As it presently exists DySSSy takes little or no notice of the existence of other professional groups but the QUAN network are adapting it for use in multiprofessional teams. Since DySSSy is free of pre specified standards in theory at least it is eminently suitable for adoption by other professions.

The American Occupational Therapy Association's (AOTA's) Quality Assurance Monitoring System

Background and Scope

The AOTA's Quality Assurance Monitoring Manual (Joe and Ostrow, 1987) was designed to help occupational therapy departments to design quality assurance monitoring procedures which would meet with the requirements of the JCAH (now JCAHO). It offers what are described as the 'basic building blocks of a system ... that has been field tested by occupational therapists who are experts in quality assurance'. It is stressed that the models and examples used are only one way of meeting JCAH requirements. While the system is primarily for use at departmental level it is recognised that it may form part of a larger system of hospital or community-wide quality assurance.

Description

The system comprises five basic steps which are as follows:

- Identify overall indicators of care and select relevant measures and criteria; set standards.
- Collect data and if standards are being met report it.
- Determine cause of problem and plan remedial action.
- Implement remedial action.
- Measure again to see if problem has been solved.

The system thus deals with each stage in the quality assurance cycle although the major emphasis is on the process of local standard setting. Indicators are related to the overall objectives of the facility or department such as assisting patients to cope with the activities of daily living (ADL) or to return to employment. Indicators are specified and then broken down into precise, concrete measurable criteria. Thus where the indicator is 'timely intake evaluation' the measure would be 'time between admission and evaluation', it would be applied to 'all patients', and the criterion might be '95% of all patients will have evaluation performed within two days of admission'. Where the indicator is 'increased level of self care for acute care patients' the measure might be 'functional level before and after five consecutive treatments', it would be applied to acute care patients for whom improved function is a treatment goal, and the criterion might be '85% will move up one level of function on ADL scale in one area of self-care'. Indicators are thus general statements, measures are practically available data and criteria are desirable but achievable levels of success. It is recommended that all staff should be involved in the establishment of criteria and that consensus should be achieved. It is also suggested that patients might be involved at this stage. Indicators selected should reflect aspects of care which are high-risk and problem prone and which demonstrate the routine quality of care (the system acknowledges a debt to Williamson's 'health accounting' (Williamson, 1978; 1988)).

It is recommended that criteria should as far as possible reflect data that are already being collected although not all routinely collected data need play a part in the quality assurance exercise. Aspects of structure (including costs) should be monitored along with process and outcome criteria although it is stressed that the most important criteria are outcome criteria. Compliance rates (e.g. 95% of patients in the first example given above) should also be set for each criterion. Records should be kept which give dates and results of each review, indicate the individuals responsible for the review and for any identified remedial action, and give dates for completion of remedial action and for the next review.

Guidance is given on sampling of cases and topics and the manual ends with a series of detailed examples of quality assurance monitoring for stroke patients, patients with physical disabilities, and mental health patients. Sample indicators and criteria and pro formas for recording review information are given in each case.

Commentary

The AOTA system is designed for use in the context of JCAHO accreditation of occupational therapy departments but could obviously be transferred to other settings and professions. The guidance given in the manual is detailed and clearly set out. More detail on techniques for consensus development and on finding or designing valid measurement techniques might have been helpful.

The system has had substantial take up in US occupational therapy and could readily transfer to UK and other contexts. To date there is no published evidence of such transfer.

Systems Giving Procedures for Local Review without Preliminary Standard Setting

Much early health care quality assurance consisted of relevant 'experts' making judgements about quality of care or, typically, quality of facilities in settings where they were not themselves professionally involved. Thus the inspection and accreditation procedures which the professional bodies employed in determining the suitability of wards or hospitals for training were based on the knowledge and experience of 'expert' individuals. They were taken to have internalised standards which they could apply and use without any need to articulate them. No doubt members of these groups discussed the judgements they made but the only requirement was that they should be able to *recognise* quality. They did not need to define or describe it. Donabedian (1985) and other authors refer to systems which rely on the unarticulated judgements of expert reviewers as systems of 'implicit' review.

An early study using implicit review was carried out by Peterson et al. (1956) who assessed quality in a group of general practices in North Carolina. Trained visitors undertook direct observation of doctor–patient transactions and consultations. Using their own implicit standards they arrived at judgements about care. Very similar procedures are currently employed in the Royal College of General Practitioners (1985b) 'What Sort of Doctor?' initiative. In this scheme GPs visit each other's practices on a voluntary and reciprocal basis. Visitors have guidelines in which it is suggested that they engage in observation and discussion; view videotaped consultations; and inspect medical records. They are also recommended to bear professional values, accessibility, clinical competence and communication skills in mind. No more specific standards are suggested in these areas and they are expected to make their own minds up about appropriate levels of quality.

In hospital settings most of the traditional mortality review committees and many of the more recent medical audit committees review cases on a similar basis of internalised practitioner knowledge of what constitutes good care. Explicit data may be available regarding the incidence of particular events but the judgements made about actual standards or appropriate levels of quality remain unarticulated. Even in the more systematic hospital quality assurance procedures of the US cases selected from records on the basis of explicit criteria (e.g. all cases of post operative death) are often reviewed on the basis of professional judgement without explicit previously determined standards.

Explicit standards and criteria have the obvious advantage of reliability. If they are properly designed they should be usable by different judges on different occasions to produce the same result when applied to the same episode of care. They also facilitate comparison between settings and over time. They are, however, both difficult and time consuming to construct and may be open to the charge of having gained specificity by having lost relevance. Major advantages of review without explicit standard setting are that it can take place immediately once reviewers are assembled and that it can take account of variation in the detail of cases or patients without going through a laborious process of standard modification. It is also perceived by professionals as respecting the uniqueness of their expertise and as being more likely to maintain confidentiality. Its disadvantages are possible bias or lack of experience among reviewers and lack of comparability between judgements, the precise basis of which is never open to scrutiny.

As noted above many formal and informal medical audit groups operate in this way without stated criteria. Their procedures are less often written up than those of more explicit standard setting groups. Two examples have been chosen for inclusion here. One is Group Peer Review as reported from UK general practice and the other is the Medical Audit Committee (MAC) system reported from the San Diego (California) Regional Trauma System (Shackford et al., 1987).

General Practice Group Peer Review

Background and Scope
The Royal College of General Practitioners first launched its quality initiative in 1983 (RCGP, 1983) and since then UK general practitioners have been involved in a wide range of pilot activities (Hughes and Humphrey, 1990; Irvine, 1990a; b). Among these are a number of schemes based on the idea that practitioners from a number of practices getting together to discuss the quality of their care will in itself lead to its improvement. Some such groups are based on existing mandatory meetings (e.g. those organised periodically by postgraduate education committees) and some are set up specifically with a view to involvement in quality assurance. They are often known as peer review groups.

In theory a peer group is a group of individuals who have common backgrounds and interests and whose status is perceived by each of them to be equivalent. The theory behind all forms of peer review is that sharing confidential or potentially threatening information with people perceived to be like oneself is more likely to lead to full disclosure, creative problem solving, and perceptions of social support than is sharing such information with people perceived to be superior or more powerful.

Description
GP peer review groups vary in their composition. Many are groups of practitioners from local or regional practices but others involve non-medical members of the primary care team employed by or attached to the various practices (Pendleton et al., 1986; Hughes and Humphrey, 1990). Some groups also involve outsiders as facilitators of discussion and review or as advisors on particular topics such as referral patterns or newly developed management information systems.

Topics discussed by groups can include all aspects of individual care and service organisation and management. Routinely available statistics such as the results of practice activity analyses (Crombie and Fleming, 1988) or Family Practitioner Service (FPS) indicators (HMSO, 1990c) can form the basis of discussions as can presentation of individual cases, response to patient satisfaction surveys or explorations of locally detected difficulties. Any of these may reflect events in several practices or events specific to one. The distinction to be made between these kinds of review and quality assurance based on more explicit standards is that as Irvine (1990a) puts it they 'have been designed basically to answer the question "What happened?" rather than "Did we do what we said we would?"'. In other words they do not refer to predetermined standards but to implicit standards thought to have been internalised in the training and experience of participants.

These standards may be articulated explicitly during discussion but they are rarely recorded or made available beyond the membership of the group.

Commentary

Since the prescription of medical audit in community care within the recent NHS reforms general practice peer review groups (and other quality related activities) have proliferated. The procedures are simple and could easily extend to other professional groups.

There is evidence to suggest that review of general practice cases using implicit standards judges treatment to be of higher quality than does review of the same cases using explicit predetermined standards (Slater, 1989). It may be, therefore, that quality assurance based on implicit peer review leads to comfort and complacency rather than disinterested scrutiny and action for improvement. There is a lack of evidence about the extent to which such review actually changes the effectiveness of practice. Freeling and Burton (1986) suggest that groups tend to keep moving on to new topics and to resist the iterative collection of data which would allow them to monitor improvement. On the other hand, that does not mean that such improvements did not take place. There is a growing body of evidence to suggest that at least attitudes change. Thus Hull (1984) and Grol et al. (1988) report diminution in perceptions of threat, greater openness to self-analysis and greater understanding of group processes. They suggest these might transfer to other working groups. On the negative side there is at least some evidence that change in both attitudes and actual care may be a function of the novelty of the procedure and therefore may be short-lived (Harris et al., 1985; Grol et al., 1988).

San Diego Medical Audit Committee (MAC)

Background and Scope

While the San Diego MAC system (Shackford et al., 1987) operates within the US system of care with its more extensive and more systematic quality assurance procedures it is similar to medical audit currently operating and recommended for extension in UK hospitals (HMSO, 1990a; b; Shaw, 1990). It is in use in a regional system for trauma care consisting of five adult trauma centres and one paediatric centre. The system serves a population of just over two million and anticipates a throughput of some 2500 cases per annum. While MAC is tailor made for that setting its basic characteristics are not dissimilar to systems in use in other areas or in other specialties. Thus there are several levels of scrutiny and some cases are reviewed more thoroughly than others; and while judgements are substantially based on implicit standards they are made within guidelines and are assisted by systematically collected data.

Description
MAC is based on a registry of trauma care which is common to all centres involved. It collates data about patients at five stages of care namely, pre-hospital, on admission, on operation, during intensive care, and at death or discharge. Admission data for example includes information on date and time of admission, mode of arrival, time and nature of consultations, treatment, laboratory tests, radiology (ordered and results), admission diagnosis, response to treatment, and final disposition (death, discharge to community, discharge to other specified facility). The registry is computerised and data are entered at the admission and discharge points. A 'trauma score' is entered at admission and an 'injury severity score' at discharge.

The audit process begins when the trauma nurse coordinator at each centre reviews the register details for all patients for completeness, accuracy and the presence of delays in treatment (explicit standards have been set for this – trauma surgeons should arrive in less than five minutes and consultants in less than 30). All cases are then reviewed by the centre's trauma director who uses his own implicit standards to prepare a report commenting on appropriateness of diagnostic procedures, timeliness of care, appropriateness of treatment, complications, morbidity, and length of stay in the centre. The director summarises deficiencies noted and steps taken to correct them and writes a short narrative comment on all deaths, major complications, and patients with an injury severity score above a set threshold. Morbidity is classified (within guidelines which clarify the classification terms) as due to delay in diagnosis, error in diagnosis, error in technique, error in judgement or patient disease. Mortality classification is also carried out within guidelines and deaths are said to be either nonpreventable, potentially salvageable or frankly preventable. Mortality guidelines both clarify terms and indicate appropriate sources of documented evidence to be used in making the classification.

The full MAC committee is responsible for audit of all trauma cases in the region and has representatives from the San Diego County Emergency Services Division, the County Coroner's Office, and multiprofessional groups from both trauma centre hospitals and non-trauma centre hospitals. The committee receives summary reports from all the trauma directors on all of the patients but sets up subcommittees to review them (again using implicit standards) and to tabulate complications, delays and deaths (it also receives autopsy reports of all trauma patients dying in non-trauma hospitals). If there is any disagreement or if there are particular problems the cases are passed on to the full committee and the responsible trauma director is informed that the case is about to be presented. Instances of particularly high quality care are also selected for presentation and trauma directors are thus given positive as well as negative feedback.

The full committee meeting (monthly) is identical to traditional surgical morbidity and mortality meetings and involves formal presentation of the cases and opportunity for question and discussion. Minutes are kept and forwarded to county level. Trend data is collated and may be passed to the county if this is required. The county may also request an on-site visit if a hospital has repetitive problems. For any given case the process takes a maximum of six weeks from patient discharge to inclusion of data in trend analysis.

Commentary

Historically autopsy has been the main method of quality assurance in trauma care. The method has been criticised because it is singularly retrospective and focused exclusively upon negative instances; because the available information is restricted; and because it commonly does not involve physicians other than pathologists and surgeons (or for that matter nurses and rehabilitation professionals) (Mosberg, 1980; Donald and Collie, 1981). MAC is concurrent, gathers data at various stages in care and is multi-disciplinary. It also refers specifically to good practice as well as bad.

Shackford et al. report on the results of MAC after its first two years of operation and almost 8000 patients. They report the identification and attempted remediation of a number of specific problems. These include inappropriate categorisation or 'mistriage' of a proportion of patients who should have been sent to trauma centre hospitals but were not; a significantly higher proportion of preventable deaths at non-trauma hospitals; and errors in judgement at trauma hospitals resulting in unnecessary treatments. On the other hand, the system identified positive features including general smoothness in communication and lack of delay, and an overall low rate of morbidity. Setting the system up, devising recording protocols and reporting guidelines was costly in time and personnel. Expenditure on computer equipment and software and other supplies was also involved but initial costs were diminishing as expertise increased and various set-up problems were ironed out.

MAC thus seems to have been successful in its own context and could probably transfer to others. It guides judgement of quality but does not predetermine it and both gathers trend data systematically and deals with the detail of individual cases. On the other hand, the extent to which it retains cases in the system through several stages of screening probably renders it more expensive than systems based on smaller samples of cases.

Case Selection Techniques

Questions of sampling arise whenever measurement for the appraisal of standards is undertaken (see Chapter 5, p. 174 for a more general discussion of sampling). They are particularly important when little preliminary selection of quality problem or patient group has taken place and the purpose of the exercise is review of overall quality of care across a large and varied group of practitioners and patients.

Most techniques for selection of cases for review have their origins in the US system of hospital-wide quality assurance and accreditation. In such systems the initial selection of cases for review is usually on the basis of retrospective screening of hospital records. The screening is often carried out by quality personnel whose background is in records or nursing. Subsequent review is generally carried out by professionals competent in the relevant areas of care but usually not those who were responsible for the care in question. Professionals' future employment or remuneration may be affected by the review results so selection of cases is of real significance. The criteria for selection must be at once simple enough to be used by individuals of limited specialist knowledge and yet sufficiently sophisticated to select cases which are representative of the population and validly indicative of the overall quality of care.

The simplest method of all is to draw a random sample of all patients receiving care. There are two important difficulties associated with that approach however. One is that departments or physicians with large throughputs will be reviewed much more frequently than those with small throughputs. The other is that given that most care is of average, that is reasonable quality very good or (perhaps more significantly) very poor cases may go quite unreviewed and thus undetected. Many of the original US systems of criteria for selecting cases from records in fact focused exclusively on instances of poor quality. The screening procedure consisted of quality personnel checking records against a long list of positive care criteria (e.g. discharge advice should have been recorded for each patient; appropriate laboratory tests should have been undertaken). Criteria could have been determined by local practitioners, by 'experts' brought in as consultants or by some outside professional or third party organisation. Each audited case record had to meet each criterion to receive an adequate quality of care rating and to escape review. Cases selected for review tended to include those where records were incomplete and those where care was in some way unusual. Lists of criteria were often long and time consuming to develop and use. Given the wide variations among patients many criteria did not apply equally to all cases and many records were selected in which subsequent review showed care to have been perfectly adequate. Even the development of different lists for narrowly defined subsets of patients failed to overcome the problem and selection continued to produce both false positives (i.e. sound quality selected for review) and false negatives (i.e. poor quality not selected for review). Three specific techniques have been developed to counter these difficulties. They are *occurrence screening, criteria mapping* and the *self-adapting focused review system (SAFRS)*

Occurrence Screening

Background and Scope
This method of identifying instances of poor care which merit subsequent review begins with a list of negative indices reflecting adverse patient events or outcomes. Sometimes referred to as *sentinel health events* they are based on the assumption that 'identification of the reasons for the *aeroplane crashes* in health is far simpler, more definitive, and less costly in time, money and personnel than the global approach of observing entire populations' (Rutstein et al., 1976, p. 583). The initial screening personnel are operating not from a list of things that should happen and identifying variations from that but rather from a list of things which should not happen and identifying instances of that. A large number of such lists of negative criteria or 'occurrence screens' are available for a range of medical conditions and care settings (Craddick, 1987). Hartmann et al. (1990) report an application developed specifically for quality assurance in nursing. The occurrences can be outcomes, e.g. unnecessary death or complications during or after treatment or aspects of process, e.g. practitioner error, system delay or confusion, or equipment failure.

Description
Specific applications vary in detail but the following reflects general practice. It is closest to the Hartmann et al. (1990) system.

First, screening criteria are developed. They may be taken from published lists or in the US system from lists mandated by various third party regulatory/funding bodies, or may be developed from 'expert judgement' which may be internal or external to the particular care setting. A case is then identified from records which instances one (or more) of the negative criteria. The record of the case is then scrutinised by a first level reviewer who is usually an individual professional with knowledge of the care area. This reviewer looks for care issues relevant to practitioner error (e.g. failure to follow orders, failure to carry out procedures, inadequate documentation, inadequate safety precautions); system deficiencies (e.g. delays in communication, inappropriate referrals, inadequate availability of staff or services); or equipment difficulties (e.g. malfunction, unavailability, or inappropriateness). Depending on the issues identified the reviewer passes the case to an appropriate second level review group (if no issues are identified the case is simply filed as a non-review). The second level review group analyses the case, rates it for practitioner quality of care and for severity of outcome. It either files the data if both ratings are above a predetermined threshold or recommends remedial action. If action has been recommended the case is passed to a third level reviewer who is generally a senior clinician in the relevant area. The third level reviewer is responsible for initiating action.

Commentary
Occurrence screening is in wide use in US quality assurance. Its value as a way of pinpointing poor quality depends on the validity of the initial criteria and on the reliability and validity of the judgements made in identifying issues and rating practitioner quality and outcome severity. Hannan et al. (1989) using a statistical model to control for a range of patient and hospital variables, applied occurrence screening based on criteria developed by 'expert judges' to cases involving death in hospital. The number of cases subsequently regarded as having been genuine instances of poor quality care was significantly greater than the number which were so regarded in a sample of cases selected at random, that is without the criteria. The study was based on a total sample of over 8000 cases.

Occurrence screening thus seems to be successful in pinpointing instances of poor care. Its value as a selector of cases for quality review is more debatable. First, it is a retrospective method which allows poor quality to occur before improvement can be initiated. Second, its emphasis on poor care may leave high quality care unconsidered and thus unremarked.

Criteria Mapping

Background and Scope
Criteria mapping is an approach to the identification of cases for review based on a representation or map of the decisions that experienced clinicians should have made when treating a particular type of case. It was developed in the context of US hospital quality assurance for use in hospital-wide review.

Description

Criteria maps represent the clinical decisions which should be made in treating given conditions in an algorithm or decision tree.

In the case of diabetes patients, for example, checks should be made to see whether they are also suffering from genitourinary tract infection. The first decision in the decision tree should be whether the patient is female. If so she should be asked about frequency and dysuria. If not the practitioner should proceed to checking creatinine levels. If the patient is male and reports dysuria or abnormal frequency then the practitioner should proceed to normal clinical procedures for a urinary tract infection. If either male or female patients have creatinine levels above 1.4 mg% then a urine culture should be obtained.

Each decision is recorded and screening personnel can determine the percentage of present and appropriate decisions. They then select for subsequent review all cases which fall below a given percentage.

Criteria mapping is based on two maps. The first of these is a physicians' map (P map) which is derived from expert judgement and consideration of relevant literature. It is a set of criteria items grouped according to the objectives of care. Thus for diabetes Greenfield et al. (1975) give objectives covering diagnosis, exploration for comorbidity through time, management of the disease itself, and prevention of both ketoacidosis and frequent hypoglycaemia. Each of these clusters of objectives then leads to an abstractors' map (A map) which consists of a branching diagram indicating the various decisions to be made and action to be taken in order to achieve the objectives. The first level abstractor scrutinises all records of patients with the condition and scores them on a simple yes/no system for appropriate decisions. Cases where there is a given proportion of no decisions (as a percentage of the total number of relevant decisions) are selected for subsequent second level review by relevant clinicians. This review can take various shapes but is usually similar to that outlined for occurrence screening above.

Commentary

Criteria maps vary in complexity and length. Demlo (1983) estimates that they vary in the number of branches from 38 to 228. Nonetheless, they have been successfully used by medical records and other non-practitioner personnel and have proved both reliable and transferable (Demlo, 1983; Law et al., 1989). Greenfield et al. (1981) validated the mapp ng method by demonstrating its superiority over traditional criteria list scores and over a number of demographic variables in predicting the appropriateness of admission and dis-charge decisions for patients with chest pain.

Criteria maps have been developed for a variety of conditions including urinary incontinence (Chambers et al., 1984), diabetes mellitus (Greenfield et al., 1975), emergency medicine (Greenfield et al., 1977; Kaplan and Greenfield, 1978), osteoarthritis (Greenfield et al., 1978) and chest pain (Greenfield et al., 1981). Law et al. (1989) also report development and use of a criteria map for use by occupational therapists dealing with patients with problems in self-care. Finally, Padilla and Grant (1982) report development of criteria maps based on Orem's (1971) model of nursing care for use in quality assurance for nursing cancer patients.

Donabedian (1985) points out that one of the major advantages of maps is the possibility they afford for empirical testing of the relationships between decision making and clinical outcome. Such testing should then be fed back into the refinement of the map itself. This kind of decision analysis based on refinement of expert judgement is very similar to the consultation and analysis which precedes the development of protocols for computerised medical expert systems. These are already in existence as aids to diagnosis (Buchanan and Shortliffe, 1984; Shortliffe, 1973; Luger and Stubblefield, 1989; Morris and Reid, 1989). There is a developing literature in the mathematics of decision analysis (Bunn, 1984) and reference to this could lead to maps in which the occurrence of inappropriate decisions at different branch points might lead to different quality weightings based on the probabilities of their relationship to serious negative patient outcomes.

Criteria mapping like occurrence screening focuses particularly upon instances of poor quality. Maps are time consuming to produce although the analyses production requires are said to induce debate and positive problem solving among professional participants (Law et al., 1989; Padilla and Grant, 1982).

Self-Adapting Focused Review System (SAFRS)

Background and Scope
SAFRS is a recently developed system (Ash et al., 1990) for identification of cases for review. It is based on sophisticated statistical analyses of the probability of occurrence of quality problems and the development of models which predict the future occurrence of such problems in terms of criteria which can thus be used for the selection of cases. Ash et al. demonstrate the technique using criteria for prediction of inappropriate hospital admissions.

Description
The first step in the SAFRS system consists of developing a model which estimates the probability that each case will instance a quality problem. This is done on the basis of reference to existing records and expert judgement (if these are unavailable probabilities can be

arbitrarily assigned). Cases are then sampled from the population of records so that those with a high probability of problem instances are more likely to be selected. The actual incidence of problems is then compared with the expected incidence and the model is mathematically adjusted to allow for the new findings. This process is repeated at intervals and the predictive power of the model is thus increased.

Commentary
SAFRS is mathematically sophisticated although once developed it is reported to be relatively easy for minimally computer skilled personnel to use. Its particular advantages are its repeated reference to the empirical basis for case selection (subsequent to initial development of criteria) and the fact that its probabilistic nature permits the use of statistical inference techniques which are not viable with other criterion based selection methods. Thus since every case has a known non-zero probability the observed problem rate in the sample can be used to estimate the rate in the population or in other samples from it. As Ash et al. (1990, p. 1038) comment their 'model guided probability sampling can increase the efficiency of the review process without sacrificing the generalisability and usefulness of the results'.

SAFRS remains a research tool at present but it could clearly be more widely applied.

Local Problem Solving Techniques

The case selection methods discussed above are in a sense ways of identifying quality problems. Each technique is a method of retro-spectively screening records of care to generate the maximum possible number of instances of poor care. These cases are subse-quently reviewed and underlying problems are traced. Their even-tual resolution is presumed to lead to future overall quality improvement. Since the early 1980s a number of commentators have thought the procedure a top heavy, ritualistic, and time wasting way of identifying opportunities for quality improvement (Skillicorn 1981a; b; Haggard, 1983). In their view a quicker route to problem identification and quality improvement consists of simply asking local groups to identify and track likely issues. This also has the advantage that practitioners themselves feel less threatened by the procedure and are motivated to seek out problems rather than to hide them for fear of subsequent sanctions. As Skillicorn (1981a, p. 21) suggests 'staff physicians are in fact the best equipped to review the problems of their peers. They know their colleagues, they know the institution, and they know the idiosyncrasies of both. And when significant things in patient care go wrong they are tough on their peers, tougher than any external group.'

A number of techniques have been developed for such 'looking for trouble' including positive solicitation of patient and employee complaints; records monitoring systems somewhat like occurrence screening (see above p. 100); and scrutiny of a range of other data sources such as committee minutes, liability proceedings, and hospital or unit log books (Skillicorn, 1981b). This philosophy of shopfloor initiation of quality improvement is also the basis of Ishikawa's (1982) quality circles and their subsequent development into the Japanese systems of company-wide quality management. Quality circles themselves have been adapted and used widely in health care in the US and UK.

The local problem solving techniques to be dealt with here are quality circles and two techniques for 'problem tracking' namely the 'quality improvement plan' (QIP) (Benson et al., 1986), and 'issue logs' (Brown et al., 1984).

Quality Circles

Background and Scope
The aim of quality circles in health care as in industry is the identification and resolution of locally relevant problems. They are designed to maximise staff participation in quality activities and to foster the development of a quality culture. They can operate in any part of the health care system.

Description
While the various quality circle schemes reported in the health care literature vary in detail they all share substantial common characteristics. They are small groups of people from a common background whose purpose is the improvement of quality in a specified area of care. The group usually has a membership of between six and 12 people but the precise details of membership can vary. Thus some quality circles consist entirely of volunteers (as in Ishikawa's original (1982) model) while others are based on the 'natural work group' principle. In the health care context this might be all staff on a ward, all staff in a given professional department, or all staff in a multi-professional team. If this 'natural group' is large then the principle for selection of members can be one of representation of interests – thus each professional group in the multi-professional team might provide a member.

One further variation in membership is the inclusion of a group 'facilitator' who is particularly skilled in the operation of quality circles. This facilitator might be brought in from an outside consultancy (Garson, 1983) or be a hospital-wide quality coordinator or member of a hospital or district quality committee (Adair et al., 1982; Dutkewych and Buback, 1982). Alternatively, the facilitator might be selected by a more senior coordinating group but still be a member of the work group upon which the circle is based (Wine and Baird, 1983). However selected the facilitator's role is to ensure maximum participation among members, maximum creativity in production of ideas and problem solutions, and minimum conflict. The facilitator is also supposed to give information and guidance as necessary (and particularly in the initial stages of the group's operation) but to do so as non-directively as possible.

Once established the health care quality circle's first task is the identification and selection of problems for attention. A number of techniques are used for this but in each the main aim is to ensure maximum contribution from members. Both brainstorming and nominal group techniques (see Chapter 5, p. 159 and 162) are popular. Such activities can be assisted by preliminary consideration of local objectives and standards (Wine and Baird, 1983) or of data routinely collected for other reasons. Once a problem is selected an analysis takes place of possible causes and possible action for remediation (again using brainstorming, nominal group or, in this instance, the Ishikawa 'fishbone' technique (see Chapter 5, p. 160)). Action plans are then either implemented or referred to some other relevant group.

Commentary
Health care quality circles have been reported in many areas of hospital based care (Dutkewych and Buback, 1982; Prothro, 1981; Kanter and Stein, 1981) in long-term nursing home care (Garson, 1983) and in nursing specifically (Haggard, 1983; Wine and Baird, 1983; Robson, 1984). In 1982 the US National League for Nursing thought the technique of sufficient applicability to publish a handbook for nurses about to establish circles (Adair et al., 1982). More recently Dalley and Carr-Hill's survey of quality management in the NHS showed that quality circles or similar problem solving groups represented a substantial proportion of the initiatives being established (Dalley and Carr-Hill, 1991).

In their health care applications quality circles tend to be relatively unsophisticated in their approach to data collection and analysis and to lack reference to specific standards. Their identification of problems is often haphazard and may reflect staff interests or preoccupations rather than severity of impact upon patients. In health care as in industrial settings they have been criticised for failure to ensure action for improvement, or to shepherd ideas through to groups who can effect improvement – in other words for becoming no more than talking shops. It is often noted that circles are more likely to be effective if senior management is committed to using the results of their activities in a broader system of quality assurance and management (Dutkewych and Buback, 1982; Garson, 1983; Wine and Baird, 1983). Despite these cautions the broad principles of 'shopfloor' participation and non-directive group leadership and decision making which underpin the quality circles philosophy has had considerable impact throughout health care quality assurance.

Benson, Wilder and Gartner's Quality Improvement Plan (QIP)

Background and Scope
QIP (Benson et al., 1986) was developed in 1982 for use in the quality assurance procedures of three community health centres operating as part of the Methodist Hospital of Indiana. Its authors describe it as a 'one-page quality assurance tool' which is designed to facilitate communication and to track problems.

Description
QIP is literally a one page pro forma which is readily available to all relevant departments in the three health centres involved. As potential quality problems emerge in any given department staff are expected to gather information which will allow them to complete the QIP pro forma. This can be undertaken by one individual or by a local quality group. The information required covers the following:

- Clear identification of the problem (in narrative form and by title to facilitate computer coding).
- Indication of the impact of the problem upon actual clinical care; of its prevalence; of its impact on costs; and of whether it is realistically solvable (yes/no answers to each of these).
- Identification of the professional or local standard which the problem violates.
- Identification of other staff or departments involved.
- Identification of the level or person from which solution is likely to come.
- Target completion date (which is a measure of the severity and thus urgency of the problem).
- Indication of the problem's status (new, revised or reopened).

Once completed the form is passed to a central quality assurance committee who are responsible for (a) setting the local problem in the context of other problem reports it has received; (b) steering the form(s) (with modifications if need be) to the relevant problem solvers and (c) logging the problem with its source, targetted problem solvers, and target date in the computerised record of quality assurance activities. The bottom half of the form has space for dated signatures of relevant department heads and of the QIP initiator. It also indicates the proposed problem solution. Once that part of the form is completed it is again logged in the computer. Unresolved problems are flagged as their target dates are passed and are notified to higher organisational levels – after three months to the vice-president; after six to the president and ultimately to the board of directors. The computer also produces data on rates of problem identification and solution for all departments and information on the range of activities is widely disseminated (although appropriate confidentiality is maintained).

Commentary
QIP is clear and simple to use and according to its authors it is a useful systematisation of local quality activities which might otherwise fail to engender action for improvement. It would be easy to adapt for other settings.

Issue Logs

Issue Logs and related 'quality profile analyses' are in use as part of the hospital-wide quality assurance programme of the Greater Southeast Community Hospital in Washington, DC (Brown et al., 1984). Like QIP they are a means of tracking and monitoring the occurrence and solution of quality problems in the various departments of the health care organisation.

Description
Issue Logs are simple documents available for completion by any member of staff in any hospital department on their own behalf or on behalf of patients. They have space for a brief description of the problem identified, the patient's (or patients') name(s), the name of the attending physician, and the date of completion. The logs can be signed by their initiator or completed anonymously. They are then passed to a central quality assurance committee. The committee considers the logs alongside other quality assurance data and information and quality profiles are prepared for each department. Problem solutions are then determined in the light of overall profiles and trends and are passed to appropriate groups or individuals for solution.

Commentary
Issue Logs are extremely simple to use and according to Brown et al. (1984) they provide a useful adjunct to other quality assurance activities. Unlike quality circles and QIP, responsibility for determining problem solution and implementing action for quality improve-

ment is clearly held by the central committee rather than the local groups. This could be a disincentive although conversely it ensures that problems are likely to be addressed by individuals with the authority to effect solutions. Issue logs could easily be adopted in other settings.

Process Measurement Techniques

The process of care comprises all the procedures and activities through which health professionals and support workers deploy their time, skills, knowledge and resources in pursuit of improved patient health and well-being. It has technical, interpersonal and moral components and includes access, diagnosis, treatment, discharge, after care, and health education and promotion.

The ultimate bench mark of health care quality is obviously the achievement of improved health and well-being. Assessment of such outcomes, however, is made difficult by their long-term nature and by confounding variables such as poverty, nutrition and social support over which the providers of care have little control. Assessment of process quality is both more immediate and less susceptible to the influence of confounding variables. Being closer to the actual delivery of care it is also more likely to identify causes of poor quality and thus opportunities for improvement.

There is a substantial literature on the difficulties of disentangling relationships between process and outcome quality. Some authors suggest that assessment of process quality is only justified when precise relationships with outcomes can be identified while others suggest that in some areas of care the process of delivering it is an end in itself (Berwick and Knapp, 1987; Ellis, 1988). Donabedian reviews the literature and concludes 'Process and outcome are therefore complements to each other in the assessment of quality, not alternatives. A preference for one over the other must be based not on causal validity but on something else – the availability of information, for example, ease of measurement, or timeliness relative to the uses to which the information is to be put' (1987, p. 77).

Judgements about appropriate standards for the processes of care are obviously made on a daily basis as care is routinely delivered. Further, the entire edifice of professional pre-service and in-service education is premised on the notion that somebody somewhere knows what constitutes 'good practice' or competence. In respect of each of the technical, interpersonal and moral aspects of process, however, medical science remains inexact and 'good practice' is a shifting phenomenon. Indeed professional education is increasingly devoted to creation of 'reflective practitioners' (Ellis and Whittington,

1972; 1988; Schön, 1991) who both recognise the imperfection of their science and consider their practice a process of hypothesis testing which may in the end advance it. It can be argued that involvement in setting and appraising process standards is a similar exercise.

The techniques which are considered in this section assume the existence of process standards. They vary considerably, however, in the extent to which their originators either indicate or comment on the origin and derivation of the standards on which they are premised. They are designed to be used in assessing whether or not standards have been achieved. In other words, they are essentially measuring instruments. Their originators often refer to the way they might be used within the overall quality cycle of standard setting, appraisal and quality improvement but the techniques themselves are clearly most relevant at the measurement stage of the cycle.

Where explicit local process standards are in place the appropriate strategy for appraising them may be the design of local instruments. Thus if the standard suggests that all physiotherapy clients in a particular unit should be seen within three weeks of referral all that is needed is a way of recording total patients and patients not seen after three weeks. Simple low level measurements of this kind are useful in indicating local problems and opportunities for immediate quality improvement. Where detailed standards do not exist or where a broad overall measure for comprehensive evaluation of quality of care or for comparison between different care settings is required more sophisticated measurement may be necessary. The instruments considered here are often adopted for such purposes.

Professions vary in the extent to which they have developed instruments for measurement of the process of care and as in so many areas of health care quality assurance nursing is in the forefront. Many of the instruments developed for nursing could however be adapted for other professions.

Most of the instruments described here have been published with a view to their being used outside of their setting of origin. Some of them lead to global scores of 'quality' which are said to provide a basis for comparison across wards, units or care settings. As noted above they rarely refer to explicit standards but rather to some implicit construct of 'quality process' represented either in the ratings and other judgments made by the users of the instrument, or in the decisions made about item inclusion and scoring during its construction. Questions of reliability (the consistency of the scores obtained) and validity (the extent to which the instruments actually measure what they are designed to measure) are therefore of particular significance (see Chapter 5, p. 180 for fuller discussion of reliability and validity).

The instruments to be considered here are as follows:

- The Phaneuf Audit (Phaneuf, 1976).
- Barney's Nursing Care Plan System (Barney, 1981).
- The Craig Audit Instrument (Stewart and Craig, 1987).
- EQAM (Ervin et al., 1989).
- Price and Greenwood's (1988) Treatment Plan System for Residential Care.
- The Slater Nursing Competencies Rating Scale (Slater, 1975; Wandelt and Stewart, 1975).
- Qualpacs (Wandelt and Ager, 1974).
- The Rush Medicus Nursing Process Quality Monitoring Instrument (Jelinek et al., 1974).
- Monitor (Goldstone et al., 1983).
- The National Association of Theatre Nurses Quality Assurance Tool (NATN, 1989).
- PA/Royal National Orthopaedic Hospital Nursing Quality Measurement Scale (Flindall et al., 1987).
- SIMP (Schmele, 1985).

The Phaneuf Audit

Background and Scope
The Phaneuf Audit (Phaneuf, 1976) is a tool for retrospective assessment of records of the process of nursing. It was devised in the US in the 1960s and is thus one of the earliest systematic measures of health care process quality. It is designed to be used monthly by an 'audit committee' of experienced nurses who review a randomly selected sample of records for recently discharged patients. While the audit is designed for typical US recording systems it has been used in the UK (Bradshaw, 1987).

Description
The first two parts of the audit schedule refer to characteristics of the setting in which the relevant episodes of nursing care took place. There are two pro formas – one for hospital or nursing home care and the other for community care.

The third and main part of the instrument is the chart review schedule. This has 50 statements describing positive aspects of care given, grouped in seven categories or 'sections' reflecting Lesnik and Andersen's (1955) 'functions of nursing'. The seven sections are as follows:

- The application and execution of the doctor's legal orders.
- The observation of symptoms and reactions.
- Supervision of patients.
- Supervision of those participating in care.
- Reporting and recording.

- The application of nursing procedures and techniques.
- The promotion of health by directing and teaching.

Thus the statements in the first section on carrying out doctor's instructions include 'Orders promptly executed' and 'Evidence that nurse understood cause and effect'.

Auditors score patient records for each of the 50 items as yes, no, or not applicable; no scores always have a value of zero but each of the yes and not applicable scores have different weightings. Thus yes scores in section one carry seven points but yes scores in section two can carry seven or five points. Members of the audit committee are allowed to consult if they are uncertain how to score an item. Scores are totalled and the total yes/no score is multiplied by a value determined by the not applicable scores. The final score has a range from zero to 200 which is accompanied by a literal grading from unsafe through poor, incomplete, good and excellent. It is suggested that one audit can be carried out by an experienced auditor in about fifteen minutes.

After each monthly meeting of the audit committee reports are prepared and feedback is given to individuals or groups as appropriate.

Commentary

The Phaneuf audit system was one of the first systems designed for nursing quality assurance. It had substantial uptake when it was first published and has had considerable influence on subsequent developments in nursing quality assurance.

The traditional criticism of the Phaneuf Audit (Hegyvary and Haussman, 1976; Mayers, 1977; Van Maanen, 1979; Openshaw, 1984; Kemp and Richardson, 1990) is that it relies on a written record. and is thus more an assessment of record keeping and language skills than of care. It has also been commented (Wright and Whittington, 1992) that the time devoted to preparation of unnecessarily excellent records may be time which would otherwise have been devoted to care itself. These criticisms of course apply to any system based on record audit. Phaneuf (1976) counters these arguments by suggesting that nurses who think about how to prepare good records are nurses who are thinking about nursing. Bradshaw (1987) recognises the problems but adds that the Phaneuf audit or something like it may be a useful adjunct to other forms of audit based on more direct observation. In that context any falsity of records would be evident.

More significant criticisms of Phaneuf surround its reliability and validity. Each statement requires a judgement before it can be scored and each auditor may be using different criteria in arriving at that judgement – what, for example, does 'promptly' mean with respect to carrying out instructions? And would it have a different meaning for a patient in intensive care as opposed to one in a long-term rehabilitation unit? Phaneuf recommends and most users report a fairly lengthy period of discussion between auditors to obtain agreements about interpretation before using the audit so that at least some degree of reliability of measurement can be obtained within a given audit team. Extreme care would have to be taken if Phaneuf scores from different teams were to be compared.

No information is available about the validity of the Phaneuf instrument, of the model of nursing upon which it is based or, importantly, of the weightings assigned to the various items. Phaneuf herself (1976) states that the weightings are the result of extensive testing of the instrument.

Barney's Nursing Care Plan System

Background and Scope
There are several case studies in the literature exemplifying the use of nursing care plans as a basis for quality assurance (Mayers et al., 1977; Gould, 1985; Montemuro, 1988; Kemp and Richardson, 1990). Barney (1981) has been chosen for inclusion here for its detail and for its (early) recourse to computerisation as an aid to monitoring. The system was developed in St Joseph Hospital in Denver, Colorado which at that time was a general and maternity hospital treating some 23,000 patients per annum in 26 patient care units.

Assessment of the quality of care process can be conceptualised as exploration of the extent to which its executants attain their own objectives – or meet their own standards. Process measures can therefore be based on any explicit statement of intention or documented plan. Fortunately, health professionals are increasingly encouraged to maintain just such records. In nursing in particular a very large part of the recent professional and educational literature has been devoted to the development of models of care designed to facilitate the explication and articulation of care planning, execution, and evaluation (Whittington and Boore, 1988). These plans form the basis of several quality assurance initiatives in nursing.

Other professions are increasingly adopting similar documentation systems. Weed's (1968) problem oriented medical recording system (see p. 154 below) is particularly popular in the rehabilitation professions and there is some evidence of its use as a basis for quality assurance (Kuntavanish, 1987; England et al., 1989; Merrall et al., 1991; Wright and Whittington, 1992).

Description
The system is designed for record based concurrent evaluation of the process of care. It is based on nurses having worked through the four

parts of the 'nursing process' (Yura and Walsh, 1988) namely assessment of patient needs, formulation of a plan of care, implementation of a plan of care, and evaluation of patient progress and achievement of nursing goals.

The instrument is divided into five sections namely, nursing care plan, patients' physical needs, patients' non-physical needs, nursing care objectives, and administrative and managerial services. Patients are divided into four groups depending on the intensity of the care they require and different pro formas are available for each. Each section of each pro forma consists of a series of statements representing positive aspects of the process of care. Thus 'The patient is protected from accident and injury' and 'The patient's rights to privacy and civil rights are honoured'.

Quality of care for three patients on each patient care unit is examined every month. Patients are selected at random, one from each classification of illness group (Diagnosis Related Grouping). Reviewers (who are experienced nurses not directly involved in the relevant care) audit care plans and records for those patients across all shifts. They also gather data by means of direct observation of appropriate aspects of care. The system is thus not entirely records based although it is premised on the existence of a particular type of recording. Having undertaken their observations and audits the reviewers complete the pro forma by writing yes, no or not applicable against each statement. Each statement has a numerical value from one to five based on a rating of 'importance in care' carried out by the instrument's originator. The information is then fed into a computer which produces, collates and analyses overall scores for patients, wards and care units over the months and years. Feedback is given to appropriate groups and individuals.

Commentary

As noted above there are several systems in the literature which use care records as the basis of process appraisal. The Barney system is a clearly set out example. The system has face validity in its close relationship to the model of care and method of recording already in use in its hospital of origin. It would have similar acceptability where related systems were in use. Concurrent audit of records and observation of care as it is delivered should improve validity of the judgments made although questions remain about the transfer of the weighting system to other settings or over time. Barney (1981) reports that 'nurse observers can be trained to achieve reliability' and states 'we expect that the tool will discriminate between patients who receive high and low quality of care'.

The Craig Audit Instrument

Background and Scope

The Craig Audit Instrument (Stewart and Craig, 1987) was developed for use by public health nurses in a Canadian Regional Health Department serving a population of some 260,000 people in urban and rural settings of varying socioeconomic character. The instrument is based on the four stages of the nursing process (Yura and Walsh, 1988) namely *assessment, planning, implementation* and *evaluation* and presumes the existence of records following that outline. In fact the nurses who now use it use a version of problem oriented medical recording (see p. 154 below) modified to allow for recording of the stages of the nursing process. The instrument is used for retrospective audit of records of care process for individuals and families whose care has either terminated or whose contract of care has been renegotiated.

Description

The Craig audit instrument is a list of 44 statements of criteria and standards grouped into the four sections of the nursing process. The assessment criteria and standards are subdivided into those applicable to assessment of the individual, to assessment of the family and to nursing diagnosis. Thus under 'Assessment: family' one criterion is 'General Health' and the accompanying standards statement is as follows.

'Recording should include: practice related to sleep and rest, diet and exercise, use of alcohol/drugs, atmosphere in home, homemaking practices, patterns of seeking health care and coping with health problems'.

Similarly, under 'Implementation' one criterion is 'Goal directed intervention' and the accompanying standards statement is 'Nursing actions documented focus on specific short-term goals'.

Scoring involves rating records against each of the 44 standards statements on a five-point scale from poor to excellent (guidelines are given for interpretation of the scale) or marking the standard not applicable. An overall score is computed making an allowance for the number of not applicable standards.

The audit committee who use the tool comprise five volunteer nurses and one nurse supervisor (also a volunteer). They meet monthly to scrutinise a random sample of records. Both new members of the committee and new staff participate in regular audit orientation sessions. Findings, scores and recommendations are discussed and reports are sent to the director of nursing. Any findings reflecting directly on individual performance are not made available to the director or to nurse supervisors other than the one on the committee.

Commentary
Stewart and Craig (1987) report general acceptability of the instrument, enthusiasm for the process of audit among the nurses involved, and a gradual improvement in audit scores. The use of the audit has also led to in-service education initiatives and to review of management programmes. It could be adapted for use in other settings.

The criteria and standards contained in the Craig Audit Instrument were developed substantially from the literature although a check was made that relevant information was regularly recorded in pre-audit records. For 14 of the 44 standards less than 50% of the pilot study records contained relevant information. Stewart and Craig report that they were retained nonetheless 'to ensure the content validity of the record' (Stewart and Craig, 1987, p. 139). They also indicate inter-rater reliability testing but do not give results. Given the relatively high level of inference required by the standards statements, audit committee member training is clearly important.

The Ervin Quality Assessment Instrument (EQAM)

Background and Scope
EQAM (Ervin et al., 1989) is designed for use in retrospective assessment of the quality of care process in public health nursing. It is based on the four components of the nursing process (Yura and Walsh, 1988) namely assessment, planning, implementation and evaluation and presupposes records of care using that structure. It focuses on 'episodes of care' defined as a sequence of visits from first referral to termination of care due to lack of further needs (i.e. it would not be suitable if episodes of care were interrupted or terminated for other reasons). Needs are defined as including health education and health promotion as well as remedial and palliative care. Completion of the nursing process in home visit nursing is said by Ervin et al. to require a number of visits and EQAM is therefore said to be suitable only for cases involving four or more visits.

Criteria for inclusion in each of the four nursing process sections of the instrument were determined by expert judges using a modified Delphi technique (Delphi involves asking individual experts to make judgements, showing them their own and other judges' results and asking them to review their judgement, and repeating the process until consensus is reached – see Chapter 5 (p. 163) for fuller description).

Description
EQAM is a simple 14-criterion instrument divided into the four sections of the nursing process. Thus the assessment section contains criteria such as 'data were documented to support identified problems' and the evaluation section includes criteria such as 'the

plan of care was evaluated with client or family'. Reviewers rate records on each criterion scoring met/not met and if scoring 'met' giving a rating from one to five indicating the extent to which the criterion was met. Space is also available for comments in each of the four sections.

Commentary

Ervin et al. obtained high (0.60 to 0.82) scores for reviewer consistency but rather lower scores for inter reviewer agreement (0.38 and 0.35 in different agencies). They argue that these low agreement scores may be a function of the records themselves (lack of completeness, different emphases in different agencies, etc.). The authors also make clear that EQAM is primarily designed for research purposes but that its use in practice 'may be possible after further testing and applications in a variety of agencies'.

Price and Greenwood's Treatment Plan System for Residential Child Care

Background and Scope

Price and Greenwood's (1988) system was designed for use in a long-term residential child care centre in Rochester, New York. It has places for approximately 150 children (mostly adolescents) who exhibit a wide variety of emotional and behavioural disturbances and for whom the most common diagnosis is 'conduct disorder often complicated by borderline personality traits or borderline to mildly retarded intellectual functioning'. The centre is staffed by a multi-professional team.

The principle underlying the system's construction is that outcome prediction and monitoring for such clients is peculiarly difficult and that appropriate process standards may vary considerably from one young person to another. Concurrent monitoring via treatment plans is thus the most viable option. Price and Greenwood also suggest that awareness of prospective monitoring encourages the multi-professional team to plan and modify plans explicitly and co-operatively.

Description

When clients are admitted to the centre they are allocated to a care co-ordinator (usually a graduate social worker) who has responsibility for preparation of the treatment plan within a specified period of time. The plan must include a series of initial health, psychological, psychiatric, educational, social, behavioural and recreational assessments; a formulation of needs highlighting strengths and weaknesses; a review of the appropriateness of admission to the centre rather than some other more specialised facility or to a system of community support; establishment of long-term goals (e.g. return to family, independent adult living, adult residential care); schedule and treatment length expectations; formulation of discharge criteria; statements on therapeutic approach, treatment goals, and associated specific objectives and tasks; a narrative rationale and justification for the plan; dates for plan review; and dated signatures of the case co-ordinator and a supervising senior member of staff. Plans exist for current residents and for those who have moved on into fostering, group homes in the community, or family based day treatment. Treatment records are also maintained which follow similar outlines to plans.

Plans and their related records are reviewed by separate quality assurance staff who also spend time in training and assisting staff with the process of treatment planning and recording. Plans are reviewed quarterly for their 'mechanics', that is completeness, timeliness and comprehensibility; and for their strategic viability. If there are problems with the strategy proposed the case co-ordinator has an opportunity to modify the plan before it is passed on to a second level review committee. Reviewers have checklists of very specific criteria which plans must meet in both the mechanical and strategic parts of the review. Thus the mechanics part of the 'initial assessment' checklist for treatment goals includes such details as inclusion of target dates, consecutive numbering, expression in behavioural terms, and expression in language clear enough to be understood by clients and their families. Strategic review is more complex and edges towards review of outcomes, involving reviewers in judgements regarding both appropriateness and quality of treatment. Again these judgements are assisted by checklists. These focus squarely on the extent to which goals may or may not have been achieved; on the extent to which objectives and tasks have been (a) realistic, (b) adequately related to goals, and (c) achieved; and on frequency and quality of contacts between providers and clients.

Data from individual case reviews are aggregated for each worker and summaries prepared regarding both mechanical and strategic quality of planning. These are passed to the programme director. Thresholds are specified for both mechanical and strategic adequacy below which the director is obliged to take action for improvement including staff development initiatives. The reviews are an integral part of biannual staff appraisal procedures.

Commentary

Price and Greenwood's system demonstrates that careful planning and recording can provide a basis for monitoring. They report that staff take the reviews very seriously and that the system has encouraged interprofessional discussion and co-operation and a generally self-questioning and self-reviewing culture. It is recognised by several outside accreditation agencies as an effective means of determining quality in an area where many clients 'leave the programme with ambiguous outcomes' (Price and Greenwood, 1988, p. 274).

The system emphasises review of staff competence to the exclusion of other potentially relevant administrative and managerial factors and could be regarded as unduly 'top down'. No indication of the reliability of reviewer judgement is given but the system seems to be acceptable to staff concerned and thus has some measure of validity in its own setting.

While the Price and Greenwood system is designed for a specific setting its underlying principle (monitoring through planning for delivery as much as actual delivery) would apply in other areas where clients are particularly variable and outcomes are often ambiguous.

The Slater Nursing Competencies Rating Scale

Background and Scope
The Slater Nursing Competencies Rating Scale (Slater, 1975; Wandelt and Stewart, 1975) was developed at Wayne State University, Detroit, for assessment of nursing competence during the process of hospital care. It is a rating scale based on concurrent observation of care although actual rating can be completed retrospectively. The scale provides both numerical and descriptive assessments which are designed to be used to compare the quality of individual nurses' performance, to provide feedback on competence and to detect areas of strength and weakness. It can be modified to suit a variety of hospital settings and it has been used as part of quality assurance programmes (Mayers et al., 1977). Hough and Schmele (1987) report a version of the scale for use in home health care.

Description
The Slater scale consists of 84 items or 'nursing actions' divided into six subsections namely psychosocial/individual, psychosocial/group, physical, general, communications, and professional implications. Thus psychosocial/individual is defined as 'Actions directed toward meeting any psychosocial needs of individual patients' and the relevant section of the scale contains items such as 'Gives full attention to patient' and 'Is a receptive listener'. Each statement is in turn accompanied by a series of 'cues' exemplifying the particular statement in a range of care settings. These are designed to assist observers to understand the statement and thus to rate it with minimum ambiguity or variation. These cues can be modified by addition, deletion or editing depending on the precise setting in

which the scale is to be used. The statements themselves may not be so modified.

Observers are encouraged to 'shadow' the nurses being rated for about three hours making notes as they do so on each interaction with patients or on behalf of patients, and comparing the nurse's behaviour with the relevant standards. Based on notes and recall observers then rate performance. Observers are asked to refer the rating to their own implicit characterisation of 'the quality of performance expected of a first level staff nurse'. They then award a rating on a five-point scale from one to five accompanied by a literal scale from 'poorest nurse' to 'best nurse'. Space is also available for coding 'not applicable' or 'not observed'. Ratings for 60 of the 84 items are sufficient for production of a normally reliable and valid assessment. A nurse's performance can be rated over any period from several days to one year. Observers derive a mean rating for each item by averaging the various observations made and compute an overall score.

Commentary
The Slater scale was widely piloted and refined prior to publication and it has subsequently been used in very many US settings. Internal consistency scores above 0.90 have been recorded (Wandelt and Stewart, 1975; Hough and Schmele, 1987) and high inter-rater reliabilities have also been reported (Wandelt and Stewart, 1975). It is essentially a scale for the assessment of individual nurse competence but can readily be used as part of wider programmes of quality assurance.

Qualpacs

Background and Scope
The Qualpacs scale (Wandelt and Ager, 1974) is a development of the Slater scale in which the focus has been shifted from the assessment of the quality of care delivered by individual nurses to assessment of the quality of care delivered to specified groups of patients. The final score is a measure of the quality of care delivered by a ward or unit. The scale is designed to be used in any nursing setting.

Description
Qualpacs is a 68-item scale divided into the same six subsections as the Slater scale namely psychosocial/individual, psychosocial/group, physical, general, communication, and professional implications. Again as in the Slater scale each item is accompanied by cues which are designed to assist the user of the scale in interpreting the item. Observers work in pairs to reduce the possibility of bias. They

are required to observe care over a period of two hours as it is delivered to 15% of the total patients on the ward or to five patients, whichever is greater. After the two-hour period of direct observation the observers spend a further hour examining charts. Each item is rated on a five point scale from poorest to best care the standard for comparison being again the average first level staff nurse. Items can also be recorded as not applicable or not observed. Wiles (1987) describes a variation in which additional note is taken of the grade (sister, staff nurse, student, etc.) of nurse delivering the care which is the basis of the item rating. Having completed the observations the observers compute a mean rating for each item and for each section, and an overall score (taking account of items scored not applicable or not observed).

Commentary

Qualpacs has been used extensively in the US for both research and quality assurance purposes. In the UK Harvey (1991) reports use of Qualpacs in 3.6% of English District Health Authorities. Its most reported use in the UK is in the Oxfordshire Health Authority where it has been used for some years as part of a peer review centred system of nursing quality assurance (Wainwright and Burnip, 1983a; b; Pearson, 1987; Wiles, 1987). Phillips et al. (1990) report the development of a scale called 'Qualcare' based upon Qualpacs but separately validated for use in nursing care of the elderly and designed to pick up instances of 'elder abuse'.

Like the Slater scale Qualpacs was devised on the basis of expert judgement and relies on the internal standards and judgements of nurse observers in its implementation. It was rigorously piloted and tested during its development and evidence of acceptable levels of inter-observer reliability, test/retest reliability, internal consistency, and discriminatory power are reported by the authors (Wandelt and Ager, 1974). Ventura (1980) and Ventura et al. (1982) describe concurrent validity studies comparing Qualpacs with other instruments designed to measure nursing quality in which significant correlations were not found. They and other authors (Openshaw, 1984; Harvey, 1988b; Kemp and Richardson, 1990) point out that both the Slater scale and Qualpacs place greater emphasis on psychosocial and communication aspects of nursing than other scales and suggest that this may account for the poor correlations.

As noted above Qualpacs is in more extensive use in the US than in the UK and it has not been modified in any way to meet the specific circumstances of UK nursing. Despite that those UK nurses who do use it seem enthusiastic and problems seem to be associated with the organisational context and managerial style with which its use is associated rather than with the instrument itself (Harvey, 1991).

The Rush Medicus Nursing Process Quality Monitoring Instrument

Background and Scope
The Rush Medicus instrument was first developed in 1972 by the Medicus Systems Corporation of Chicago, the Rush Presbyterian–St Luke's Medical Centre, Chicago and the Baptist Medical Centre, Birmingham, Alabama (Jelinek et al., 1974; Hegyvary and Haussman, 1975; Haussman et al., 1976; Haussman and Hegyvary, 1977). It was devised on the basis of expert judgement and is premised on the execution of nursing care based on the 'nursing process' model (Yura and Walsh, 1988). Rush Medicus is designed for use in a range of nursing care settings including medical, surgical, obstetrics, recovery room, accident and emergency, psychiatric, and paediatric units. Rajki et al. (1985) also report the development of a variation on the Rush Medicus instrument for use in dialysis care.

Rush Medicus has been used extensively in the US and elsewhere and Kemp and Richardson (1990, p. 68) call it 'probably the best known methodology to measure the quality of nursing care in the world'.

Description
Rush Medicus is structured round six main 'objectives of care' which are derived from the 'nursing process' model. They are as follows:

- The plan of nursing care is formulated.
- The physical needs of the patient are attended.
- The non-physical needs of the patient are attended (psychological, emotional, mental, social).
- Achievement of nursing care objectives is evaluated.
- Unit procedures are followed for the protection of all patients.
- The delivery of nursing care is facilitated by administration and managerial services.

Each of the six objectives subsumes a number of sub-objectives. Thus the objective for the formulation of a plan yields five sub-objectives including 'The patient is assessed on admission' and 'The nursing care plan is coordinated with the medical care plan'. Each sub-objective then yields a range of specific care criteria. These are grouped according to a classification of patients by medical conditions and severity of illness.

Nursing staff and observers work together on classifying patients and the results are fed into a computer which then produces worksheets based on criteria which are appropriate for patients in that ward or unit. Worksheets contain from 30 to 50 criteria questions to be answered on the basis of direct observation, chart review and interviews with patients and nurses. The total system contains 257 criteria questions 205 of which are patient specific and 52 of which refer to the nursing unit.

Observers are experienced nurses not directly involved in the unit being assessed and who have been given training in the use of the instrument. They work in pairs and are given assistance in choosing data sources for arriving at the answers to the questions on the worksheets. Answers are recorded in the form yes/no/not applicable. Observations are made for a sample of 10% of one month's admissions and are spread randomly across time during that month. Completion of each questionnaire takes about one hour. Scoring involves expressing the number of yes responses for each item as a percentage of the total number of yes and no responses for that item. Overall scores can then be computed for each sub-objective and objective and for the whole exercise.

Commentary

As already noted Rush Medicus is in wide use and must therefore be judged a generally acceptable tool for use in quality assurance. Hegyvary and Haussman (1976) report extensive testing for validity and reliability although Openshaw (1984) points out that content and concurrent validity testing was substantially limited to comparisons with other measures also based on the execution of care according to the nursing process model. The validity of the Rush Medicus is thus dependent upon the validity of that model as a representation of best practice in nursing.

Despite the widespread use of Rush Medicus both Van Maanen (1979) and Kemp and Richardson (1990) suggest that it is time consuming in use and difficult to score. Smeltzer et al. (1983) describe an attempt at implementing the system which had difficulties associated with its perception as a 'top down' management tool rather than a more locally based adjunct to professional quality assurance.

Monitor

Monitor (Goldstone et al., 1983) was the first instrument for the measurement of nursing quality to be developed specifically for use in the UK. It is an adaptation of the Rush Medicus instrument developed as part of a nursing staffing levels project carried out in the North West Regional Health Authority.

Monitor was first developed and used in medical and surgical wards but several modifications have now been developed for other settings. The available versions are medical and surgical; geriatric; district nursing; paediatric; neurological; nursing home; midwifery (three versions – pregnancy, labour and post-natal); health visiting; psychiatric; accident and emergency; and mental handicap. Guides and manuals are also available and there is computer software for the medical/surgical, geriatric and paediatric versions. David and Pritchard (1987) also report a local modification of Monitor for use in oncology nursing.

Description

Monitor assesses the quality of nursing in four areas of care related to the nursing process model (Yura and Walsh, 1988) namely, planning and assessment; physical care; non-physical care; and evaluation of care. These areas are then subdivided as follows:

Planning and Assessment

- Assessing the patient on admission.
- Information collected on admission.
- Assessment of patient's current condition.
- Coordination of nursing care with medical care plan.

Physical Care

- Protecting the patient from accident and injury.
- Provision of physical comfort and rest.
- Needs for hygiene.
- Needs for nutrition and fluid balance.
- Needs for elimination.

Non-physical Care

- Orientation to hospital facilities on admission.
- Nursing staff courtesy.
- Patient's privacy and civil rights.
- Consideration to patient's emotional and psychological well-being.
- Measures to promote health maintenance and illness prevention are taught.
- Involvement of patient's family or carers.

Evaluation of Care

- Appropriateness and evaluation of objectives.
- Patient's response to treatment is evaluated.

Separate lists of questions related to each of these sub-areas are available for patients in each of four dependency groups (minimal care, average care, above average care, and maximum or intensive care). Thus for dependency four patients there are eight separate questions to be answered with respect to the patient's nutrition and fluid needs. They cover detail of fluid intake and output, intravenous therapy and so on. For dependency one patients there are only two questions dealing with special dietary needs and availability of any necessary help with eating. The number of questions to be put regarding the quality of care delivered to a particular patient thus varies depending on both the severity of their illness and the area of care which is being explored. The maximum dependency care questionnaire has 65 physical care items and 17 non-physical care items for example while the minimal care questionnaire has 16 physical and 28 non-physical. A separate 43-item questionnaire addresses issues of ward environment and management.

Two assessors (experienced nurses not associated with the ward being assessed) complete questionnaires either for all patients on the ward or for a random sample of three patients from each dependency group. Their answers are based on a mixture of direct observation, chart review, and interviews with nurses and patients. Each answer is recorded as yes, no, or not applicable (for some questions a 'partly yes' answer is possible). Scores are allocated one for yes, 0.5 for partly yes and zero for no and the total for each patient is expressed as a percentage of all yes, partly yes, or no answers. These percentages can then be averaged for each dependency group, for each area of care, and for the ward overall. Detailed analysis of areas of low scoring or comparison between wards can then ensue. It is suggested that an experienced pair of assessors can complete assessment based on all patients in a 25-bed ward in about two days. It is also recommended that Monitor be applied roughly once a year.

The Monitor material contains careful explanation of the questionnaires and scoring system and suggestions for pre Monitor preparation including consultation with trade unions, ethical committees and so on. It also emphasises the importance of discussing results with ward staff.

Commentary

Monitor is in wide use throughout the UK. Harvey (1991) undertook a survey of nursing quality assurance in English District Health Authorities which showed a 35.7% uptake of Monitor – by far the largest uptake for any one method or approach. Its widespread use is a clear testament to its face validity and acceptability in practice. Several authors (Slack, 1985; Pullan and Chittock, 1986; David and Pritchard, 1987; Hilton and Dawson, 1988) report that using Monitor has proved a simple, acceptable and cost-effective method of examining the quality of nursing care and that actual improvements in care have been effected as a result of analysis of Monitor scores. Harvey (1991) comments that using Monitor is often the first step in implementing a 'top down' nursing quality assurance system within a Regional or District Authority. She notes that Monitor results are frequently used as 'management information' as much as for feedback to individual wards or units.

Other authors have been more critical. Barnett and Wainwright (1987) point out that Monitor has not been subjected to the range of reliability testing to which the Rush Medicus was subjected and that the lack of emphasis on observer training in the material may lead to bias and unreliability in assessments. A further potential source of such unreliability lies in the nature of many of the questions which leave room for more than one interpretation or for relatively high levels of inference in arriving at conclusions (Whelan, 1987). Kemp and Richardson (1990) also point out that some patients may be too ill to understand and answer the questions put while others may answer questions positively for fear of offending staff with whom they have a continuing relationship. Barnett and Wainwright (1987) also highlight the anomaly that while Monitor and its precursor the Rush Medicus are clearly premised on the existence of a nursing process approach, the authors of Monitor suggest that it can be equally well applied in wards where some other model is the basis for care.

A particularly important criticism which Barnett and Wainwright begin to explore concerns the focus of the Monitor measurements and thus the meaning and comparability of the scores which it produces. Barnett and Wainwright point out that the nursing process model is a sequentially dependent model. Thus the execution and evaluation of high quality care is conceived as contingent on the existence of a sound plan for care which in turn is based on adequate assessment of patient needs. Put crudely a patient diagnosed as suffering from mild stomach ache who in fact has appendicitis does not receive high quality care however well the procedures appropriate to care and evaluation of care for stomach ache are carried out. It is thus difficult to understand ward scores on Monitor which are high on execution of care but low on planning and assessment.

Another issue of measurement concerns the number and distribution of 'not applicable' responses. Rush Medicus gives a threshold for the proportion of such responses above which measurement should be abandoned but Monitor does not do so. Given that both the frequency and distribution of these responses may vary from ward to ward averaging and comparison may be statistically perilous. Similarly, comparison between wards where the 'all patients' procedure rather than the sampling procedure has been used may be unadvisable since the proportions of patients in the various dependency groups (and thus the range of questions put) will vary from ward to ward. If, on the other hand, the 'sample of three' method is adopted that may not be a sound representation of the typical distribution of dependency levels in each ward.

Finally, Barnett and Wainwright (1987) discuss the extent to which Monitor fails to take account of variation in quality over time. Rush Medicus scores are based on time sampling over a period of a month whereas Monitor observations are completed in rather less than 48 hours. These two days may have been an atypical period for the ward concerned.

In summary Monitor is a popular instrument which can undoubtedly contribute to the generation of concern for quality and to identification of local scope for quality improvement. It is simple to use, it is applicable in a range of settings, and in many cases its availability has been instrumental in getting nursing quality assurance started. Its use as a global measure of quality from which comparisons between wards and groups are made without reference to other evidence may not however be advisable.

The National Association of Theatre Nurses Quality Assurance Tool

Background and Scope
The National Association of Theatre Nurses instrument (NATN, 1989) has been developed over a period of years on the basis of consultation with a cross section of the membership of the UK National Association of Theatre Nurses. It is designed for use in the assessment of the quality of care process in operating theatres.

Description
The NATN QA tool is divided into five sections as follows:

- Preparation of personnel.
- Pre-operative patient care.
- Operating room care.
- Recovery patient care.
- Departmental organisation.

Each section contains a series of standards statements which in turn subsume a list of criterial statements. Thus under 'Recovery patient care', one of the standards is 'Nurse/patient communications are effective in minimising fear, embarrassment and anxiety'. That standard is then associated with a list of criteria including 'Verbal reassurance is given to the unconscious patient' and 'There is tactile communication with the patient'. Each of these criterial statements is presented on a scoring sheet on which observers are asked to record yes/no/not applicable. They are also given guidance on how to obtain evidence to support their judgement, e.g. 'observe' or 'ask patient'. Observers work in pairs and it is recommended that they should be experienced theatre nurses one of whom is associated with the unit being assessed and one of whom is not. The Association have a panel of people experienced in using the instrument who can be made available to act as the external observer and to give general advice to units or authorities who are beginning to use it. Annual assessment is recommended.

Commentary

The NATN QA tool is simple, clearly set out, and easy to use. It has had extensive use among theatre nurses since its construction although there are as yet no published accounts. While it is designed specifically for theatre nursing contexts the general principles of its construction and use could transfer to other areas of nursing or even to other professional settings.

The NATN tool is said to have been validated in a number of hospitals during its development but no details are given of formal testing for validity or reliability. Interestingly the Association are engaged in a kind of continuous validation in that the members of their panel of assessors are encouraged to keep records of their use of the instrument in each setting they visit with a particular view to improving it. A second edition incorporating modifications based on this feedback is currently in press.

PA/Royal National Orthopaedic Hospital Nursing Quality Measurement Scale

Background and Scope

The PA/Royal National Orthopaedic Hospital Nursing Quality Measurement Scale (NQMS) (Flindall et al., 1987; Wheeler, 1991) was developed by a group of senior nursing consultants in association with PA Management Consultants. It draws on ideas from a number of other scales including Monitor, Qualpacs and Phaneuf. It includes a section on the resources available for care and gives guidance on using the results of measurement in determining quality action. Its originators make it clear, however, that the primary focus of the scale is measurement of the process of nursing care (Wheeler, 1991).

It is designed for use in a number of nursing specialties on the assumption that whatever the patient group, nursing has a core component. It is not designed for comparisons between wards or units but rather for assessing trends in quality in one ward over a period of time.

Description

The PA/RNOH scale is designed to be used by two trained assessors who are qualified nurses with experience relevant to the ward to be assessed but not associated with it. It is divided into five sections. The first two ask the assessors to make and record judgements about the profile of ward activities (including numbers of patients, beds, consultants, skill mix), and about the adequacy of available resources (including levels of nursing cover, availability of paramedical services, physical environment, catering). Only the second of these is transformed into a numerical rating (on a percentage scale).

The third section of the scale concentrates on observation of the process of care. Both assessors observe care delivered to four randomly selected patients and rate care on a four-point scale for each item on a checklist. Observations take place over a period of not less than two hours. Cues are given to assist assessors in their ratings and a 'not applicable' category is also available. The assessors also scrutinise records of ten randomly selected recently discharged patients and again rate them on a four-point scale for each item on a checklist.

Section four of the scale is a 42-item questionnaire to be administered to a random sample of ten patients or their representatives. Section five is an overall summary section in which the assessors are expected to discuss their findings highlighting both shortcomings and positive features, and recommending action for improvement. The scale thus produces both a descriptive judgement and a numerical rating.

Finally the scale contains space for the development of action plans resulting from the exercise of assessment. These are to be developed by the ward teams in conjunction with the relevant quality co-ordinator. One action plan deals with quality action which can be undertaken entirely by the ward team and the other with quality action which requires co-operation or approval from others.

Commentary
The PA/RNOH NQMS is a simple system which is said to have face validity in the orthopaedic settings in which it has been used (Wylie, 1989; Kemp and Richardson, 1990; Wheeler, 1991). It is specifically designed for transfer to other nursing settings. Its general principles of construction and use could transfer to other professions.

No information is available on systematic testing for reliability and validity of the PA/RNOH scale. Kemp and Richardson (1990) comment that some parts of the record based observation checklist 'seem to be ambiguous'. Sampling of patients and records also seems somewhat *ad hoc* and no guidance is given on control for severity of illness/degree of dependency or for time of observation.

The Schmele Instrument to Measure the Process of Nursing Care (SIMP)

Background and Scope
SIMP was developed in 1979 as part of an assessment of the quality of community health care being provided by the American Native Peoples Health Service in Shawnee, Oklahoma (Schmele, 1985). It focuses on measurement of process quality in community nursing. It is premised on the American Nurses' Association standards for home health nursing, which in turn are based on the application of the nursing process model (Yura and Walsh, 1988).

Description
SIMP contains three self-contained data sources namely, observation of nurse/patient interaction (30 items); chart audit (23 items); and client satisfaction (17 items). For each of these data sources there is a list of questions which is subdivided into the four components of the nursing process namely, assessment, planning, implementation and evaluation. Thus under 'nurse/patient interaction observation' the 'assessment' section contains the question 'Did the nurse involve the family in the assessment?' while under the 'client satisfaction survey' section the implementation section contains the question (to be put to the client) 'How well do you understand what you need to do to keep healthy?' The criterial questions were developed from the ANA standards by means of expert judgement and consultation with both practising nurses and nurse educators.

SIMP assessors are experienced nurses who accompany the observed nurses on home visits and observe and make notes. Following visits they complete the observation and chart audit parts of the instrument. Patients are asked to complete the client satisfaction instrument immediately after the relevant visit. Each data source can yield a maximum score of 100 (maximum 300 for the whole instrument) and each of the four sections within each source can yield a maximum score of 25. A yes response to any individual question gives a score which is a proportion of 25 depending on the number of questions in that section. No and non-applicable answers are both given a score of zero. Scores are then summed for each section and each data source and for the whole instrument.

The sample of nurses and patients chosen for observation in the studies reported was selected opportunistically and no guidance is given on either patient selection or frequency of assessment.

Commentary
SIMP is a US instrument which does not seem to have been taken up elsewhere although the nursing process is widely accepted as a model in the UK and Europe and the ANA standards for home health care

which Schmele refers to are very closely tied to it. It seems to have been easy to use and to have been acceptable in community nursing contexts. It could possibly be adapted for use by other professions practising in community contexts.

SIMP has been validated in a study carried out with the assistance of the Visiting Nurse Association in Oklahoma City. Patient groups were said to be 'very representative of the types of clients that make up the caseloads in home health care' (Schmele and Foss, 1989a, p. 57). Internal consistency coefficients for the first two data sources were high (0.87 for observation and 0.75 for chart audit) although the coefficient for the client satisfaction part of the instrument was very low at 0.25. Schmele and Foss attribute this to general difficulties of measurement in patient satisfaction studies. Construct validity was tested by asking observers to complete the Slater scale (Wandelt and Stewart, 1975) for the nurses who had been observed using SIMP. No positive association was found, however, and the authors discuss this in terms of the Slater scale's broader content and emphasis and suggest that it would be useful to retest SIMP's validity against the unpublished version of the Slater scale which is more closely tied to the nursing process model (Stewart, 1984).

Schmele and Foss make it clear that SIMP is in its initial stages and that it will undergo further validation and modification but consider that 'it will have practical value in measuring the process aspect of nursing care in home health' (Schmele and Foss, 1989a, p. 62).

Quality Control Techniques

Background and Scope
Quality control techniques were first developed in manufacturing industry in the 1930s. They preceded the development of quality assurance techniques as such (see Chapter 3, p. 39 for fuller discussion). Quality control involves setting a precise standard for a product or process, monitoring its achievement and either rejecting defective products or remedying ineffective processes. Statistical techniques are often used to determine the amount of variation which can be allowed before quality falls below a predetermined threshold. Statistical quality control techniques thus accept that some variation is inevitable but facilitate its control. Quality control can thus be distinguished from simple inspection of product quality by its emphasis on processes as well as products and by its acceptance of a level of variation. It remains an important part of wider systems of industrial quality assurance and quality management.

Similar techniques are in widespread use in health care quality assurance in areas where the aim is to produce or in some way manipulate physical (including biological) objects rather than to treat people directly. Quality control thus has its major applications in pathology, radiology, nuclear medicine and medical laboratory science.

Description
Quality control techniques are designed to control not just the quality of products but also the quality of the process which led up to their production. Careful description of each step in the relevant process and of the sequence of steps is a necessary precursor of quality control. This is often done by constructing a flow diagram. It can include indication of the various points at which resources are required and of the time it is expected each step will take. Oakland (1989) points out that this exercise alone can often produce opportunities for improved process quality as unnecessary or duplicate steps are revealed.

Once the flow chart is established and accepted as an accurate picture of the process it becomes possible to analyse adverse events or below standard products in terms of the frequency with which they can be attributed to the various steps in the process.

The most important feature of quality control systems is the 'control chart'. Such charts are designed in various different ways but they all facilitate the easy determination of limits of variability beyond which a product or process is not allowed to go. If it does go beyond them it is the employee's duty to either halt or modify the process in some way. The control chart is thus a kind of traffic signal signifying go, caution or stop depending on the degree of variation from the predetermined standard. There are different types of control charts for different situations but the most frequently used are charts showing means and ranges for variables known to be significant in the relevant process, and charts showing number or proportion of defective products. There is now a wide variety of statistical techniques for process analysis. These are more fully discussed in Oakland (1986) and Ross (1988).

In health care quality control standards have been set in pathology and other related areas in a number of countries. Thus in the US there is a College of American Pathologists (CAP) scheme (Koepke, 1974) and in the UK the National External Quality Assurance Scheme (NEQAS) has been in existence since 1969. These schemes establish guidelines and standards for the establishment and implementation of quality control procedures. They refer to such matters as staff qualifications, equipment and instrumentation, accommodation, and safety, as well as making recommendations for frequency and content of quality control surveys and procedures. The bodies concerned also carry out visitations and inspections.

Commentary

Despite the well-established procedures for laboratory oriented quality control there is limited evidence of their extension to other areas in health care although some authors (Laffel and Blumenthal, 1989; Dagher and Lloyd, 1991) have suggested wider application. In the laboratory context there is universal acceptance of the need for quality control procedures. There is debate about particular techniques and about the range of activities over which they are appropriate.

Several authors who are themselves radiologists or pathologists have suggested that the processes of ordering, delivering and commenting on test and laboratory results might be subjected to flow analysis and process control (Friedman, 1986; Rickert, 1986; Lamki et al., 1990). Thus standards would be set for the time of delivery of samples and results to specified individuals and locations and undue variation from standard times would be subject to review. Dagher and Lloyd (1991) describe the extension of flow analysis to the activities of an Accident and Emergency Department.

Outcome Appraisal Techniques

The outcomes of care are its various effects on patients. These effects can be physical or psychological and can be assessed in individual patients or in groups of patients. They include mortality; health status (in general and in respect of specific conditions); level of function; freedom from pain and discomfort; well-being and attitudes to self, health and illness; and response to care delivered including understanding, participation, compliance and satisfaction.

The existence of sound techniques for the measurement and analysis of outcomes might be thought essential to health care quality assurance. Regrettably, however, the literature reflects the extreme difficulties encountered by researchers, clinicians and quality assurance specialists in (a) agreeing what appropriate indicators of good and bad outcomes are (b) disentangling the results of health care interventions from the confounding effects of other variables and (c) demonstrating relationships between measures of the process of care and measures of related outcomes.

As Berwick and Knapp (1987, p. 51) comment 'we simply know too little today about what in health care actually does produce good health to rely on the measurement of outcome quality as an indicator of the process quality of the care delivered'. In similar vein the US Institute of Medicine notes that despite the great wealth of clinical research less than 20% of current medical practices (other than the prescription of drugs) have ever been validated in blind clinical trials (Institute of Medicine, 1985). The other 80% are thus adopted on the basis that clinicians *think* they work. Even given validation in clinical trials such validation addresses only the 'efficacy' of a procedure or treatment in ideal circumstances and not its 'effectiveness' in the real world of day-to-day health care. If little is known about the clinical efficacy of much medical care even less is known about its effect on particular patients. The appraisal of outcome quality explores just these effects.

Berwick and Knapp go on to suggest that in many cases (particularly in ambulatory care) the patient's objectives in seeing a physician are better described in terms of feelings and attitudes than in the conventional categories of cure or palliation of 'illness'. In other words the patient may be well satisfied to be given reassurance or just to be listened to despite having been provided with little in the way of more interventionist care. Thus they argue that what health care provides in some contexts is 'not outcome in the sense of increased longevity or function – but rather process itself'.

The difficulties of examining relationships between process and outcome are well detailed by Slater (1989). He reviews a range of studies in ambulatory care among which he finds half demonstrating a positive relationship and half demonstrating none. He concludes that 'it has not been possible to demonstrate with consistency a relationship between assessments of process and outcome' (p. 359). He also points out, however, that the failure may be methodological rather than substantive. The one study which was able to employ a fully experimental design with random allocation of subjects and longitudinal outcome follow up did demonstrate a relationship between type of care and outcome (Hypertension Detection and Follow-up Program, 1979).

Donabedian (1987) recognises the difficulties and suggests that process and outcome measures should be regarded as complementary rather than as alternatives. He also suggests that deficiencies highlighted by outcome measurement can profitably lead to more detailed examination of process quality. Hanks and Kramer (1984) describe a quality assurance initiative in which the source of divergent outcomes for two virtually identical groups of Hodgkin's disease patients who had been treated in the same way in similar care settings was eventually tracked down to a consistently occurring technical failure in a pathology laboratory. Previous less detailed investigation of laboratory procedures had not identified the failure. The results of outcome measurement do not always lead to such investigation of process however. Without a reasonable indication of the relationship between the processes of care and their outcomes it is often difficult to know where to look for the causes of poor outcome quality. Remedy and improvement may thus be impossible.

Despite the undeniable difficulties outcome measures do have several basic advantages. First, they reflect the totality of care received from the point of first admission or request for treatment to final discharge or death; second, they are readily understood and accepted as valid by both patients and practitioners; and finally, they can be used to indicate not just the quality of care received but needs for further or compensatory care. All of these advantages obtain whether the outcome measures being considered are of care quality for individual patients or aggregated measures of care quality for specified settings or geographical areas.

Many outcome studies concern clinically specific local outcomes determined as important by the practitioners involved. Thus published accounts of medical audit as described by Shaw (1990) have included local outcome evaluations as means to the improvement of quality in X-ray identification of carcinoma of the colon (Stephenson, et al., 1984); follow up procedures in respect of women with abnormal cervical smears (Cotton et al., 1986); management of acute myocardial infarction patients (Frangley and Corkill, 1984); prescribing of anti-microbial drugs to maternity cases (Pridmore and Gunthorpe, 1985); use of blood fractions (Rutherford, 1987); notification to GPs of hospital deaths (Neville, 1987); identification of fractures (Tachakra and Beckett, 1985); and prevention of deaths from asthma (Eason and Markowe, 1987). The 'Lothian Audit' (Gruer et al., 1986) which is the longest standing systematic local audit in the UK also makes substantial use of outcome evaluation.

These and similar medical outcome audit procedures are very clinically focused and are specific to the settings of the audits concerned. The measuring tools employed are the traditional tools of clinical observation, investigation and diagnosis. They will not be dealt with in detail here. Readers with similar interests may wish to pursue the references.

In nursing, too, a number of specific local initiatives have developed and used outcome standards and many of the general systems developed for local nursing quality assurance give explicit guidance on so doing (Mayers et al., 1977; Daugherty and Mason, 1987; Pearson, 1987; Kemp and Richardson, 1990; Kitson, 1990). With a few exceptions the rehabilitation and other professions allied to medicine have tended to focus on process standards and measurements. Where outcomes have been addressed they have been patient satisfaction outcomes (England et al., 1989).

For obvious reasons patient death is an outcome which has been the subject of considerable interest. There is a well-established tradition of comparing regions, hospitals and services on the basis of mortality data, particularly where death can be said to have been avoidable or untimely (Hooker, 1933; Kohl, 1955; Shapiro et al., 1958; Royal College of Physicians, 1978; Lunn and Mushin, 1982; Charlton and Lakhani, 1986; HMSO, 1986; Buck et al., 1987). Use of such data in isolation without correction for the mix of cases being handled or for a variety of exogenous patient factors such as class, ethnicity, nutritional status or social support networks has been heavily criticised. Conversely, it has been argued that if allowances were made for such confounding variables there would be so little variability left between hospitals or regions as to make comparison pointless (Lohr, 1988).

It has also been pointed out that death is a relatively rare event in health care and thus virtually irrelevant as an indicator of quality in the treatment of the majority of conditions. One aspect of the unavoidable mortality data which has been demonstrated repeatedly, however, is the relationship between low mortality figures for a given condition and high volume of such cases treated (Hughes et al., 1987). This is often interpreted as a specialism or 'practice makes perfect' effect. As Lohr (1988) points out however causality may be in the reverse direction and low mortality rates may lead to high rates of referral and thus high volume rather than the other way about.

'Avoidable morbidity' data (including data on inappropriate treatments and avoidable complications) are also available for some conditions (Lakhani, 1985), and for readmission after surgery (Lakhani, 1985; Roos, 1986; Wennberg, 1987). As Cleary and McNeil (1988) point out, however, such measures are also subject to the confounding influences of case mix and other variables. Also, like mortality measures, they give little indication of where to initiate changes in process with a view to improvement in outcomes.

Outcome evaluation is also a feature of the various regional comparisons facilitated in the UK by the regular publication of health statistics from the Office of Population Censuses and Surveys and of data based on the various NHS performance indicators. Again such data can only be used with caution since as the UK Standing Medical Advisory Committee (HMSO, 1990b, p. 32) point out 'interpretation (must) take into account factors such as the validity of the data, variations in the incidence and prevalence of disease in the community being served and other confounding factors including case mix'. They conclude that the usefulness of such indicators in carrying out medical audit is limited.

In the US recent 'small area studies' (Wennberg and Gittelsohn, 1973; Keller, 1988; Spitzer and Caper, 1989) and comparisons of access to care among differing socioeconomic and ethnic groups (Woolhandler and Himmelstein, 1988) also make use of outcome evaluation alongside consideration of demographic and other variables. While these service level studies are of obvious importance in the overall pattern of health care quality assurance the specific techniques employed in ensuring valid comparisons are essentially those of statistical epidemiology and public health and will therefore not be dealt with here. Studies at this level are also even further from identification of opportunities for quality improvement than more local outcome audits.

The techniques which will be considered here will include a number of instruments for the measurement of general (i.e. clinically non-specific; applicable to a range of conditions) health care outcomes. They will also include techniques for control of confounding variables. Thus techniques for making allowances for the severity of illness of the patients whose care is being considered will be included. Patient satisfaction as an outcome of care will be considered briefly but readers will be referred to other sources for detailed consideration of the very extensive literature on the subject (a subsequent section in this chapter will return to patient satisfaction surveys in the context of techniques for consumer involvement; general issues of questionnaire design and survey methodology will be dealt with in Chapter 5). Psychometric and other approaches to the assessment of health status and general well-being will also be dealt with briefly and issues surrounding the design and use of psychometric tests will be returned to in Chapter 5.

The techniques to be considered will be grouped as follows:

- General health indicators.
- Quality of life measures.
- Measures of disease and disability.
- Pain measures.
- Patient satisfaction measures.
- Severity of illness classifications.

Since a large number of instruments are available in each group they will not be dealt with one by one. References to other sources will be given.

General Health Indicators

Background and Scope
General health is taken here to mean overall positive health without reference to any particular condition or diagnosis. It would be possible for physicians to make judgements about patients' levels of health on the basis of records of past illness and consultation or on the basis of a profile of physical indicators. The scales considered here do not adopt that approach but rely instead on self-report of perceptions of health. They are a systematisation of the physician's traditional question 'How do you feel?'.

Measurement of general health has gradually increased in significance as articulation of the aims of care has moved beyond statements about increase in life expectancy and prevention and cure of disease to include subtler concepts. Thus the World Health Organisation

(1958, p. 459) describes the aims of care as 'physical, mental and social well-being and not merely the absence of disease and infirmity'. A large number of general health scales have been devised and several articles and textbooks provide annotated listings and reviews (Bergner, 1985; Lohr and Ware, 1987; McDowell and Newell, 1987). The scales have been used in many health research contexts and to a lesser extent in outcome quality appraisal (Davies and Ware, 1981; Lohr, 1988). Some scales have been developed for use with particular groups in the general population such as the elderly (Kane and Kane, 1981) and children (Johnson, 1976). Others such as the arthritis impact measurement scale (Meenan, 1982; Meenan et al., 1982) and the physical and mental impairment of function evaluation for the chronically ill scale (Gurel et al., 1972) are designed to be used with groups of people with specified diagnoses although still assessing general health.

Description

These scales are essentially self-report questionnaires designed for use in both clinical and research contexts. They are developments of techniques previously devised in psychological testing and attitude scaling. They vary in sophistication but most have been piloted and developed with appropriate populations, are based on an explicit model or approach to the definition of general health, and provide information on validity and reliability.

The available scales vary in their length, emphases and subdivisions. Thus among the best established scales the Nottingham Health Profile (Hunt et al., 1981) has 38 questions grouped into six sections on energy level, pain, emotional reactions, sleep, social isolation, and physical abilities; the Sickness Impact Profile (Bergner et al., 1981) has 136 questions grouped into physical and psychosocial dimensions; and the General Health Ratings Index (Davies and Ware, 1981) deals with perceptions of past health, current health, future health, worry and concern about health, and belief about susceptibility to illness.

Many general health measures have subscales on mental health and social adjustment and a number of measures are available which concentrate exclusively on these aspects of health in general populations (i.e. among people not previously diagnosed as requiring psychiatric care or support). Significant among these are the General Well-being Schedule (Dupuy, 1978), the Mental Health Inventory (Ware et al., 1979) and the General Health Questionnaire (Goldberg, 1978).

Commentary

McDowell and Newell note that the well-established scales of general health have proved their worth in respect of standardisation, reliability and validity and conclude that they 'are in many ways the showpiece of current health measurement technology' (1987, p. 320).

Measures of general health have had more use in research contexts than in quality assurance but could profitably be more frequently adopted in outcome assessment. They can be used at service or local level and provide a sound basis for studies comparing outcomes in different groups or at different points in time. Lohr (1988) suggests that they might be particularly pertinent in assessing the quality of care in long-stay settings.

As with all self-report measures administration and data collection can present problems (e.g. respondent literacy, motivation, availability) and consideration should be given to the practicality of the measures alongside consideration of their validity and reliability.

Quality of Life Measures

Background and Scope
As general health has come to be accepted as a significant outcome of health care subtler aspects of 'health' and 'wellness' have assumed greater importance. Specifically, attempts have been made to examine the effects of health care on quality of life. This has involved health professionals, social scientists and others in considerable contention regarding appropriate definitions and operationalisations of 'life quality'. Quality of life scales and techniques have nonetheless been developed for general populations and for specific groups such as the chronically ill (Spitzer et al., 1981) and the elderly (Lawton, 1975).

Quality of life measures have four main areas of use each of which impinge on outcome quality assurance. First, they are used in the evaluation of particular treatment programmes or settings (e.g. nursing home care); second, they are used in the assessment of the cost effectiveness of particular treatments and thus in resource allocation; third they are used in selecting treatments for individual patients; and fourth, they are used in selecting patients for treatments where waiting lists are long and resources scarce.

Description
The available measures vary widely but an initial distinction can be made between measures which are conventional scales designed to measure respondents' quality of life status at a given point in time and those which are designed to be used in conjunction with an assessment of life expectancy. The latter techniques yield a prospective measure of the number of 'quality adjusted' years of life a particular treatment is likely to provide for an individual patient or for a group of patients. Thus a treatment which gave 10 years of life

with 50% function might be regarded as equal in value to a treatment which gave five years of life with 100% function.

McDowell and Newell (1987) review quality of life measures not related to life expectancy. They note that there is considerable confusion in the literature and recommend clear distinction between measures of quality of life per se, of life satisfaction, of morale, and of happiness. They define measures of quality of life as combinations of measures of material circumstances and of people's perceptions of the adequacy of these circumstances. Measures of life satisfaction are defined as comparisons of perceived quality of life with external standards or with aspirations. Morale measures are said to assess an aspect of mental orientation (and are thus close to personality assessments); and happiness measures are concerned with transient states of well-being in response to events.

Other authors (Zautra and Goodhart, 1984; Holmes, 1989) have suggested devising scales which assess adjustment to changing circumstances and scales which measure perceptions of mastery and control. Cohen (1982) examines the idea of satisfaction and adjustment over the life-span and proposes a definition in terms of satisfactory realisation of 'life plans'. He suggests that some features of an individual's life plan will be unique while other features will be substantially universal. Valid scales would thus have core questions which addressed the universal features of such plans while other optional questions would allow for individual variation.

Given the slipperiness of the quality of life construct it might be expected that attempts to use such measures in determining or evaluating treatment would be undertaken with great hesitation. In fact the concept of the 'quality adjusted life year' in which assessments of quality of life are associated with life expectancy is in considerable vogue. There are two main sources of this methodology namely the Quality of Well-being Scale (QWB) (Kaplan and Bush, 1982) and the Quality Adjusted Life Year (QALY) technique developed by Williams (1985).

The QWB scale was developed specifically for purposes of cost benefit analysis and resource allocation. It 'quantifies the health output of any treatment in terms of the years of life, adjusted for their diminished quality, that it produces or saves' (Kaplan and Bush, 1982). A 'well year' is defined as a year free from illness and thus of optimum quality. If disease reduces the quality of life by one half then during a year of chronological life only 0.5 'well years' will be obtained. Conversely, a health care intervention which restores the quality of life from 0.5 to 1.00 produces 0.5 'well years'. If the treatment is given to a number of people then the number of 'well years' increases accordingly and the cost effectiveness of the treatment can be derived by dividing the total number of 'well years' produced by the total cost. If resources are scarce it will be appropriate to deploy them on treatments which produce the maximum number of 'well years' for a given outlay. Spending money on expensive treatments which can only be given to a few people may therefore be less appropriate than spending the same amount of money on a large number of less immediately dramatic treatments which produce more 'well years' for the same expenditure.

The QWB classifies individuals who have received particular treatments in three stages. First, a structured interview lasting about 15 minutes is administered during which information is elicited on mobility, physical activity, and social activity including self care. The individual is then rated on a five-point scale on each of these dimensions. Each possible permutation of ratings by dimensions (excluding those which are said not to occur in the medical literature or to be logically impossible reduces this to 43 'function levels') is then related to a 'level of well being' value derived from judgements of 'undesirability' undertaken by a population sample in which 867 subjects rated some 500 items. Finally, adjustments are made to the rating to reflect any prognoses which the patient has for future transition to better or poorer health. This is combined with life expectancy to give the 'well life expectancy'. Simple averaging produces figures for populations and the total years of 'well life expectancy' which treatments or programmes are producing can be calculated.

Williams' (1985) QALY technique is a similar but much simpler procedure based originally on questioning 70 healthy individuals on their evaluation of various states of loss of mobility and presence or absence of pain. These assessments are related to the likely results of various treatments and combined with life expectancy data to yield the number of 'QALYS' likely to be produced by the intervention for one or several patients. As with QWB 'well life years' the results are combined with cost information to provide an indication of the most cost-effective treatments. It is suggested, however, that the results of QALY calculation can also be used to assist practitioners to decide which patients to prioritise for treatment and, in circumstances of less resource scarcity, to counsel patients as to the optimum choice of procedure.

Commentary

McDowell and Newell (1987) review a number of scales which assess quality of life without relating it to life expectancy. They conclude that the scale for which the best evidence on reliability and validity can be found is the Life Satisfaction Index (Neugarten et al., 1961). They note, however, that its theoretical basis has been criticised and that there is uncertainty as to what it actually measures and thus as to interpretation of scores. This uncertainty chimes with Campbell's (1981) finding that when healthy individuals are questioned about the quality of their life they respond differently in relation to different domains. Thus satisfaction with family life might be high, with health might be moderate and with material circumstances might be very low. Respondents provide a satisfaction profile rather than a global assessment of satisfaction and scales which do not allow for this have limited validity. Ferrans and Powers' (1985) observe that the relative importance of satisfaction domains varies over a lifetime and that each does not influence overall perceptions of life quality equally. Variation in individual perceptions of life quality are also emphasised in the sociological critique that current assessments ignore cultural plurality and reflect the value systems of the white, middle class, western world (Holmes, 1989; Mulkay et al., 1987).

There is thus a variety of definitions and approaches and it is not surprising that the literature does not reflect a clear relationship between perceived quality of life and either material circumstances (Najman and Levine, 1981) or health status as measured by conventional means (Robinson and Shaver, 1973; Freedman, 1978; Najman and Levine, 1981). On the other hand, health status has often been shown to be an important dimension of perceptions of life quality (Knapp, 1976; Flanagan, 1982).

Despite the uncertain status of measures of life satisfaction and other aspects of quality of life their use in outcome quality assurance is increasing and it is likely that new scales will be developed for use in particular settings such as care of older people.

Both QWB and QALY measures have been subject to considerable criticism on both ethical and methodological grounds. QWB has also been criticised for its impracticality, although it has in fact been used in the evaluation of a range of screening programmes and other treatments (McDowell and Newell, 1987).

QALY methodology has been criticised for the smallness of the sample of judges upon whose evaluations it is based (Goodinson and Singleton, 1989); for the limited number of quality of life dimensions upon which it is based (Goodinson and Singleton, 1989; Holmes, 1989); for its failure to take account of individual variation in preferences and utilities and for ignoring the ethical implications of not doing so (Harris, 1987; Mulkay, et al., 1987; Holmes, 1989); and for invalid calculation of preferences (Gafni, 1989).

In addition to the criticisms already cited it might also be noted that both QWB and QALY techniques assume that treatments are always provided in similarly propitious circumstances and are thus uniformly effective.

Despite these many criticisms there is clearly something simple and attractive in the notion of calculating health care outcomes in terms of increased quality of life. At an implicit level it is likely that many individual practitioners and patients already use some such assessment in deciding whether or not to give or ask for treatment. The uses to which the explicit methodologies are likely to be put, however, include the assessment of quality at service or regional levels. They are also likely to be used in establishing care priorities and, as resources become scarcer, in the rationing of care. In that context they should be used with caution in their present form.

Disability Measures

Background and Scope
When quality assurance is being carried out for a group of diagnostically similar or identical patients one obvious source of outcome assessment is the range of physiological and other measures which have been clinically validated as indicators of disease. Thus the quality of management of diabetic patients might be assessed in part at least by regular measurement of blood glucose levels, or of treatment of chronic respiratory disorder by assessment of vital capacity and so on. These measures are clinical indicators of disease, and by implication disability.

Explicit measures of disability fall into two categories. First, there are indirect measures such as number of days away from work, number of days of restricted activity, enforced unemployment or premature retirement. Measures of this kind are often used in evaluations of large scale health programmes or of entire services.

The second category contains the very large number of scales and questionnaires which have been designed by rehabilitation specialists to assess the extent of functional disability or handicap suffered by patients before, during and after care. Scales are available for screening, clinical, and research purposes and have been designed for use with patients suffering from specific disorders, with severely and mildly disabled groups, and with groups drawn from the general community. The concept and model of disability underlying such tests varies considerably but it is possible to trace in their development the increasing emphasis on independent living for disabled groups. Thus the earliest tests tended to be based on clinical descriptions of types of impairment whereas later tests assess patients' capacity (or lack of capacity) to carry out 'activities of daily living'. Similarly, the activities selected for emphasis have increasingly come to be those associated with life in the community rather than in sheltered care.

While there is little evidence of the use of these assessments in outcome quality assurance they are regularly used by the rehabilitation professions in the evaluation of individual and group treatment programmes and it is only a matter of time until they are employed in quality assurance as such. Bair and Joe (1989) note that the American Association of Occupational Therapy sees the development and evaluation of standardised assessments of functional disability as an area of special emphasis in their response to the need for improved quality assurance systems.

Description

Clinical indicators of disease are both numerous and beyond the technical scope of this book. They will not therefore be described in detail, although it is clear that they have a significant role to play in health care quality assurance. This section, then, will be limited to description of explicit measures of disability, specifically those which go beyond the relatively straightforward assessment of days of generally defined restricted activity to the assessment of what is generally known as 'activities of daily living' (ADL).

McDowell and Newell (1987) comment that 'there has been a proliferation of scales to measure physical disability and handicap' and indicate that they found descriptions of more than 50 in the literature (they go on to review 13). Were a similar search to be carried out today the number would be higher and yet more have undoubtedly been developed locally without subsequent publication. Unfortunately, as several authors have commented (Gresham and Labi, 1984; McDowell and Newell, 1987; Eakin, 1989a; b), the quantity of these scales is not matched by their quality.

ADL scales are generally assessments of patients' abilities to carry out a number of tasks which are thought to be significant aspects of independent life, self-care and integration in the community. They often combine questionnaire and direct observation techniques and almost without exception are administered to individual patients on a one to one basis. Those which are designed specifically for use with patients who are (or are about to be) living in the community are sometimes referred to as 'instrumental activities of daily living' (IADL) scales. They are more likely to contain items on activities such as shopping or use of public transport than are the more restricted ADL scales.

The most frequently used scale (in the UK as well as the US) is the Barthel Index (Mahoney and Barthel, 1965). The Barthel Index is an ADL scale originally intended for use with long-stay patients, although it has been used in a wide variety of other contexts. It is a rating scale completed from records and by direct observation. Scores of zero, five, 10 or 15 are assigned to each of 10 topics (or 15 in the extended version) including such items as feeding, toileting, bathing, dressing, continence, and various aspects of mobility.

Commentary

Despite their immediate attractiveness clinically relevant indicators of disease have disadvantages in quality assurance outcome measurement. Lohr (1988), for example, suggests that they are intrusive and difficult to collect (particularly if their collection is over and above the regular provision of care); that they provide at best a partial assessment of the quality of care (particularly if the patients concerned suffer more than one ailment); and that they are unsuitable in areas where the optimal therapeutic approach is unclear.

Measures of restricted participation in normal employment or other activities also have their disadvantages. They are difficult to collect, are rarely condition specific, and do little to indicate either sources of poor care or potential for improvement.

The more specific ADL and IADL measures have had some limited use in quality assurance and, as noted above, more extensive use in programme evaluation. Unfortunately, many of them are unsatisfactory. McDowell and Newell (1987), for example, lament their lack of theoretical foundation. They suggest that the scales show little evidence of refinement or elaboration of concepts of disability and handicap and that their content and coverage may be inappropriate. They also regret the lack of reliability and validity data for most scales. Eakin (1989a; b) reviews 15 scales and finds that they vary considerably in the definition and operationalisation of content; that their reliabilities are often suspect; that their users often assume unwarranted generalisability of results from hospital to home care settings; that validity studies are limited; and, finally, that many scoring procedures are inappropriate for the type of scale. As noted above the Barthel Index is the most popular ADL scale. It too has limitations however. McDowell and Newell (1987) comment that it is restricted in both scope and content since deterioration and improvement can occur beyond either end of the scale and since it includes nether mental nor verbal function. Nonetheless, they also note that evidence for the reliability and validity of the Barthel Index is more substantial than for other ADL scales.

In summary, it seems that while measures of disease and disability have obvious potential for employment in outcome quality measurement their current status suggests that they should be used with caution.

Pain Measures

Background and Scope
Reduction in pain is an obviously desirable outcome in many areas of health care and formal assessment of pain can be used in overall assessment of care quality or as part of local initiatives with groups of patients or even individual patients for whom reduction of pain is particularly important. Pain, however, is a subjective phenomenon and measurement is therefore difficult. Pain is related to tissue damage but not directly, since minor damage can lead to intense pain

and major damage to relatively little pain. A range of biological, psychological and social factors have been shown to influence the way in which pain is reported and thus to render self-assessment suspect.

Despite these difficulties a number of techniques for pain measurement have been developed. Those in wide use are mostly questionnaire measures. Measures based on behavioural observation and measures similar to those used in laboratory studies of signal detection are also in use but so far they have had limited clinical application.

Description

The most frequently used assessments of pain are questionnaire measures assessing the intensity of pain experienced. These use either adjectives, a numerical scale or a visual analogue to which the patient is expected to match the severity of the pain experienced. This is variously elaborated to incorporate assessments at different times, over different durations and in response to different aspects of treatment (e.g. provision of analgesic medication). The best established pain inventory of this kind is the McGill Pain Questionnaire (Melzack, 1980). The MPQ is based upon a list of 102 words describing pain which are grouped into three major classes namely those associated with the sensory qualities of pain (e.g. burning, throbbing); those associated with the affective qualities of pain (e.g. blinding, annoying); and those associated with the overall intensity of the experience of pain (e.g. mild, vicious). Respondents tick the words which apply to them and note is taken of other aspects of the patient's condition. Each word is associated with a value for intensity in its subclass (sensory, affective, overall) and scoring based upon simple addition is used to obtain totals for the subclasses or overall. The intensity values are based on expert judgements of students, patients and physicians obtained during the development of the test. Acceptable reliability and validity coefficients are quoted in McDowell and Newell's (1987) review of the technique.

Commentary

While there is little current evidence of use of pain assessment measures in outcome based quality assurance there is certainly scope for their employment. Ferrell et al. (1991) discuss the importance of pain management in oncology nursing and describe an approach to the record based audit of pain management procedures.

Patient Satisfaction Measures

Background and Scope

Patient satisfaction measures are among the most frequently used techniques in health care quality assurance. Dalley et al.'s (1991) survey of quality assurance initiatives in the NHS found that they were the most frequently mentioned techniques being cited by over 20% of respondents. They have also had very substantial use in programme evaluation and in other areas of health care research. There is thus a substantial literature and a relatively refined method-ology and several extensive reviews can be found (Cleary and McNeil, 1988; Hall et al., 1988; Hall and Dornan, 1989; McIver and Carr-Hill, 1989; Evason and Whittington, 1991). There is a separate but related literature on the use of questionnaire and survey techniques for the assessment of patient compliance with instructions and treatment regimens (Ley, 1988; Sbarbaro, 1990) findings from which might also be interpreted as assessments of outcome quality but not necessarily of satisfaction.

Patient satisfaction measures have been used for a variety of purposes and in a wide range of settings. Some are designed to identify problems and potential improvements, some provide an overall estimate of satisfaction with a given service or episode of care and some are used as part of an initiative in increasing patient participation in care. Administration can be by postal survey, by aided or unaided group or individual completion in the care setting, or as part of a structured or unstructured interview carried out in the care setting or in the patient's home. Respondents can be patients or their relatives or other representatives and administration can take place during or after care. Almost all specialties have been the subject of patient satisfaction measures although the Dalley et al. survey of NHS patient satisfaction activities (1989) showed that maternity care was the most frequent setting.

Description
Patient satisfaction measures vary in reflection of the wide variety of purposes and settings for which they are designed. Thus some are substantial documents providing a structure for hour long interviews while others are extremely simple instruments with half a dozen closed or even yes/no questions targeted at very specific groups of patients. Some are detailed, multi-dimensional scales designed to assess the overall construct of satisfaction and have been tested for reliability and validity (Ware and Snyder, 1975; Locker and Dunt, 1978) while others are simpler one off questionnaires designed for specific settings and do not aspire to such sophistication.

Commentary
Despite the large number of patient satisfaction studies which have been undertaken and the increasing use of patient satisfaction measures in quality assurance a number of methodological difficul-

ties must be noted. First, the definitions and operationalisations of satisfaction underlying the various scales designed to assess the global construct vary considerably. Comparisons between studies or generalisations to new settings are therefore perilous. Second, it has been shown that individual variables such as age, social class, sex, race, level of education and type of medical insurance influence satisfaction (Locker and Dunt, 1978; Weiss, 1988; Zastowny et al., 1989). This may be a function of care provided for different groups but it may equally be a function of different expectations or different susceptibility to answering questions in a 'socially desirable' i.e. positive way. Social desirability has also been suggested as an explanation of the frequently noted phenomenon that most patient satisfaction enquiries produce very positive results. Patients still receiving care may not wish to offend their carers by responding negatively (Halpern, 1985; Jefferson and Storm-Clark, 1989). Finally, patient satisfaction surveys have been criticised for their restricted content. A number of reviewers (Cleary and McNeil, 1988; Hall and Dornan, 1989) point out that satisfaction with the interpersonal aspects of care is assessed much more frequently than satisfaction with technical aspects. Other authors (Pollitt, 1988; 1989; Calnan, 1989; Evason and Whittington, 1991) suggest that some patient satisfaction surveys are superficial exercises restricted to 'wallpaper and waiting rooms (and avoiding) the harder issues surrounding treatment priorities, quality of life and equity of access' (Evason and Whittington, 1991, p. 74).

Severity of Illness Classifications

Background and Scope

A frequent criticism of early record based medical audits stemmed from the inflexibility of the criteria used for selection of cases for subsequent in-depth review (Demlo, 1983). In particular audits were criticised for failing to take account of the differences in the nature and severity of patients' illnesses and thus in the care they required. A number of responses to this criticism emerged including 'criteria mapping' (Greenfield et al., 1975; Kaplan and Greenfield, 1978) which was dealt with on p. 101 above; and disease 'staging' (Gonnella and Goran, 1975; Gonnella and Louis, 1988) in which the sequential development of patients' illnesses is taken into account.

The US Medicare system pays health care providers according to the number and types of patients they treat rather than according to the care they actually provide. Until 1983 they had paid for services provided and the establishment of the new system required classification of patients into types. This was done by the adoption of the Diagnosis Related Groups (DRG) classification system. With increased competition for scarce resources the DRG system was subjected to rigorous scrutiny and was found wanting in several respects. Specifically, it was observed (Van Cleave, 1989; Douglass and Batchelor, 1989) that significant variation in patient needs occurred within DRGs. They were thus unsuitable for the quality assurance systems required by Medicare and other third party purchasers. A number of alternative classification systems designed to reflect the severity of patient illness were therefore developed.

In the more substantially state provided health care systems of Europe and the UK patient classification has been less of an issue. Shaw (1990), however, notes that the clinical data capture (CDC) extension system which is a feature of the most frequently used computerised medical record system in the UK (Patient Administration System – PAS) uses the International Classification of Diseases (ICD) automatically. He stresses the importance of using such a classification system in medical audit so as to ensure internal consistency and valid external comparison. The Department of Health have commissioned a number of investigations of possible systems of patient classification for use in these and other contexts.

Description

The various classification systems vary in complexity, specificity, coverage and purpose. The Diagnosis Related Groups and International Classification of Diseases systems are essentially taxonomic groupings of related diseases and do not place particular stress upon individual patient variation in severity or stage of disease. Horn and Buckle (1989) describe five alternative classification systems which they suggest are improvements on DRGs. They are the Acuity Index Measure (AIM) (which elaborates the DRG system by defining subgroups); Acute Physiology and Chronic Health Evaluation (APACHE II) (which assesses the risk of morbidity or mortality for patients admitted to intensive care on the basis of 12 physiological variables, age, and the presence/absence of chronic disease); Computerised Severity Index (CSI) (which, used in conjunction with DRGs produces case mix groups on the basis of diagnostic data and clinical observations); Medical Illness Severity Grouping System (MEDISGROUPS) (which defines severity on the basis of 241 key clinical findings); and Patient Management Categories (PMCs) (which defines approximately 800 clinically homogeneous groups on the basis of a range of diagnoses and clinical procedures). All of the systems are designed for retrospective quality assurance based on selection of cases from records. Several are premised on the use of the Uniform Hospital Discharge Data Set (UHDDS) which is a commonly used method of recording patient information at the point of discharge from hospital.

'Disease Staging' (Gonnella and Goran, 1975; Gonnella and Louis,

1988) was an earlier response to the same problem of variation in case mix and severity of illness in patients treated. Staging is based on the assumption that classification of illness can best be carried out in four dimensions. The first dimension records the location of the disease (e.g. cardiovascular system, respiratory system); the second the etiology of the disease (e.g. autoimmune, degenerative, infectious); the third the pathologic change characteristics of the disease; and the fourth its 'stage'. In staging diseases are divided into four levels of increasing severity. First level conditions are conditions with no complications or complications of minimal severity; second level conditions have problems limited to one organ or system and a greater probability of complications than level one; level three conditions have multiple site involvement, generalised systemic involvement and a poor prognosis; and finally level four is death. Staging criteria are available for over 400 diseases.

As noted above classification of diseases has been less of an issue in Europe than in the US. Nonetheless, a number of quality assurance initiatives have taken severity of illness into account. Thus Fernow et al. (1981) describe a method for measuring the performance of clinicians treating patients with inguinal hernia and with myocardial infarction in which demographic and physiological risk factors in patients were identified and controlled. Similarly, Selbmann et al. (1982) controlled for confounding patient variables in the quality assurance of obstetric care in Bavarian hospitals.

Commentary
Allowance for case mix and severity of illness is clearly more advanced in US quality assurance than in its UK equivalent. It is likely that it will become more widespread. Available techniques have been criticised for lack of reliability and validity and for failure to take account of variations in hospital and practitioner practices in the timing of admission, referral and diagnostic testing (Van Cleave, 1989).

Consumer Involvement Techniques

Background and Scope
In some senses all quality assurance is consumer oriented. In health care, however, there is considerable debate as to the extent to which consumers can or should be involved in appraising and improving the quality of care (Pollitt, 1988; 1989; 1990; 1991; Youll and Perring, 1991). It is generally agreed, though, that while there are many areas of health care quality assurance which require professional knowledge and experience there are also substantial areas where consumer involvement is both feasible and desirable. There is also a developing

consensus that there is room for more consumer involvement than has been traditional (Youll and Perring, 1991; McIver, 1991).

Youll and Perring (1991) discuss consumer involvement in long-term residential care settings and outline a continuum of possibilities ranging from no involvement at all to full membership of governing bodies. Hatfield and Smith (1988) discuss the role of the consumer in psychiatric quality assurance and identify four methods of involvement. They are as follows:

- Providing more quality information and education.
- Offering membership of appropriate professional quality groups, boards of management, commissions, etc.
- Instigating and working with mutual help groups.
- According such groups a role in the processes of referral to specific care settings or practitioners.

As both sets of authors agree such schemes are relatively rare. The overall pattern in health care (and health care quality assurance) is one of more assertion of consumer rights to involvement than actual involvement.

Description

By far the most frequent type of consumer involvement in health care quality assurance is the administration of patient satisfaction instruments. Their results can be used as global measures of outcome quality or to identify potential problem areas or opportunities for improvement. Their use as outcome measures was discussed above (p. 146) and it will therefore be their use in problem spotting which is covered here.

An early account of a patient satisfaction system using telephone interviews (Zimney et al., 1980) details 1954 problems collected from 1110 interviews. In order of frequency the most significant were problems with access and waiting times, with services (including charges), with failure to understand instructions or explanations, and with failure to comply with treatment regimens. The staff of the medical centre involved conducted regular surveys and tackled problems as they emerged. Kind (1989) documents a similar problem focused scheme in which volunteer community practices agreed to undergo an extensive review by groups of patients who rated the practice as a whole, its facilities and the skills of individual practitioners and went on to identify potential for improvement. Kroshus and Abbott (1988) describe a series of telephone surveys designed to tap response to an information and education pack for arthritis sufferers in which a particular focus was not just the degree of non compliance with treatment suggestions but the reasons for non compliance. The education pack was regularly up dated to take account of patient comments.

While comment on care was of course anonymous in each of these initiatives the practitioners knew when and how they were to be assessed and arguably could have 'polished' their performance accordingly. A more 'hidden' system borrowed from the service industries is described by Berwick and Knapp (1987). In this system (in use in the Harvard Care Plan) quality assurance 'stooges' role-play patients seeking information, making appointments and arriving unannounced in reception areas, and make notes and records of the way the practice treats them. The various employees and practitioners of course assume they are real patients. They know that such simulation may occur at some point but not when. According to Berwick and Knapp good feedback is obtained and the Harvard Care Plan intend to develop the idea further.

It was noted above that mutual self-help groups might be involved in the referral of psychiatric patients (Hatfield and Smith, 1988). One or two examples exist of the actual involvement of such groups. The National Coalition for Recognition (NACOR) is an independent quality assurance organisation composed of representatives of the US diabetic community (i.e. of patients). It has set detailed standards and review criteria for diabetes education programmes (NACOR, 1986) which cover needs assessment, programme planning, programme management, communication and co-ordination, access to the programme, curriculum content, instructor standards, and evaluation and review procedures. Criteria are spelt out under each of these headings for the institution delivering the programme and for the programme itself. NACOR grants recognition to diabetes education programmes which meet the standards and it is obviously in the interests of providing institutions to do so. Consumers are thus involved in a quality assurance system in a fashion analogous to the involvement of many professional bodies.

Finally, recent changes in funding patterns in the US have led to increasing concern for the quality and costs of health care among US business interests. A number of developments have thus occurred in which the business community have involved themselves alongside professionals in ensuring quality care for their local community. One such system is detailed in Woods (1990) account of the Greater Cleveland Health Quality Choice Project. In the Cleveland project a voluntary consortium of local business, hospital and physician interests have produced quality indicators for local hospitals and are promoting preferential purchase of care from participating hospitals. Savings from the system will be devoted to ensuring access for underprivileged groups. The quality indicators include a substantial degree of patient consultation and satisfaction measurement.

Commentary

While consumer involvement in health care quality assurance

remains limited it is clearly increasing and a number of novel initiatives have already been documented. If quality is, ultimately, that which satisfies the consumer, more are needed.

The techniques which have been described vary in focus and scope. They are all relatively simple, however, and could well be adapted for use in other settings.

Records Techniques

Background and Scope
The maintenance of adequate records is an essential feature of quality assurance. Retrospective audit would be impossible if patient records were not available for reference and even concurrent audit would be difficult without relevant records of patient assessments and care plans. Records and documentation are similarly essential once observations and measurements have been made. Without them discussion of gaps between standards and practice and of possible action for improvement would degenerate into vague or even argumentative assertion.

US medical record systems have been used for quality assurance purposes for a very long time and are in any case more detailed than their European equivalents due to the requirements of the various payment and billing procedures. In the UK several authors comment on the need for improved and preferably computerised record systems for the establishment of sound audit procedures. Shaw (1990) for example suggests that 'accurate, timely, well-presented data are essential' (p. 32). He stresses that this may mean the involvement of information specialists and possibly statisticians and will certainly mean the co-operation of the district medical officer and general manager. He goes on to detail the information management systems typically available in NHS hospitals and concludes that they are a suitable basis for quality assurance. Secker-Walker et al. on the other hand regard current DHSS required recording systems as 'hopelessly inadequate for the task of providing comprehensive descriptions of clinical care or allowing meaningful case mix analysis' (1989, p. 169) and recommend the use of other systems. In UK general practice, too, it seems that record keeping must improve if quality assurance is to be put in place. Irvine (1990a, p. 53) for example states that 'it is acknowledged that the records in British general practice are generally insufficient for reasonable performance monitoring'. He goes on to note that the problem is not just a problem for quality assurance but rather for all aspects of systematic practice and community unit management. Many practices are now actively installing computer recording systems and quality assurance activities should be facilitated by this development.

Description

As in so many areas of health care quality assurance the nursing and rehabilitation professions have well established systems. Thus almost all UK nursing units maintain some kind of care plan or nursing process record which can without too much difficulty be adapted for quality assurance purposes (Mayers et al., 1977; Kemp and Richardson, 1990). Of particular significance in the nursing and rehabilitation professions in both the US and the UK has been the adoption of the Problem Oriented Medical Record (Weed, 1968). POMR is a way of collecting and organising patient data and structuring it according to patient problems so as to facilitate documentation of patient status and care. It can be used by a single profession but is particularly suitable for interprofessional use. The five main components of the POMR are the data base; the problem list; the initial plan; the progress notes; and the discharge summary. The *data base* is a systematic collation and summary of all information available and relevant at the point when the patient's clinical problems are articulated. The *problem list* is a comprehensive list of all of the patient's problems including diagnoses, abnormal laboratory results or other clinical observations, emotional, family or financial problems, etc. Problems can be entered by any member of the interprofessional team and are numbered, thereby becoming an index to the rest of the chart. The *initial plan* is a written statement representing the treatment team's agreed approach to care. It is completed as explicitly as possible and contains specific instructions regarding timing of medication and other procedures. *Progress notes* vary in different users of the POMR system but many users (Mayers et al., 1977; Gatere, 1985) recommend use of the 'SOAP' format where S refers to the patient's *subjective* account of what is happening and of their response to it; O refers to the professionals' *objective* observations of the progress of care; A refers to the professionals' *assessment* following these subjective and objective accounts; and P refers to the resulting *plan* for subsequent care. The *discharge summary* section of the POMR system often follows the same SOAP format. POMR has been used as a basis for quality assurance procedures in nursing (Mayers et al., 1977; Allison and Kinloch, 1981; Gatere, 1985; Kemp and Richardson, 1990) and in the remedial professions (England et al., 1989; Merrall et al., 1991; Wright and Whittington, 1992).

Commentary

As already noted the maintenance of adequate records is a vital part of any quality assurance exercise. Any improvement on the currently rather *ad hoc* nature of medical recording for quality assurance purposes is to be welcomed. Comparisons across clinical firms, units of management, districts, regions or even nations would be greatly assisted by moves towards greater uniformity.

5

Techniques for Quality Assurance in Health Care

Part Two: *Generic Techniques*

Introduction

The last chapter dealt with techniques specifically developed for use in quality assurance in health care. This chapter deals with techniques originating elsewhere but in general use in health care quality assurance. They are grouped as follows:

- Consensus development.
- Surveys.
- Psychometrics.
- Interpersonal skill analysis.

Quality assurance was characterised in earlier chapters as a cycle of activity. The cycle begins with the agreement and setting of standards and proceeds through measurement and appraisal of quality, identification of potential for improvement, action for improvement, and finally return either to reappraisal or to reconsideration of standards. The techniques to be considered in this chapter have been used at various stages in this cycle. Thus setting standards, determining action for improvement and conceivably other stages in the cycle depend on a group of people agreeing – i.e. on consensus development. This often happens relatively unselfconsciously and informally but systematic and explicit techniques have also been used successfully. These will form the core of the guidance given here. Survey techniques (including questionnaires) have been widely used in quality appraisal, particularly in the assessment of patient satisfaction but also in appraisal of the process of care and in the determination of standards. Psychometric tests have had more limited use in outcome and process appraisal but the principles underlying test construction and interpretation are relevant across the spectrum of quality assessment. Interpersonal skill analysis has had only limited use in the appraisal of quality but the principles which underlie it are of considerable relevance in assessment of the process of interaction between professionals and patients which is at the heart of care.

Each of the four types of technique to be considered is well represented in the social and behavioural science and health research literatures, and each has been brought to a high level of technical refinement. This chapter will provide an introductory outline of each type of technique and will explore actual and potential applications in health care quality assurance. Readers who seek more advanced or detailed coverage will be referred to more specialised technical manuals and textbooks. The sections and subsections of this chapter will not be subdivided into background and scope, description, and commentary, in the manner of the previous chapter, but information on these topics will still be provided.

Consensus Development Techniques

Consensus development is a feature of several stages of the quality assurance cycle. It often takes place entirely informally and virtually unremarked. Thus when physicians engaged in peer review of individual cases find similarly socialised colleagues to be of like mind they may give little thought to the way they arrived at agreement. The process is more one of consensus identification and articulation than of consensus development. More explicit procedures for consensus development are likely to be called upon when group members have dissimilar backgrounds; when little is known about the area under discussion; where there is genuine debate in the area; or when the consensus arrived at is to have wide implications or to be given much publicity.

Standard setting is one area where many health care groups have had recourse to explicit techniques for consensus development. The Royal Australian and New Zealand College of Psychiatrists for example developed very detailed specifications of standards for the treatment of schizophrenia, anxiety and other disorders (Andrews, 1984; 1985) based on careful analysis of the literature, sampling of opinion among practitioners and reference to the views (anonymously provided) of a nominated panel of experts. Despite this care there was considerable subsequent correspondence in their journals regarding the validity of some of their suggestions – and indeed of their temerity in undertaking the exercise in the first place. The argument put forward was that consensus procedures do not necessarily produce the *right* conclusions but just the popular ones. Standard setting groups like other committee or work groups are subject to interpersonal conflict, dominance by the powerful or merely noisy, and a tendency to 'group think' or going along with what they have said before (Janis, 1972). Even where decisions are made anonymously judgements are not necessarily free from bias.

Interestingly, only very few reports exist (Enderby and Davies, 1989; Van der Gaag and Davies, 1991) of analysis of actual observed professional practice as a basis for consensual standard setting. Several authors, however, (Ellis, 1988; Neufeld and Chong, 1984) have argued that empirical analysis and observation of competence (and perhaps particularly of interpersonal competence) is a logical precursor of health care standard setting.

Consensus development in any context involves interaction between people. This often takes place in face to face groups. There is a very substantial psychological literature on group discussion, problem solving, negotiation and decision making (Argyle, 1963; 1969; Janis and Mann, 1977; Fisher and Ury, 1981; Blumberg et al., 1983; 1986; Luft, 1984; Morley and Hosking, 1985; Morley, 1986; Whittington, 1986) much of which is at least potentially relevant to the technology of consensus development. Thus in classic studies of group problem solving (Shaw, 1932; Davis and Restle, 1963) groups were given simple problems to solve, their performance was observed and variables which were thought to predict early and accurate problem solution were identified. Lewin (1947) for example suggested that democratic approaches to group discussion and problem solving produced better results than more autocratic approaches or having individuals work in isolation. Later studies have been less sanguine about the clarity of such results however and indeed Hackman and Morris (1983) concluded that 'the few general findings that have emerged...do not encourage the use of groups to perform important tasks'. They stressed, however, that the studies they reviewed may not have done enough to encourage their groups to maximise the potential benefits of being a group. These include having access to a larger pool of information, being able to generate a larger number of potential solutions to the problem in hand, and developing a high level of motivation for the implementation of problem solutions.

Other studies of real and laboratory groups have noted that group performance varies depending on how well established the group is (Tuckman, 1965); that the presence of disruptive individuals or of individuals particularly skilled in leadership or facilitation has an influence on the success and maintenance of the group (Argyle, 1969); and that individuals in groups are more likely to express extreme opinions than those working alone (Stoner, 1968; Moscovici and Zavalloni, 1969).

Irving Janis' studies of 'group think' (Janis, 1972; Janis and Mann, 1977) are particularly pertinent to consideration of the group processes underlying consensus development. Janis and his colleagues began by studying real life government policy formulation groups whose deliberations had led up to 'historical fiascos'. These included Chamberlain's appeasement decision, Kennedy's Bay of Pigs decision, and Johnson's decision to escalate the war in Vietnam. From these case histories and subsequent laboratory studies Janis and his colleagues identified what were termed the 'adverse effects of concurrence seeking' – going for agreement at any price because 'something must be done'. These adverse effects included incomplete survey of alternatives; failure to examine the risks of a preferred choice; failure to reappraise initially rejected alternatives; poor information search; selective bias in processing information at hand; and failure to work out contingency plans. Janis and his colleagues also identified problem ambiguity and complexity and group solidarity and cohesion as factors likely to lead to 'group think' and ready acceptance of inappropriate solutions. All of these factors are likely to be present when groups of professionals set about the development of health care standards or the determination of action for quality improvement. The problems in hand will be complex and difficult to understand, and the quality group is very likely to share a common background and to have common interests. If the group concerned also excludes other legitimate quality stakeholders (e.g. consumers or members of other professions) then 'groupthink' processes in combination with the protection of vested interests could lead to uncritical and possibly inappropriate standard setting.

In summary, the advantages of using groups to develop consensus in health care quality assurance include the potential for a wide canvass of opinion; the notionally higher level of creative generation of ideas; and (significantly) the fact that individuals who have been involved in developing a consensus are more likely to understand its implications and to champion its implementation. The disadvantages are largely those of potential bias, failure to consider all the relevant information, and being too easily persuaded that achieving group consensus is the same as solving the problem. Each of the techniques which will now be considered tries to preserve the advantages by consulting numbers of people but at the same time to counter the disadvantages by somehow overcoming the deleterious influences of face to face interaction. As will be seen this often means keeping participants apart for some at least of the time. The techniques are as follows:

- Standard Committee Procedure.
- Brainstorming.
- Nominal Group Technique.
- Delphi.

Standard Committee Procedure

The most obvious procedure and the one most frequently adopted by professional bodies in determining national standards is the creation of a working party, committee, commission, board or other group with a designated membership and remit. Such groups typically review relevant literature, consult with 'experts', develop networks, and hold workshops with representative practitioners. Through a sequence of meetings (using normal committee procedures) they consider drafts and redrafts of proposals until they finally arrive at a consensus document. Chassin (1988) reviewing standard setting activities in the US medical profession notes the predominance of committees and working groups and comments that such procedures are 'haphazard...without any attempt to be certain of covering all relevant literature...there is often little attempt at critical evaluation...the clinical experience of the authors is often added in to the brew anecdotally and unsystematically'. He concludes that the 'unscientific process does not give one confidence in the validity of the conclusions it produces' and that 'the statements of guidance emerging from this haphazard process are often unusable'. Earlier chapters of this book have noted blandness, lack of specificity and limited guidance on use in several professional standards documents developed through straightforward committee discussion and consultation.

Despite their disadvantages committee procedures are familiar, easy to establish and have considerable face validity. Given that the individuals who chair and participate in committees are aware of the potential hazards and that they have developed appropriate interactional and organisational skills (Whittington, 1986) these benefits may outweigh the disadvantages.

Brainstorming

Brainstorming was first devised by an advertising executive as a way of increasing the number of creative ideas produced in discussion of product advertising campaigns (Osborn, 1957). The basic premise was that the greater the number of ideas produced the more likelihood there was of producing a novel and potentially profitable one. Osborn considered that normal group interaction inhibited the production of ideas as more junior or reticent members of the group deferred to more assertive colleagues. He also noted that proposed ideas were often ignored or condemned out of hand before being properly considered. Brainstorming techniques are designed to counter these difficulties. They have been popular in a range of management training and organisational development contexts and are a particular feature of industrial quality circles.

In basic brainstorming sessions group leaders or facilitators begin by explaining to group members that the aim is to produce as many ideas or problem solutions (which in health care quality assurance might mean approaches to quality improvement or areas for quality appraisal) as possible. They stress the importance of including all possible ideas however silly or trivial they may seem. Contributions are made orally, one by one, and recorded by the facilitator on a master list which is usually compiled on a blackboard or flip chart so that all members can see it. All members have to contribute and if necessary the facilitator will encourage slow contributors. During this contribution phase no comment, evaluation or criticism is allowed and each idea is simply accepted and recorded. Discussion of the ideas contributed only begins once creativity has been exhausted and no more new ideas are being put forward.

Once ideas have been collected they are categorised according to the aims of the group. If for example the group is using brainstorming to identify possible areas for quality appraisal it would be sensible to remove from the list all suggestions which are clearly beyond the powers of the group, and then perhaps to categorise ideas in terms of ease of appraisal, or time and resources needed to carry out the exercise, or seriousness of poor quality, before eventually deciding on one or more areas.

In industrial quality circles brainstorming is often used in conjunction with Ishikawa's fishbone cause and effect analysis diagrams (Ishikawa, 1982; Hutchins, 1990). Here brainstorming is being used at a later stage in the quality cycle to decide on likely causes of poor quality and thus to identify possible action for quality improvement. The fishbone diagram works back from the existence of a given quality problem to analyse the possible contributory causes. The

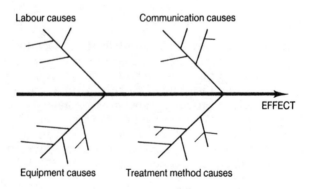

Fig. 5.1 An Ishikawa fishbone cause and effect diagram

initial analysis might begin by identifying either the logical possibilities or the steps in a process. Thus a problem regarding delay in an Accident and Emergency Department might produce an initial analysis as set out in Fig. 5.1. Here possible causes are grouped under labour force, equipment, treatment methods and communication.

Brainstorming sessions would then be carried out to identify possible causes under each of the four headings and the group would rank such causes for perceived importance. If subsequent investigation confirmed the group's analysis then quality action would be determined and initiated.

Process fishbone diagrams begin by identifying the stages in a process as in Dagher and Lloyd's (1990) analysis of quality problems in a Florida emergency department (see Fig. 5.2). Here each step in the process and each sub-process has been mapped and as undue variance (deviation from predetermined standards) is discerned the map provides a focus for brainstorming (and investigating) potential causes.

Brainstorming has remained a popular group problem solving technique for almost 40 years and it is tempting to conclude that it must have some validity. Unfortunately, systematic studies comparing its effectiveness with techniques involving individuals working

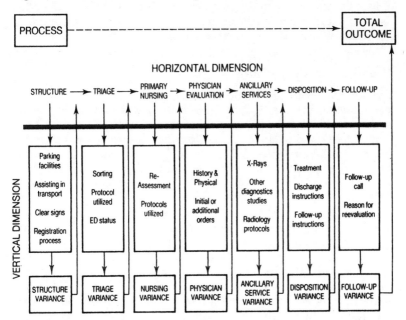

Fig. 5.2 Chart mapping the entire sequence of processes through subprocesses (vertical dimension) of each major step (horizontal dimension) in the Accident and Emergency system and indicates types of variances to anticipate at each step

on their own do not entirely bear the conclusion out. Thus both Taylor et al. (1958) and Dunnette et al. (1963) have shown that a given number of individuals working in isolation produce more and better solutions to set problems than do the same number of similar individuals working together in a brainstorming group. It might be observed, however, that the real issue is not whether brainstorming groups are better than brainstorming individuals but whether brainstorming groups are better than non-brainstorming groups. Oddly enough studies addressing this question do not seem to have been undertaken. It has also been pointed out in defence of brainstorming (Maier, 1967; Hutchins, 1990) that laboratory studies generally use groups who do not usually work together and problems which have no real implications for them. They are thus poor analogues of real life problem solvers such as health care quality assurance groups. Maier (1967) also stresses the value of participation in decision making and suggests that subsequent uptake and implementation of ideas developed in groups is likely to be more successful than that of ideas developed and put forward by isolated individuals.

In summary it remains debatable whether the quality of ideas produced in brainstorming groups is likely to be any better than that of ideas produced in other groups. Brainstorming does, on the other hand, maximise participation and may thus foster motivation for problem solving and, conceivably, a quality culture.

Nominal Group Technique

The nominal group technique was developed in 1968 by Delbecq and Van de Ven from studies of decision making in laboratory groups, of problem solving at the National Aeronautics and Space Administration (NASA), and of citizen participation in environmental planning (Delbecq and Van de Ven, 1971; Van de Ven and Delbecq, 1974). It has had many applications since then including several in health related areas (Van de Ven and Delbecq, 1972; Van der Gaag and Davies, 1991).

Nominal group technique (NGT), like brainstorming, is a structured technique for improving decision making in a face-to-face group. In NGT group members are first introduced to the problem or task and then spend a period of time sitting silently with as little collusion with other members as possible while producing a written list of possible solutions or ideas. This period of silent individual activity is followed by a 'round robin' in which the group leader asks each member in turn to contribute an idea. Each idea is recorded on a master list without comment and the round robin continues until all ideas are on the master list. Group members are allowed to expunge ideas from their lists if they think they are the same as previous ideas and to add ideas to them if they have further thoughts during the round robin phase. Once all ideas are on the master list ideas are discussed for clarification and evaluation. The meeting concludes with a voting procedure in which ideas or solutions are ranked (or rated) silently, independently and anonymously by each group member and the 'group consensus' is the pooled outcome of the votes.

Van de Ven and Delbecq (1974) compared NGT groups with normal chaired interaction groups using mixed groups of university staff, students and parents working on a problem thought to be genuinely contentious namely drawing up a job description for part time student residence warden/counsellors. They found the NGT groups to be superior both in quantity of ideas put forward and in the degree of satisfaction with both process and outcomes expressed by members. They concluded that NGT groups fostered consistency in decision making (the structure providing discipline for groups which might otherwise just waste time); a balance between task and socioemotional group support activities; equality of participation by group members; and a perceived sense of closure, accomplishment and interest in future activities.

As noted above NGT has been used in health related areas and it is likely that something akin to it has been used in health care quality assurance although no systematic exploration of its value in that context seems to have been undertaken. It has obvious potential at each stage in the quality cycle where the development of consensus is important.

Delphi

The Delphi technique originated in the Rand Corporation's involvement in the development of US defence strategy and specifically in technological forecasting (Helmer and Rescher, 1959; Dalkey and Helmer, 1963; Gordon and Helmer, 1964). Its use since then has spread through management science and practice, policy studies, engineering, educational research, health and social service research, and quality assurance. Writing in 1988, Reid identified over 400 references to use of the Delphi technique in education, social science and health.

The Delphi technique avoids the confounding influences of face-to-face groups by the simple tactic of keeping group members apart from each other. It is designed to collect, aggregate and refine judgements made by notional 'experts' on specified problems or topics. The basic steps in conducting a Delphi are as follows:

- Identify and involve a suitable group.
- Design a package of relevant information identifying problems to be tackled or issues to be addressed.

- Post the package to each group member with a 'return by' date and an assurance that their responses will be anonymised in subsequent analyses.
- Collate and analyse responses.
- Design a further package of information giving feedback on the responses to the first package and again requesting responses.
- Post the second package with a 'return by' date.
- Repeat the procedure until an acceptable level of consensus has been achieved (or until available time or resources will not run to further rounds).

Within these basic parameters many variants on Delphi have been developed. A particular distinction can be drawn (Turoff, 1970; Linstone and Turoff, 1975; Strauss and Zeigler, 1975; Reid, 1988) between Delphis which are based on numeric judgements and feedback and those which require verbal responses and thus more qualitative analyses and feedback. Numeric Delphis are often used in forecasting activities as when experts are asked to estimate the date by which a particular event is likely to have occurred. Feedback in each round would consist of distribution characteristics of the responses in the previous round. This is often restricted to statements of averages and ranges but is sometimes rather more complex. There is debate about the relative effectiveness of different forms of numeric feedback (Donegan and Dodd, 1991). Numeric Delphis are often computerised thus increasing the complexity of the data which can be handled and the feasibility of conducting several rounds of consultation.

Verbal Delphis demand more of the investigator in the development of qualitative frameworks for the coding of responses and in the presentation of cogent but unbiased feedback for further rounds of consultation. Many criticisms of Delphi are in fact criticisms of the way this stage of the process has been handled. Second and third round verbal Delphis often try to overcome the difficulties by asking respondents to rank or rate responses for importance or feasibility and thus try to achieve an optimal compromise between qualitative and quantitative methodologies.

In health care quality assurance Delphi has been used to develop consensuses on concepts of 'wellness' (Mullen and Gold, 1988); on objectives and activities in a paediatrics department (Loughlin and Moore, 1979); and on standards for ambulatory care (Holmes et al., 1978; Romm and Hulka, 1979; Hastings, 1980), for child health (Osborne and Thompson, 1975), for tuberculosis prophylaxis (Inui et al., 1979), for general nursing (Farrell and Scherer, 1983), and for community nursing (Ervin et al., 1989). Wright and Riley (1991) used Delphi to compare consensuses developed by experts with those developed by practitioners with respect to the importance of elements of a therapeutic recreation service as indicators of overall quality of the service.

Reid (1988) considers the status of the Delphi technique as science and concludes (p. 242) that 'Delphi is best used when no more scientific or social scientific method can be used and when the problem being studied is not amenable to more standard approaches...if, as is often the case the alternative is an anecdotal or entirely subjective approach, the Delphi method shows clear advantages.' She goes on to discuss the various published critiques of the Delphi method and concludes that while many criticisms are either valid for a particular Delphi exercise but not for the technique per se, or a function of inappropriate comparison with rigorous scientific study, some criticisms do stand up. These are essentially criticisms of the procedures adopted for the selection and sampling of participants or 'experts' and thus of the replicability and generalisability of the consensus they develop. It should be noted, however, that these criticisms would also apply if different consensus development techniques were adopted since groups would still have to be selected.

The Van de Ven and Delbecq study discussed above in the context of NGT groups also compared both the normal interaction groups and the NGT groups with similarly constituted Delphi groups (Van de Ven and Delbecq, 1974). They found that Delphi groups produced slightly fewer ideas than NGT groups but significantly more than normally interacting groups. NGT groups reported considerably more satisfaction with their involvement than did either the Delphi or normally interacting groups between which there was no significant difference in the degree of satisfaction expressed. They concluded that Delphi offered little advantage in the way of involvement and socio-emotional reward; that lack of opportunity for verbal clarification and comment created communication and interpretation difficulties; and that averaging numeric responses ignored the subtleties of response which might have been aired in a face-to-face context (it should be noted, however, that the more sophisticated numeric Delphi techniques go some way to counter this particular criticism). On the other hand Delbecq and Van de Ven also reported that the process of writing responses rather than merely discussing them encouraged thought; that the anonymity of the Delphi process achieved its objective of removing the influence of group conformity pressures; and that participants concluded the process with a modest feeling of closure and achievement but also with detachment.

In summary then, Delphi is a generally popular and well-established technique which has had some use in standard setting in health care quality assurance. Its advantages lie in its attempt to overcome the pressures and potential biases of face-to-face interaction and in the opportunity it affords for involving larger numbers of individuals (or more prestigious individuals) than could be assembled regularly in one place. Its particular disadvantages lie in the time involved in postal consultation and in the potential for attrition in the subject group. Other potential dangers reside in failing to select and sample a suitably representative or otherwise appropriate group of participants and in providing either biased or confusing feedback. There appear to have been no studies of the reasons for the very substantial sample attrition rates reported (90% by the second round of the Farrell and Scherer (1983) study) but it may be that some kinds of feedback are so confusing as to put respondents off entirely. Finally, it might be observed that while Delphi seems to free respondents from the immediate conformity pressures of face-to-face interaction they are unlikely to disappear completely. Social desirability is a pervasive response set and even in anonymised surveys respondents are likely to respond as they would wish to be represented (or indeed see themselves) and may not therefore voice (or write) a true opinion.

Surveys

Surveys have been widely used in health care quality assurance. There is a substantial literature on the assessment of patient satisfaction by means of survey questionnaires and on the role of such assessment in both process and outcome quality assurance. Questionnaires have also been used in the assessment of 'staff satisfaction' as an aspect of health care quality (Pelletier and Poster, 1988) and many techniques for the assessment of process quality include questionnaires for patients, staff or other significant groups as part of their procedures (see the Sunset Park/Lutheran Medical Centre System p. 81; the Heatherwood Hospital system p. 83; and SIMP, p. 130; for examples). Surveys also play a part in the development of standards and in deciding on action for quality improvement (as for example in the Delphi procedure described above). They have a role in the establishment of standards, in the appraisal of various aspects of quality and in the determination of quality action. In other words, they can be useful at almost any stage in the quality assurance cycle.

The Dalley et al. (1991) survey of quality management initiatives in the National Health Service in England and Wales found that the largest single category of initiatives reported was 'customer relations' and that 58.6% of these initiatives (i.e. some 12% of all initiatives) were in fact patient satisfaction surveys. In a slightly earlier study McIver and Carr-Hill iden ified 230 customer feedback studies which had been undertaken in England and Wales between 1984 and 1988 (McIver and Carr-Hill, 1989). They included population and locality studies, surveys of inpatient and outpatient groups, and studies of accident and emergency departments and focused on a wide range of topics from hospital food and transport to terminal care and geriatric services. Many of the District Health Authorities who supplied information for the survey described these feedback exercises as part of wider strategies for the improvement of customer relations and the development of quality assurance. Most such exercises are carried out on a one off or relatively infrequent 'snapshot' basis but some UK health authorities and US health care organisations are moving towards a system in which patient opinion is regularly solicited by means of standard questionnaires. This has the additional advantage of giving some indication of changes in patient satisfaction over time or of the gradual emergence of a quality problem.

Surveys are standard procedures in social and behavioural science and there are very many textbooks at all possible levels of sophistication and complexity. The guidance which will be given here will be specific to the use of the techniques in health care quality assurance and will be relatively basic. It is subdivided into guidance on questionnaire design, on data collection, and on sampling. Readers seeking a more general introduction are referred to Payne (1951), Oppenheim (1992), and Dillon (1990) on questioning and questionnaire design; to Brenner (1981), Brenner et al. (1985) and Millar et al. (1991) on interviewing; and to Moser and Kalton (1971) and De Vaus (1986) on sampling and general survey methodology. Cartwright (1986) and Dixon and Carr-Hill (1989) provide guidance particularly focused on health related investigation.

Questionnaire Design

Health care quality assurance questionnaires are normally designed for particular contexts. Dixon and Carr-Hill (1989), however, report activities in some UK health authorities where 'questionnaire modules' are being prepared so that anyone considering, say, a questionnaire for Accident and Emergency patients would be able to adopt suitable questions from the relevant pool of modules. They would also have access to comparative data since, by definition the questions would have been put to other similar patients in different areas or contexts. In most cases, however, the decision to 'do a questionnaire' means designing one.

The process of questionnaire design can be divided into three stages namely initial preparation, writing and piloting. The initial preparation phase should include careful consideration of whether a questionnaire is really the best way to find answers to the quality questions being tackled (other methods such as informal interviews with key individuals, group discussions, or short periods of observation may be quicker or cheaper). It is advisable to set out carefully what the objectives of the survey are. Clarification at this stage helps subsequent decisions about the sample of people to be involved in answering the questionnaire and about its length and content. Many questionnaires contain questions the answers to which never appear in published results because they were in the event irrelevant to the topic being investigated.

Over-long questionnaires are both more expensive than shorter ones and more likely to produce low response rates. On the other hand, a very brief questionnaire may omit relevant areas of enquiry. Even though existing questionnaires may not be transferable to new contexts scrutiny of their coverage can often reveal relevant topics. Consideration should also be given in the initial preparation stage to methods to be adopted for data collection and coding. Questionnaires administered by interviewers can be more complex than those designed for self-completion and they are also likely to produce higher response rates. On the other hand, they are more expensive since interviewers' training and time costs money. Access to computer coding facilities can also increase the quantity and complexity of data which can be handled and thus of questions which can be included.

Once the question writing phase has begun it is helpful to remember that a questionnaire is simply a kind of communication. It should therefore catch and maintain respondents' interest and motivation; should have a clear logical structure; should cover all the relevant points; and should neither underestimate nor overestimate respondents' knowledge and experience.

More specifically, attention should be paid to lay-out and presentation and introductions and instructions should be clear and friendly (Dixon and Carr-Hill (1989) report a study in which response rate increased by 10% when a glossier lay-out was employed). It is also sensible to make the initial questions easy ones although 'classification' questions asking for respondents' personal details are generally left until the end as they can seem threatening if put at the beginning. Motivation is also likely to diminish if the questionnaire is too long or very convoluted in structure. In general questionnaires which rely on 'filter' systems (e.g. If 'no' go to question 22; if 'yes' go to question 30; and if 'maybe' use the pink form instead!) are best kept for occasions when interviewers are available to help respondents through the labyrinth.

Coverage and logic in the questionnaire can be assisted if designers begin with a few broad general questions which can then be broken down into more specific questions for inclusion in the actual questionnaire. Gallup (1947) suggests a five-stage sequence leading respondents through each topic. It begins with questions about general awareness of the topic and proceeds through questions on general feelings to questions about specifics followed by questions on reasons for the views expressed and on strength of feelings. Thus 'Have you thought at all about the quality of the décor in the waiting area?' might lead to 'Do you think it is generally suitable?', and to

'Now please rate each of the following aspects of the décor on a five-point scale', and to 'Can you please tell me why you rated the following aspects at only one or two?', and finally to 'Now please rate the strength of your feeling that the décor is suitable/unsuitable on a five-point scale.'

The sequence of questions will also be influenced by whether the questionnaire is to be administered in an interview or to be completed by respondents on their own. In an interview the respondent can answer early questions without knowing what later questions are, whereas respondents who have a copy of the entire questionnaire in front of them may decide to answer early questions in the light of later parts of the questionnaire. Thus respondents being interviewed may be led gently into making criticisms of staff or facilities whereas self-completing respondents may stick to positive responses when they observe later questions inviting criticisms directly.

Decisions also need to be made about the balance between open and closed questions. Closed questions in which respondents have a fixed choice of alternative answers are easier to code and analyse but are heavily dependent on designers having drawn up a list of comprehensive, clear and discrete options. Open questions where respondents can comment freely make allowances for novel or unusual responses but are both more difficult and much more laborious to record, code and interpret.

Note also has to be taken of the possibility of bias being introduced as a result of respondents' predisposition to various kinds of 'questionnaire completion' behaviour. Dillon (1990) for example cites the widespread tendency to respond more favourably to positively framed questions than to negatively framed questions with the same apparent meaning. Thus respondents are more likely to answer positively to 'The décor is suitable ....Agree/Uncertain/Disagree' than negatively to 'The décor is unsuitable ....Agree/Uncertain/Disagree'. Respondents also tend to over-report socially desirable behaviour or opinions and to under-report socially undesirable behaviour or opinions. Interestingly there is evidence (Dillon, 1990) to suggest that open questions are more likely to elicit socially undesirable responses than are closed ones. Social desirability and a general disposition to please the interviewer or question designer are particularly cogent considerations in health care questionnaire design. Patients are generally favourably disposed towards their carers and feel that they have a vested interest in maintaining good relationships. They are therefore more likely to respond with a positive bias to health care questionnaires than to questionnaires about soap powder or television programmes.

At the level of individual question design obvious pitfalls include questions which lead the respondent into the answer or which ask for information or opinions which can be deduced from earlier questions. Double-barrelled questions, questions expressed in unnecessarily formal or technical language, and ambiguous questions should all be avoided. A surprising number of words can render questions ambiguous. Payne (1951) and Belson (1981) give long lists including 'usually', 'weekday', 'household', 'appropriate', 'about', 'all', 'always', 'any' and even 'you' – once 'you' is perceived as a plural it can mean almost any group. Dillon (1990) also points out that sociolinguistic variation and ethnicity can wreak havoc with apparently simple questions. In some cultures, for example, asking how many children there are in a family will be interpreted exclusively as a request for information about sons.

Once the questionnaire is drafted the next stage is piloting or testing it out. It is usually recommended that piloting should go through at least three stages. Initial piloting can often mean no more than asking a few friends or colleagues to read the material through and to complete answers as if they were genuine respondents. Once the modifications indicated in this initial pilot run have been effected the more significant part of the exercise consists of identifying a small group of genuine respondents and getting them to complete the questionnaire in circumstances as close as possible to those of the full study. This might be followed up by a group discussion with these people to help to clarify their responses and to give them an opportunity to identify any difficulties they may have had with questionnaire completion. It may also be useful at this stage to pilot the intended coding procedures as difficulties can emerge which may not have been evident in the administration and completion stages.

Coding itself is obviously simpler where the questionnaire is largely in the form of closed or pre-coded questions. Pilot analysis of open questions may reveal sufficient regularity of response to allow designers to turn some open questions into closed ones. It is also useful to conduct some pilot analyses before launching the main questionnaire as the results produced may generate ideas for modification.

Data Collection

The most common types of data collection are interviews, postal surveys, telephone surveys, and opportunistic surveys. Each have advantages and disadvantages.

Interviews like questionnaires are appropriate tools for use at several stages in the quality assurance cycle. They can be informal and unstructured requests for information or aspects of quality related negotiations among colleagues. Alternatively, they can be more formal investigations carried out as aspects of quality appraisal or of evaluation of possible action for quality improvement. Even in the more formal context interviews can be structured or unstructured. In its most extreme form an unstructured interview is one where the interviewer has an overall idea of the areas to be investigated and topics to be covered but has no clear notion of the way in which questions are to be put or of the order in which topics are to be introduced. It thus allows the respondent more freedom in structuring the presentation of information and it is often suggested that the unstructured interview accesses individual 'realities' and perceptions which would remain closed to more predetermined questioning. Unstructured interviews are often used in the initial stages of an enquiry to identify suitable questions and topics for inclusion in subsequent structured interviews. In structured interviews the interviewer has a very clear idea of the shape of the interview and of the questions which must be answered. In its purest form the structured interview follows a written questionnaire and the interviewer is only present to create rapport and to ensure that the respondent understands the procedure.

The presence of an interviewer increases questionnaire response rates but also increases costs. McIver and Carr-Hill (1989) report that only about a third of the patient satisfaction studies they identified in their survey of NHS health authorities had employed interviewers. The types of interviews and the background of the interviewers varied considerably. Student researchers carried them out in some studies, volunteers did much of the work in the studies which had been carried out on behalf of Community Health Councils, NHS staff carried them out in other studies, and in isolated instances professional survey organisations were employed.

While the presence of an interviewer undoubtedly increases respondents' involvement and motivation there is evidence to suggest that it can also be a powerful source of bias. Brenner (1981) reviews the evidence and suggests that it falls under two headings. First, bias can be introduced as a function of interviewer incompetence. In the extreme case interviewers can fill in forms themselves and ignore or deliberately distort responses. In the less culpable case they can simply misrecord responses, mumble questions or appear so off putting that respondents lose interest or fail to participate. Brenner's second and subtler source of interviewer bias resides in the fact that their very presence is a communication to respondents and may induce inappropriate response dispositions. Thus in the cases cited above where NHS personnel were involved in patient satisfaction interviewing there must be some possibility of patients having supplied 'socially desirable' responses. Even when interviewers have been selected for neutrality and have been trained to develop rapport and participation and to avoid bias, subtle differences in the way they use non-verbal behaviour can be enough to introduce distortion. Marquis and Cannell (1971) carried out a series of studies using different interviewing behaviours while trying to elicit information about health status. One group of interviewers was trained to use reinforcement techniques, that is to smile and nod and to make comments like 'uh huh' or 'I see' or 'thank you' after each response and the other group of interviewers was trained to use only the words of the questionnaire and to remain as impassive as possible throughout. The reinforcement interview produced more information overall and significantly more reference to classes of conditions and symptoms known to be much under reported in normal household surveys of health status.

While these are real sources of potential bias they should be weighed against the fact that the presence of a helpful interviewer can reduce bias which might otherwise be present in a self-completion exercise. This could be brought about by respondents' lack of motivation, level of literacy, linguistic background, sensory problem, or general tiredness, discomfort or distress brought about by illness. In each case the interviewer could either take steps to overcome the difficulty, make notes to indicate that the particular set of responses might be regarded as invalid, or abandon the interview.

As noted above the McIver and Carr-Hill (1989) study of NHS customer studies found that only a third of the investigations they identified used interviews as the means of data collection. Alternative methods included postal surveys, telephone surveys and surveys conducted by asking patients to complete questionnaires at discharge, while waiting to be seen, or at a given point during care. For each of these methods the two major hazards are reduction in response rates and the introduction of various biases resulting from the lack of interviewer supervision and encouragement of questionnaire completion.

Response rates in postal surveys vary very considerably depending on the precautions taken and persistence exercised by the investigators concerned. Moser (1958) suggests that response rates depend on the population, the subject of the investigation, its sponsorship, and the success of the covering letter in arousing interest. Length, ease of completion and 'glossiness' of presentation have already been noted as variables likely to influence respondents' motivation. De Vaus (1986) suggests that special purpose surveys addressing issues in which respondents have a particular interest can often yield response rates close to 95% or even 100%. Response rates improve if follow-up letters are sent but each follow-up produces proportionately fewer additional responses.

Telephone surveys are particularly common in the US where telephone ownership is more common than in the UK and where local calls are often very cheap or even free. Response rates in such surveys are generally high (Dillman, 1978 gives 91% as typical) and it has even been suggested that the technique affords the best possible trade-off between the interviewer supervision and support of the face-to-face interview and the perceived anonymity of the postal survey. Given low telephone costs it may also be less expensive than the alternatives since mailing and printing costs can be minimised (especially if responses are fed directly into a computer) and interviewers do not have to spend time and resources in travelling.

Health care surveys involving unassisted self-completion at some point during care are particularly prone to low response rates. Questionnaires just left lying or haphazardly distributed along with other documentation may literally not be noticed in the flurry and anxiety of arriving, departing or waiting to be seen or may just seem unimportant in the context of personal distress.

A low percentage response may not be a particular problem if the initial sample was large and if the group of non respondents is essentially similar to the group of respondents. The real problem is the possibility of systematic bias arising because non-respondents are in some way different from respondents. The views of an identifiable minority group would thus be under-represented in the survey results. Many authors report, for example, that health care postal surveys (and for that matter other postal surveys) are more likely to be completed by better educated and higher socio-economic groups. Conversely the relatively young, the elderly and housewives with children are likely to be under represented. Literacy and language community are other obvious factors which may introduce systematic biases.

Each of the potential biases discussed above for postal surveys are equally likely to distort responding in surveys undertaken during care. Again the better educated and the more middle class are more likely to be motivated to provide feedback and to regard questionnaire completion as a familiar and not particularly arduous task. Arguably too, social desirability may have a particular influence on response rates in this setting. Thus while the articulately indignant may welcome the opportunity to express grievances a rather larger group of mildly dissatisfied but diffident patients may find it easier just to ignore the request for feedback. Investigators would thus be left with an odd distribution of responses consisting of predominantly favourable answers combined with a small minority of very dissatisfied 'outliers'.

Despite their other advantages telephone surveys do introduce substantial systematic biases in that they automatically exclude potential respondents who do not own telephones. These include high proportions of the poor, the homeless, the geographically mobile and people in rented accommodation. These biases are more likely to occur in the UK than in the US.

Sampling

However data is to be collected a series of vital decisions must be made about the way in which respondents are to be selected from the total pool of all possible respondents, in other words, about sampling. Sampling is a technically sophisticated area of social and behavioural investigation and readers who seek detailed guidance are referred to the many suitable textbooks and in particular to the sources mentioned earlier in this chapter (p. 167). If the proposed survey is to be extensive or will be expensive to carry out or if it has major policy implications it may also be sensible to seek advice from a professional statistician. Discussion here is deliberately limited to basic ground rules for sampling for simple surveys undertaken as part of an overall system of health care quality assurance.

Sampling rules are designed to help investigators judge how far the answers they have obtained from a sample of respondents are much the same as those they would have obtained had all possible respondents answered their questions. They fall into two categories namely rules for estimating the number of respondents to select (sample size) and those for making the group of selected respondents as similar as possible to the whole group of possible respondents (the representativeness of the sample).

Sample size depends on two key factors, namely the amount of confidence in the results required and the extent to which respondents are likely to answer the questions put in similar ways (or conversely to produce a wide range of different answers). A regional survey of opinion on the siting of a new hospital might be sufficiently important for the relevant health authority to demand 95% confidence that the views of respondents are very similar to those of the whole population. Results might be expressed as 65% in favour of the new location with a margin of error of 2% and a 95% level of confidence – in other words the investigators are sure (and can demonstrate statistically) that 95 samples in 100 drawn from the relevant population would produce a response somewhere in the range 63–67% in favour of the new location. For other less vitally important surveys a lower level of confidence might be acceptable. Dixon and Carr-Hill (1989) suggest that 68% confidence is typical in health related surveys. The higher the confidence level required and the lower the margin of error required the bigger the sample must be.

The second factor influencing the size of the sample required is the extent to which answers are likely to vary. Since sampling decisions have to be taken before the survey is done this is a matter of judgment based on previous work, consultation with experts and comparison with similar surveys conducted elsewhere. If respondents are likely to split 90/10 on the issue in question a smaller sample is required than if they are likely to split 50/50. Tables are available which indicate appropriate sample sizes for given margins of error, variability in response and confidence levels. It should be noted that it is the absolute size of the sample that is important rather than its size as a proportion of the population of all possible respondents. A representative sample of 1000 drawn from a population of 100,000 is just as good as a representative sample of 1000 drawn from a population of only 10,000. Thus a low percentage of respondents is not necessarily a bad thing so long as it is not also an unrepresentative group of respondents. Finally, once a suitable number of respondents has been determined allowance should be made for the probable level of non-response and the sample size should be increased accordingly.

There are two basic approaches to the issue of representativeness in the sample. They are simple random sampling and the various types of stratified sampling. Random sampling involves selecting respondents at random from a list (or sampling frame) of all possible respondents. Incompleteness or bias in the list itself can be a particular problem in population surveys based on lists of electors or even on general practitioners' lists of patients, but where a reliable list of, say, all patients discharged from a particular ward can be obtained random sampling is a suitable technique. It can be carried out using tables of random numbers or by drawing a 'systematic' random sample in which every fifth, tenth, 22nd or 'nth' person is selected depending on the size of the population and the required sample size.

There are various types of stratified sampling but in its simplest form the population of all possible respondents is divided into groups or 'strata' known to be important to the survey. Thus in a hospital based survey it might be important to gather data from each ward or department – which might not happen if the list of patients was alphabetical and each tenth patient was selected. The danger would be that some wards would be under-represented and others over-represented. In that case the appropriate technique would be to draw up alphabetical lists from each ward and to random sample within each of these lists or 'strata'. A more sophisticated version of the same technique would deliberately select more patients (e.g. every fifth instead of every tenth) from wards with small throughputs thus making sure that each ward was equally represented and that comparisons could be made. If an overall result was then to be calculated for the hospital as a whole, however, the data could only be combined with suitable weighting adjustments. Similar stratification principles are also applied where the time of sampling is important. Thus it might be important to know which responses came from patients being treated in an Accident and Emergency department in peak Saturday night periods rather than in the relative calm of Tuesday mornings.

However the sample has been drawn it will be important to check for bias (or unrepresentativeness) once results are in. In interview surveys interviewers can often identify potential sources of bias but in postal or other surveys it is advisable to check general characteristics of the sample (e.g. age, sex, condition, ward in which treated) against the known characteristics of the population of all possible respondents.

It has been assumed throughout this section that sample size could be determined on purely methodological grounds. In fact, it is much more likely that variables of cost and convenience will also have a role to play in determining how large a sample can be dealt with. In some areas of health care quality assurance even a few unrepresentative responses may be valuable. If a threshold standard has been set involving safety or privacy for example, even one patient reporting a breach of the standard may be the occasion for action to improve quality. Also if a questionnaire has been designed for repeated use in a continuous programme of quality assurance monitoring it may be possible to aim at a 'whole population' response rather than a sample. Relevant comparisons across time would be feasible but would require different statistical techniques.

Psychometrics

Psychometrics is defined as the scientific measurement of psychological variables such as intelligence, aptitude, motivation, extraversion. Measuring instruments are often in questionnaire form and have usually been subjected to extensive piloting and modification before being released for general use. As will be explained below psychometric instruments lay claim to high levels of reliability and validity.

Psychometric techniques were introduced and exemplified in the 'Outcome Appraisal' section of Chapter 4 (p. 133) where a number of instruments for the assessment of general health status, quality of life, disease, disability and pain were discussed. Each of the instruments included was an established scale with a record of use in health related research and clinical practice and, in some cases, in programme evaluation and outcome analysis. This section will examine possible uses for psychometric techniques at other stages in the quality assurance cycle and, in particular, will discuss the transfer of principles underlying psychometric test design and construction to all aspects of quality measurement.

Setting explicit standards and monitoring their achievement are central features of quality assurance. In manufacturing industry there is no question but that that means detailed operationalisation of the relevant standards and careful control of variation from them. Such control involves making repeated measurements. When the standard is a standard for the physical characteristics of a product (as in the very first British Standards Institution standards for the precise dimensions of steel section for use in railway lines) measurement does not present particular problems since standard scales exist (e.g. feet or metres) for assessment of the relevant variables (e.g. length). In setting and appraising standards of health care quality or indeed in assessing health itself measurement is more problematic since the variables involved (e.g. patient well-being, patient satisfaction, empathetic communication by professionals) are often abstract constructs which cannot readily be assessed by reference to some universally accepted standard scale. There is no 'well-being' equivalent of the standard piece of metal locked in a Paris vault upon which all measures in metres were originally based. Measurement depends on the identification of a series of indicators which can be explicated and measured and which when taken together constitute a 'best guess' as to the state of the construct itself. Thus while visiting one's physician infrequently, being in employment, having a wide social network, and giving positive responses to specified questions about one's attitudes to self may not be the same as being well and healthy they are probably fair indicators of such a condition. Furthermore, they are each of them susceptible to observation and measurement. The identification of relevant indicators, the construction of scales based upon them and the interpretation of measurements made using such scales are basic problems in health care quality assurance. They are precisely the problems also confronted in the construction and use of instruments for the assessment of such abstract constructs as intelligence, aptitude and personality – in other words in psychometrics. It follows therefore that psychometrics has relevance for health care quality assurance not only in the availability of ready-made tests and assessments but also in the extension of the principles underlying test construction and use to many aspects of quality measurement.

Psychometrics is a major area of psychological science which has reached a level of technical sophistication well beyond the scope of this book. Readers who seek a detailed exposition are referred to the many available textbooks and particularly to Anastasi (1988) and Cronbach (1985) for general principles and techniques and to McDowell and Newell (1987) for discussion of the theoretical and technical foundations of psychometrics in the measurement of health.

Many of the techniques for health care quality assurance described in previous chapters are essentially (or at least involve the use of) scales developed for the measurement of indices of health care quality. They vary in complexity and scope but should nonetheless stand up to the basic standards of measurement developed in psychometrics. Four aspects of these standards of measurement will be discussed below, namely, basic characteristics of scaling; category scaling; scale reliability; and scale validity.

Basic Characteristics of Scaling

A scale is a series of numbers each of which has a distinctive meaning. To talk of a 'scale' for size, temperature, intelligence, or quality of life is to imply that numbers can be meaningfully attached to instances of these attributes. All scaling methods are based on one of four ways of using numbers in measurement. The arithmetical manipulations which are possible without rendering conclusions meaningless depend on which of the four ways is being used.

The least powerful way of using numbers (or least powerful level of measurement) is not really measurement at all but is just classification or labelling. Here wards might be numbered one to 12 but this would simply be using numbers as the names of the wards. There would be no implication that ward 12 was better, bigger or in some other way systematically different from ward one. When numbers are used in this way it is not possible to carry out any arithmetical manipulation – no addition, subtraction, multiplication or division can be done. It is clearly meaningless for example to say that the average ward in the twelve discussed above is 6.5.

The second level of measurement is the 'ordinal' level of measurement. Here again labels are attached to events but this time in such a way that the labels are arranged in some order. Thus a disability might be described as mild, moderate or severe or agreement or disagreement with a given statement might be expressed as strongly agree, slightly agree, neither agree nor disagree, slightly disagree, strongly disagree. Numbers would then be attached to each label, for example 1 for mild disability, 2 for moderate and so on. There is no guarantee that people using labels and numbers in this way mean the same thing by mild, moderate and severe or that their concept of the gap between each of them is the same. It is therefore not technically possible to carry out even addition and subtraction on this type of scale. Despite that there is considerable debate among statisticians about the underlying regularities of human judgement when faced with a scale of this kind and (as can be observed in several measures of health care process and outcome quality) responses on such scales are frequently added to produce overall scores. They should not however be subjected to multiplication or division, or to operations such as averaging based upon them. Thus to compare wards for quality of nurse patient interaction on the basis of averages of patients' placings of their nurses on a five-point scale would be perilous. The patients in one ward may have a quite different idea of what the values 1–5 mean to that of the patients in the other ward and, indeed, each individual patient may have a unique idea of the scale's meaning.

The third level of measurement does allow meaningful use of addition and subtraction. Scales at this level are known as interval scales. Here the attachment of numbers to scale values indicates a regular progression up or down the scale with intervals between each point which are known to be identical. Temperature scales are good examples of interval scales. It is possible to add and subtract them because it is clear that the difference between 10 degrees and 20 is the same as the difference between 20 and 30. Multiplication and division are still not possible, however, since the scale has no true zero point. It is not possible to have no temperature at all and zero can be placed artificially at any point in the scale (thus zero Celsius is the same as 32 Fahrenheit). Many health measurement scales claim this level of measurement although as noted above some may actually be ordinal scales in disguise.

The fourth level where all four arithmetical operations are meaningful is the ratio scale. Here not only are there equal intervals between each scale point but also there is a true zero. Length, weight, volume and density can all be measured on ratio scales. Variables such as patient satisfaction, quality of life, and professional competence might theoretically never be able to achieve this level of measurement since, as with temperature, the zero point does not represent non-existence of the phenomenon being measured but merely the transition from positive to negative (satisfaction to dissatisfaction, good quality to bad quality, competence to incompetence etc.) and could be placed at different points by different users of the scale.

Category Scaling

As noted above many health care quality assurance scales are essentially ordinal scales in which judgements and responses are ranked in order (e.g. of severity of disability, of appropriateness of care delivered). A refinement of this approach which is designed to justify the use of such scales as interval or ratio scales is known as category scaling. There are two main types of category scaling known respectively as the 'equal appearing intervals' technique and the 'magnitude estimation' technique. In each technique a group of relevant judges is assembled and they are invited to sort examples of the statements or judgements which are to form the basis of the scale concerned. In the equal appearing intervals technique they are asked to place each example in one of a fixed set of some 10 to 15 ranked categories (e.g. degrees of severity, degrees of appropriateness). A median score (defined as the middle score when all scores are arranged in order of magnitude) is then derived from their judgements and that becomes the score attaching to that particular response. In magnitude estimation the judges are given a similar sorting task but are asked to judge relative severity, appropriateness or whatever with no limits placed upon the values they attach. It is argued that this improves on the equal appearing intervals technique by determining an implied zero and thus moving the scale from the interval level of measurement to the ratio.

Despite the well-established history and use of these techniques in psychometrics it has to be noted that many scales used in health care quality assurance make little use of either and may therefore be laying illegitimate claims to levels of measurement beyond the ordinal.

Scale Reliability

Scale reliability was briefly discussed with reference to several of the techniques detailed in Chapter 4. It can be broadly defined as the consistency with which the scale provides measurement. The classic example of the unreliable scale in the measurement of physical objects is the ruler made of metal which expands and contracts with temperature and thus measures in inches of one size when used inside the refrigerated lorry and of another size when used beside the furnace. The intangibility of the constructs measured in psychometrics and health quality measurement renders reliability of measurement even more problematic.

Two types of consistency/inconsistency are commonly discussed. They are inter-rater reliability and test repeatability. Inter-rater reliability is the extent to which different raters (or observers, or judges, or users of the test or instrument) would produce the same results when asked to use the measuring instrument in the same circumstances. As has been discussed in several sections of the previous chapter, measures which rely heavily on the subjective judgements of their users or which contain ambiguous items are likely to produce low inter-rater reliabilities since there will be many opportunities for different interpretations and judgements even though the phenomena being observed may be identical. There are several approaches to the assessment of inter-rater reliability. The most common technique is probably the statistic known as Kendall's Index of Concordance. In each case the technique involves assessment of the relationship between the scores obtained by different raters and its expression in a correlation coefficient (a number from −1.0 to +1.0 where the closer the number is to 1.0 the stronger the relationship is and sign indicates its direction, for example good health and poverty are likely to be negatively related while good health and taking exercise are generally said to be positively related). McDowell and Newell (1987, p. 32) suggest that inter-rater reliability values from 0.65 to 0.95 are typical and that 'values above 0.85 may be considered satisfactory'.

Test repeatability is essentially the extent to which a test or instrument can be assumed to be measuring the same thing when used on different occasions. This is obviously important if the test is to be used on more than one occasion as part of an ongoing system of quality monitoring. Again there are several approaches to the assessment of repeatability some of which involve actually using the test on separate occasions and some of which involve splitting the test in two (e.g. by taking each odd and each even item) and assessing the extent to which the two halves produce similar scores. A commonly used technique based upon estimating relationships between all possible splittings is Cronbach's measure of internal consistency (known as Cronbach's alpha). As with inter-rater reliability values around 0.85 and above are regarded as acceptable.

Scale Validity

Reliability is in many respects a technical matter – an instrument either produces consistent results or it does not. Validity is a much more slippery concept. It is defined as the extent to which a test or instrument measures what it is intended to measure – which is fine so long as those intentions are clear and unambiguous. Even momentary consideration of the constructs typically assessed in health care quality assurance will reveal the fact that they are often ill defined and only partially explicated. It is thus singularly difficult to be clear and unambiguous about what it is that measuring instruments are supposed to be measuring. Again, however, these are difficulties also confronted in traditional psychometrics when determining the validity of tests of intelligence or personality and the techniques developed for overcoming them should therefore be transferable.

Four aspects of test validity are generally considered before a test is regarded as fit for its purpose. They are as follows:

- Face validity.
- Content validity.
- Concurrent/predictive validity.
- Construct validity.

The face validity of a test is essentially the extent to which it appears 'on the face of it' to be valid to the people who are likely to use it or to be required to complete it. It is perfectly possible that competence in orthopaedic surgery is positively related to competence in carpentry, but a quality audit tool which required senior consultants to wield hammer and nails might be less immediately acceptable than one which looked at results of actual surgery. Face validity is often dismissed as a trivial matter not worth much time or consideration by test designers but if a test is unacceptable or seems 'silly' to its users they will be under-motivated or even obstructive and results will be distorted. Even where the results produced are perfectly sound the people who receive them may not believe they are important. This could be particularly important in quality assurance where professionals and managers are expected not merely to appraise quality but to have enough faith in the process to go on to effect quality change. A particular source of lack of face validity is the development of measures without involvement of people with an intimate knowledge of the professional and clinical contexts in which the tests are likely to be used.

Content validity can be defined as the extent to which the measure encompasses all relevant aspects of the variable to be assessed, or how adequately it reflects the aims of its designers and users. It was noted, for example, that several of the instruments claiming to assess nursing process quality described in Chapter 4 were criticised for over emphasis of one particular model of nursing care (Yura and Walsh's, 1967, 'nursing process'). That was essentially a criticism of the content validity of these measures. Content validity is often not formally tested although a typical procedure involves consultation with relevant 'experts' during the design and piloting stages of the instrument's development.

Determining a test's concurrent/predictive validity gets round the problem of not knowing exactly what the test is designed to measure by comparing results from it with some other measure which is generally accepted as doing the same thing. Thus a new and conveniently short test of intelligence might be compared with a longer but generally accepted test. Predictive validity is assessed when the results of a new test are compared with related later events. Comparing the results of a measure of health care process quality with patient outcomes would be an assessment of predictive validity (and a stiff one given the often noted difficulty in the assessment of outcomes).

One of the problems with the determination of test validity in health care quality measurement is the relative recency of development of many measures. In traditional psychometrics there are 'gold standard' tests of constructs like intelligence which provide useful comparators, but it is difficult to identify such generally accepted measures in health care quality measurement. It is often necessary therefore to use techniques known as tests of construct validity. Construct validation involves test designers in unpacking the theoretical basis of their test and identifying variables to which test scores should theoretically be related. Thus a test of intelligence should, theoretically be related to school achievement and a measure of quality of nurse communication should theoretically be related to patient satisfaction. There are several technically sophisticated approaches to construct validation and there is considerable debate as to their relative powers and ranges of application. Readers are referred to other sources for fuller discussion. Despite these complexities it is worth noting that the difficulties of definition, operationalisation, isolation and measurement of relevant variables in health care quality may mean that in the end complex analysis of construct validity is the only really appropriate technique for ensuring that measures measure what they purport to.

As with reliability, measures of test validity are expressed as coefficients of correlation. Given the difficulty of rigorous establishment of validity it is not surprising that the levels reported are rather lower than those for reliability. A further problem is that correlations between two tests (as in concurrent validation) is influenced by the respective reliabilities of the two tests. The maximum correlation that can be obtained can be calculated by multiplying together the square roots of the reliability coefficients of each test. The obtained validity coefficient can then be compared with the maximum possible. A number of techniques are also available which allow test users to calculate the extent to which using the test to predict a criterion (e.g. to predict some other health outcome) is an improvement upon just guessing. The simplest way to determine acceptable levels of test validity is to determine the validities typically quoted for tests in related areas. McDowell and Newell (1987, p. 30) concede that the concurrent validity correlations between the measurements of health reviewed in their book are low, 'typically falling between 0.20 and 0.60, with only occasional correlations between very similar instruments ... falling above 0.70'.

Interpersonal Skill Analysis

All authors on health care quality assurance recognise that health care is only in part a technical process and that however complex the medical technology it is delivered by a person to a person. No patient's treatment is devoid of face-to-face contact with a practitioner. Interpersonal interaction is thus central to the delivery of care and its quality contributes significantly to overall health care quality. As Ellis and Whittington (1988, p. 264) put it:

> One of the problems a physician must face is that he must treat patients as objects subject to the laws of physics, chemistry and biology while at the same time considering them as persons subject to the less clearly defined laws of psychology. Thus a general practitioner may take temperature, pulse and blood pressure with complete competence but his interactional style itself may have an effect upon these readings. Further whatever treatment he prescribes will have to be communicated to the patient, and its success will depend on the motivation and cooperation of that patient.

There is a very substantial literature on practitioner–patient communication and on relationships between communication variables and a range of health care outcomes. There is a clear relationship, for example, between aspects of practitioner–patient communication and patient satisfaction. Ley (1988) gives 40% of patients across a range of medical specialisms citing poor communication as a source of their dissatisfaction with care while Hall and Dornan (1989) put poor communication in the top four causes of dissatisfaction. Hall et al. (1988) review 41 studies which employed observation of physician–patient interaction in order to explore the relationships between communication variables and patient satisfaction, recall and understanding, and compliance with instructions. They clustered the communication variables identified in the studies they reviewed into information giving, questioning, appearing competent, partnership building, social conversation, body movements, positive talk, negative talk, and total communication. The analysis showed that satisfaction was consistently related to information giving, appearing competent, partnership building (i.e. making the patient feel a participant in the consultation), immediacy in body movement (i.e. more eye contact, open posture, standing or sitting closer to and turning towards the patient), more positive talk than negative talk, and more overall communication. Compliance was associated with more information giving, fewer questions, and more positive talk than negative talk. Recall and understanding was also related to these three variables with the addition of more partnership building.

A good deal is thus known about the importance of practitioner–patient interaction, about its relationships to relevant outcomes and about ways of observing and categorising it. Much has also been written about the importance of interpersonal skill training in professional education for health care (Ellis and Whittington, 1981; 1988; Pendleton, 1983; Kagan, 1985; McGuire, 1986; Furnham, 1988; Dickson et al., 1989). Surprisingly little of this body of knowledge seems to have worked its way into quality assurance in health care. Indeed it is positively alarming to note the naivety of many of the assessments of communication quality which appear in instruments for the appraisal of process quality. Likewise almost all statements of predetermined professional standards give much more specific and detailed guidance on standards for the technical aspects of care than for its interpersonal aspects. These are often expressed in the most general of terms using expressions like 'communicate appropriately' or 'respect the patient at all times'. Both the novice professional and the quality appraiser could justifiably enquire 'but how will we know?' when asked to ensure that these standards are met.

There is need for further systematic observation of interpersonal aspects of care and for detailed analysis of what constitutes good practice so that standards can be set. This is no different from the more conventional activity of refining professional judgement and arriving at consensus on standards of technical care or, more rigorously, trying to relate such judgements to actual outcomes. Techniques for the observation and analysis of interaction might be borrowed from the studies of practitioner–patient interaction and patient outcomes cited above or, perhaps more profitably, from the literature on the analysis of professional competence in the 'interpersonal professions' (Ellis, 1980; 1988; Ellis and Whittington, 1981; 1988).

The analysis of interpersonal communication has a long history (Argyle, 1963; 1969; 1975; Ekman and Friesen, 1972; Hinde, 1972; Richmond et al., 1991). Specialists have only recently turned their attention to professional interaction, however, and observation and analysis of such activity is still relatively rare. The one exception to this is the observation and analysis of teaching behaviour. Here there is a tradition stretching back to the 1920s and possibly earlier and it is not surprising to find that work in other professional areas tends to emulate it.

Medley and Mitzel (1963) review the early work on teaching and offer step-by-step guidance on the construction of observation systems. Their approach remains exemplary and translates easily to other professional settings. The systems they describe involve the observation of classroom behaviour as it occurs (or on videotape) and recording and coding events into predetermined categories. Information is thus obtained about which types of behaviour occurred or how often they occurred during the period of observation. Medley and Mitzel stress the importance of reliability and validity in constructing observation systems. Reliability is generally achieved by the usual means of describing categories in as clear and behaviourally specific a form as possible. Thus 'faces the blackboard' and 'turns away from the patient' are better than 'seems disinterested'. The more behaviourally specific the category description is the less inference observers need to use in determining whether or not the behaviour has occurred. The lower the degree of inference the more likely observers are to agree and the more consistent or reliable the system is.

The problems presented by ensuring validity in such systems are somewhat more taxing. A major difficulty resides in the richness of the potentially observable data and the limits of human information processing. Thus the observer might start off with the ambition of 'looking at everything that happens' but inevitably when faced with the stream of varied behaviour produced by even two individuals talking, looking, changing facial expression, gesturing, moving about and so on, selection becomes imperative. Only 'relevant' behaviours can be coded and it thus becomes necessary to set up working hypotheses as to what these might be.

Medley and Mitzel suggest two approaches to the design of relevant observation systems namely the 'category' approach and the 'sign' approach. In a category approach the system designer draws up a list of categories which is taken to include everything which can possibly happen in a given period of observation. Thus in a system for practitioner–patient interaction the categories 'practitioner speaks', 'patient speaks' and 'nobody speaks' would provide a reasonably watertight account of everything that happened. Such a simple system might not be particularly informative, however, and the system designer might decide upon subdivision of categories. Thus in what is probably the most influential of category systems for the analysis of teaching behaviour Flanders (1970) subdivides teacher talk into seven categories as follows:

- Accepts feeling.
- Praises or encourages.
- Accepts or uses ideas of pupils.
- Asks questions.
- Lectures.
- Gives directions.
- Criticises or justifies authority.

Pupil talk is subdivided into 'responds' and 'initiates', and 'silence and confusion' remains an undivided category. The observer notes the predominant category of behaviour taking place every three seconds. This can be done by accumulating tallies for each category or by writing the category numbers down in a time line thus preserving the order of events. It is not too difficult to deduce that the system omits a number of teacher behaviours associated with provision and use of materials, and that it is devoid of reference to the content or subject matter of lessons. Also it seems to be based in a belief that pupil participation and involvement is an important attribute of 'good' teaching. The more detailed a category system becomes the more it will reflect the working hypotheses of its designer about the relative significance of various events.

Sign systems are not designed to encompass the totality of the events observed but rather home in deliberately on those taken to be significant. Thus if the focus of the study in hand was the relationship between practitioner questions and patient satisfaction a sign system might be developed in which the observer would note only the occurrence of particular types of questions and would subsequently relate their frequency to the degree of satisfaction expressed by patients. This would have the advantage of allowing detailed observation of questions themselves but would entail loss of context.

As it happens category systems have been rather more popular in the observation and analysis of teaching behaviour (Wragg, 1984; Ellis and Whittington, 1988) while analyses of practitioner–patient interaction have more often used sign systems. Given the existence of recorded category or sign observations post hoc analyses become possible. Flanders himself was particularly interested in the sequencing of categories (Flanders, 1970) and recommended the use of matrices showing the number of occasions one category of event was likely to be followed by another category. Thus a teacher in whose lessons category five (lecturing) behaviours have a high probability of being followed by other category five behaviours has a different style from the teacher whose category five behaviours are equally likely to be followed by the pupil talk categories, eight and nine. Both teachers might have the same overall frequencies of fives but their lessons would be very different. This kind of sequential analysis would lend itself readily to the study of the 'partnership building' variables identified as significant in several studies of practitioner–patient interaction (Hall et al., 1988; Robinson and Whitfield, 1988; Rost et al., 1989). Flanders (1970) also makes recommendations for category clustering, multiple coding and some sophisticated calculations of transitional probabilities each of which could improve the sophistication of the methods generally adopted in studies of health professionals' interpersonal skill.

As noted above standard setting and quality appraisal for the interpersonal aspects of health care seem relatively insulated from any of these techniques. What is needed is explication of the standards which undoubtedly exist in the minds of professionals. This should preferably be coupled with empirical observation of practice and exploration (as in the studies noted above) of relationships between particular kinds of interpersonal behaviour and patient outcomes. The basic procedure would not be too different from those employed in developing consensuses about other more technical areas of 'good practice'. It also has parallels in the analyses of medical decision making which form the basis of computerised health care 'expert systems'. In these systems inexperienced practitioners are guided through diagnosis (for example) by a computerised protocol based on refinement of the judgements of more experienced colleagues (Shortliffe, 1973; Buchanan and Shortliffe, 1984; Luger and Stubblefield, 1989). In each context experienced practitioners are encouraged to move from judgements based on unarticulated, implicit rules and demanding high levels of inference to judgements based on explicit statements rooted in manifest events and demanding low levels of inference.

In this instance, however, it might be important to precede the activity by helping the professionals (or consumers) involved to be more self-conscious and analytical about communication – to provide them with what has been termed a 'meta-language' to facilitate discourse about discourse (Simon and Bowyer, 1970). Saunders and Caves (1986) developed just such an approach in devising an assessment instrument for use in the professional education of speech therapists. Videotapes were made of previously identified 'good' practitioners across a sample of relevant professional settings.

Groups of relevant professionals were then involved in identifying specific instances of 'good interpersonal practice' with the aid of the video and using techniques akin to those of the 'nominal group' method of consensus development (see p. 162 above) derived a refined list of types of behaviour for inclusion in the assessment schedule. The technique is currently being used in a similar way in investigations of competence in physiotherapy and in teaching in higher education being carried out in the University of Ulster.

The aim of the technique developed by Saunders and Caves is primarily the development of empirically grounded assessment schedules but it is easy to see how it could also lead to the production of consensual quality standards for interpersonal aspects of care. Cameron-Jones (1988) traces the development in Scottish teacher education of related criteria for selection of entrants to the profession; for assessment of classroom performance during training; for inclusion in a profile awarded on qualification and used as a basis for subsequent employment and in-service development; and, finally, for inclusion in public statements about teacher responsibilities and duties. As she notes, these statements are an embryonic form of quality assurance and are likely to be developed further. The criteria are very specific and include statements about teachers' competence in elicitation of pupil responses, responsiveness to and rapport with pupils, and timing, pacing and organisation of activities. Again teaching seems to be leading the way, in as Cameron-Jones puts it (1988, p. 78) 'offering a model of teaching, in deriving criteria from the model and in valuing consensual definitions and judgments, as well as empirical research evidence about how the essentials of teaching are to be defined'.

Conclusion

This chapter and the one preceding it have identified, exemplified and discussed a very wide range of techniques for health care quality assurance. It has been emphasised throughout that choice of technique depends on the purpose and circumstances of the proposed quality initiative. Above all choice of technique must be reflective and, in the spirit of all quality assurance, the value of chosen techniques must be subject to monitoring and review.

Choice of appropriate techniques is clearly important, but however carefully choice is made the eventual impact on quality of care will depend on the management of the overall quality system in which they are to be used. The next chapter will discuss quality management.

6

The Management of Quality Assurance in Health Care

Introduction

The industrial quality movement developed alongside and as a consequence of the emergence of mass production. As the organisation of production became more complex quality procedures evolved from simple product inspection to company wide quality management. In health care too there is increasing recognition that quality is not just a matter for individual practitioners, units or professions. Jessee (1981) actually defines health care quality assurance as planned organisational change, and Kagan (1984) emphasises that health care quality initiatives will be short lived unless they are integrated with general management. In similar vein, the World Health Organisation's 1983 working group on the principles of quality assurance note that effective quality assurance must be seen as an agent of organisational change and that quality assurance staff 'will need to develop extensive skills in the identification of the causes of resistance to change in organisations, and in strategies and tactics of organisational change' (WHO, 1985, p. 17). Many other authors (Isaac, 1983; Williams, 1989; Coad and Hyde, 1986; Berwick and Knapp, 1987; Schmele and Foss, 1989b; Koska, 1990; Berwick, 1990; O'Leary, 1991; O'Sullivan and Grujic, 1991) note the importance of organisational factors and advocate the adoption of industrial quality management techniques. Several of these authors, however, fail to note that health care organisations have distinctive characteristics which may make the management of quality more difficult or at least very different from apparently analogous activities in manufacturing and service industries.

This chapter will focus on the management of health care quality assurance and will treat the establishment of quality systems as an example of organisational innovation. It will provide a brief account of relevant models of organisational change; give an indication of the distinctive characteristics of health care organisations which may or may not be conducive to quality innovation; develop a framework for health care quality assurance management; and present a number of examples of health care quality assurance management systems.

Organisational Change

Approaches to organisational change are coloured by the models of organisational function and effectiveness to which their advocates adhere. Such models have themselves developed (like quality assurance) in reflection of wider social and technological changes. Thus the development of mass production techniques depending on the systematic division of production into component processes was parallelled by the development of scientific models of organisation and management. These emphasised the analysis of tasks, the division of functions, and the development of clear, authoritarian chains of command. Similarly, the more recent need for market responsive, idea driven organisations in the informatics industries has fostered models in which organisations are characterised as learning systems or even intelligent organisms which form and reform in adaptation to external and internal pressures.

Morgan (1986) identifies eight different models or, in his term, images of organisation. Thus organisations have not only been represented as machines and as adaptive organisms but also as brains, as cultures, as political power systems, as psychic prisons, as constant flux and transformation, and finally, as instruments of domination. Morgan concludes by suggesting that this is a complex area in which science is in short supply and it is difficult to determine which models are most valid. They are best considered as metaphors. The skilled interpreter and operator within organisations is the one who can read the organisation imaginatively using the various metaphors as appropriate. Such a skilled and eclectic reader is also more likely to be able to manage organisational innovation.

The various approaches to health care quality assurance can be associated with different organisational models. For example, retrospective audit of records of care with reference to externally developed standards and application of sanctions to individuals or units whose work is not up to standard can be characterised as an example of mechanistic or scientific management. Quality management through local quality circles on the other hand might be better described by the various adaptive learning models in which the human needs and aspirations of individual employees are seen as part of the system.

Many recent authors on health care quality assurance stress the importance of creating a quality culture. The organisation is conceived as a microcosm of society itself; its members construct their reality according to its norms and values and their behaviour is at one with this constructed reality. The culture manifests itself through formal and informal status hierarchies, through the way communication networks are organised, through the language of policy documents and mission statements, and through the myths and images which become attached to the organisation's past history. The introduction of a new approach (such as quality assurance) will not succeed unless it fits into the culture. If the disjunction is too marked the culture itself will have to change. Thus innovators may have to attend to change at more profound levels than might at first seem to be required.

Zaltman and Duncan (1977) accept the plurality of organisational models and suggest that different change strategies are needed in different organisations. The success of innovation depends on the goodness of fit between the predominant organisational style, culture, or structural characteristics and the change strategy adopted. They identify a repertoire of four strategies which the skilled manager of innovation is expected to deploy as circumstances require. They are *reeducation, persuasion, facilitation* and *power*.

Reeducation
This strategy assumes that employees operate rationally on the basis of the information available to them. If the problem and the available options for solution are presented clearly they will arrive at commitment to change. For successful operation this strategy requires very specific information and feedback on the development of new skills and attitudes. Zaltman and Duncan also suggest, rather oddly, that providing rewards for involvement in change is part of the reeducation strategy. Rewards can include money, status, and self-esteem, and also the intrinsic rewards of participation in change related activities which are both challenging and achievable.

Persuasion
This strategy depends on skillful presentation of the message that change is both necessary and feasible. It requires charismatic and inspirational leadership throughout the organisation and probably works best when the organisation is already value driven so that change in line with the existing organisational mission is easily accepted. Persuasion consists largely in raising people's expectations of what the proposed innovation can achieve and of the part they can expect to play in it. Its obvious snag is that if the innovation fails to deliver the anticipated benefits not only will it be rejected but the credibility of future persuasive statements and of the overall mission may also be damaged.

Facilitation
In this strategy the main focus is on the individuals involved in the change. Techniques such as team building, sensitivity training and other group methods are used to enhance solidarity in groups of people most likely to be affected by the change. Group methods are also used to promote creative problem solving about relevant aspects of the change.

Power
In the last of Zaltman and Duncan's strategies change is effected through the use of the organisation's power of coercion. Employees are compelled to participate by manipulation of change related rewards and punishments.

Other authors have tried to develop models of organisational change more empirically. Both Peters and Waterman (1982) and Kanter (1983) derive characterisations of the innovative organisation from case studies of successful organisations. In Peters and Waterman's version the company organised for innovation has the following features:

- A bias for action.
- Closeness to the customer.
- Emphasis on autonomy and entrepreneuriality.
- Productiveness through people.
- A value driven motivational climate.
- Concentration on strengths.
- Simple structures.
- Simultaneous centralisation and decentralisation.

They are explained as follows.

A bias for action
The company is organised to devote human and other resources to new projects as and when they arise; there is a commitment to learning and staff development; project teams are small, fluid and organised on an *ad hoc* basis; communication is emphasised.

Closeness to the customer
There is a commitment to customer service, quality and market-led development.

Emphasis on autonomy and entrepreneuriality
Power is decentralised and authority delegated to the level where it is needed; champions of particular ideas or innovations are encouraged and a healthy level of failure is tolerated.

Productiveness through people
Organisational units are small and people are encouraged to take responsibility for their own activities; employees are trusted and encouraged to be winners.

Value driven motivational climate
The organisation is guided by a strong sense of corporate mission and inspirational leadership rather than by control.

Concentration on strengths
The organisation exploits its niche and concentrates on the things it does well.

Simple structures
Bureaucracy is avoided and staff are deployed by projects rather than by formal, stable divisions and functional structures.

Simultaneous centralisation and decentralisation
Core policy making and strategic planning are very centralised but day to day implementation and control are carried out at the lowest feasible level in the hierarchy.

Innovation for Quality in Health Care Organisations

Health care quality assurance presents several distinctive challenges. First, there is the relative intangibility of the health care product and of the interactions between people which constitute much of its delivery: there are considerable difficulties associated with measurement of the physical, social and psychological processes and outcomes of health care. Second, the uncertainty of relationships between the process of care and its outcomes is a potential obstacle to the establishment of clear and universally acceptable standards. Third, where the determination and appraisal of quality rests substantially upon judgement, conflicts are likely to arise as to whose judgement should be accepted: government's, management's, professionals', or consumers'? Finally, the typical characteristics of health care organisations may not be immediately conducive to innovation.

Health care organisations have two major distinguishing features. First, both their costs and their effectiveness are difficult to determine. This applies regardless of the particular mix of central and local governance and private and public sector funding. Second, they are the largest and most complex conglomerate organisations devoted to the practice and support of professional activity. (Educational institutions come a close second but other professions such as engineering, architecture, law, and accountancy have tended to operate either in small free-standing groups or in enclaves within organisations devoted to broader purposes.)

The management of quality in industrial contexts is often assisted by careful accounting of quality costs. Thus the costs of poor product quality associated with waste of raw materials or with additional labour required to modify defective goods can be calculated relatively easily. The costs of quality assurance procedures in labour, time and materials can also be identified. The information can then be used to convince both management and workforce that the costs of quality procedures will be recouped from the reduced costs of poor quality. Cost information of this kind can also be used to identify quality priorities. Quality initiatives are most likely to succeed where the costs of poor quality are high and those of quality procedures low.

The costs and benefits of health care quality are not so easy to calculate. In Williamson's (1978) health accounting model the costs and benefits of quality assurance are established in terms of a health currency. This includes financial factors only as part of a complex of other factors associated with improvements in personal and societal health and wellbeing. Attractive though the establishment of such a health currency may be the exercise is bedevilled by the familiar problems of intangibility of both process and outcome variables, uncertain relationships between them, and traditional reliance on professional judgement.

The pressures of resource scarcity have in fact led to increasing scrutiny of the narrow financial efficiency of health care organisations as a substitute for evaluation in terms of quality. Thus as Ellis (1988) points out measures of inputs such as material and staff resources and outputs such as number of patients treated or bed occupancy rates take the place of the more difficult measures of care process and outcome. Even this narrower scrutiny is difficult given the many sources of funding, the complex structures of budgetary control, and the uncertain relationships between supply and demand which characterise health care finance.

The second distinguishing feature of health care organisations is their dependence on professional activity. In organisational terms professionals can be distinguished from other employees by their frames of reference. Their anticipated rewards, status and self-esteem derive as much from comparison with the norms, values and traditions of their profession as from their performance in the organisation in which they find themselves. They are thus less easily managed by managers who only have access to organisational incentives and disincentives. Innovation and change are as often developed in the professional context as in the organisational and again the manager's task is to persuade professionals to see the point of the organisational mission and of specific tasks and initiatives within it.

Carnall (1990) discusses management of professionals for change and emphasises consent and persuasion as opposed to obedience and control. Thus professionals are more likely to embrace change if its instigators are themselves professionally credible. The change must be described in appropriately professional language and as a response to recognisable professional problems. Appeals should also be made to the intrinsic satisfactions of problem solving as much as to financial reward, and expert contributions should be respected and encouraged. Finally, the organisation should be value driven and its statement and development of mission should be congruent with professional aims.

Quality related innovations are particularly likely to provoke professional resistance as they inevitably impinge on professional values and traditional practices. Clear and explicit quality procedures are always easier to establish in the less professionalised areas of the organisation. In health care quality assurance car parks, waiting rooms and receptionist service are much easier targets than clinical practice.

The health care professions have characteristics which distinguish them not only from non-professional groups but also from other professions. Donabedian (1991) identifies a number of special features of the medical profession which must be taken into account if effective quality assurance is to be established. First, he suggests that medical practitioners have developed a singular degree of interdependence and group cohesion. This he interprets (1991, p. 88) as a response to the 'intrinsically hazardous and uncertain nature of clinical practice' in which it is recognised that 'every physician at one time or another is liable to be mistaken, sometimes with disastrous results'. Physicians have thus banded together to protect their mutual interests. They have developed arcane processes for professional induction and discipline which enhance their concern for maintenance of high standards but also militate against their involvement in the open and explicit processes of quality assurance. As Ellis (1988) points out they have tended to gain power through mystification rather than explication. Pollitt (1988; 1991), Lees et al. (1987) and other sociological commentators interpret the same phenomenon less charitably as the natural defence mechanism of an élite threatened by boundary disputes with other professional groups, with health care managers and even with increasingly knowledgeable patients. The medical profession has been notably unwilling to participate in quality assurance and once persuaded of its value has been very creative in setting up separate systems in which its ownership can be clearly established. It is even possible to discern this ownership dispute in the development of two separate terms namely medical audit which is carried out by medical practitioners and is often heavily dependent on implicit judgemental standards; and 'quality assurance' which is the term accepted by managers for wider and, on the face of it at least, more explicit procedures.

Donabedian's (1991) second distinctive feature of the medical profession is specialisation. This he suggests has traditionally been a source of improved quality. Admission to the various types of specialised practice has been restricted to people who have relevant qualifications. A side effect, however, has been the fragmentation of care and of its organisation. It is thus difficult to hold any one individual responsible for what is done with resulting problems for quality assurance and improvement. This fragmentation is made worse by the relative lack of dialogue between medicine and the other health care professions, which is as evident in matters of quality assurance as elsewhere. Inter-professional clinical audit where it exists is much more likely to consist of nurses with rehabilitation professionals than of medical practitioners with others. Management engendered quality assurance might seem likely to foster inter-professionality but in fact it is likely to stick to the notionally safer territory of throughput efficiency, resource utilisation, and the environmental or hotel aspects of care.

A further result of specialism and organisational fragmentation in UK health care is the relative lack of consistent and comprehensive record systems. Records and measurement are central to quality assurance. US health care quality assurance has benefited greatly from the fact that payment was traditionally tied to treatment given so that there was every incentive to maintain records of what happened. This has not been so in the UK. Despite the apparent advantage of a state supported system in which every patient is registered 'from the cradle to the grave' hospital and general practice records are neither comprehensive nor compatible and computerisation is still very much in the development phase.

The initiation and management of quality assurance in health care thus takes place in organisational contexts which are less than propitious. Despite that, as Donabedian notes (1991, p. 70), there is an increasing number 'of examples of reasonable, even remarkable success'. The remainder of this chapter will discuss health care quality assurance management systems in general and will go on to describe some such examples of success.

A Framework for Health Care Quality Assurance Management

This chapter is based on the premise that the management of quality assurance can be distinguished from its execution. Most of the techniques and approaches described in previous chapters are ways of carrying out quality assurance rather than managing it. Several are merely tools for one part of the quality cycle such as setting standards, identifying quality problems, or measuring process or outcome characteristics. Where committee structures or communication channels for quality decisions have been described they have been presented as established systems. Little attention has been paid to the way they were set up, to the reasons for deciding on these particular arrangements, or to their strengths and weaknesses.

While there is a great deal of exhortatory literature commending the adoption of a management approach in health care quality assurance the literature on specific health care quality management systems is extremely limited. Harman (1992) points out that while both TQM and BS 5750 are often advanced as suitable frameworks for health care quality management, they in fact require considerable adaptation and translation before they are either applicable or acceptable.

James (1992) reports research in progress which identifies eight common components or 'themes' in health care quality management systems. They are as follows:

- Demonstrable top management commitment.
- Securing the support of professionals (especially clinicians).
- Developing quality culture and empowering staff.
- Training.
- Customer sensitivity.
- Processes for continuous quality improvement.
- Quality specifications (qualitative and quantitative standards).
- Effective communications.

While these are themes derived from consideration of health care systems it can be observed that (with the exception of the second) each is also evident in the central features of TQM as set out by Oakland (1989) and recapitulated in Chapter 3 of this book (see p. 48). BS 5750 can be seen as a codification of the TQM approach. Thus both TQM and BS 5750 require the articulation and expression of a quality policy; and the definition, documentation and implementation of detailed quality procedures. TQM goes beyond BS 5750, however, in setting out methods for motivating and involving the entire workforce. This creation of a quality culture is said to be essential for becoming a prevention oriented, continuously improving organisation.

In summary, health care quality assurance management has much to learn from general approaches to the management of organisational change, from the broad principles of TQM, and from the commitment to the explication and review of quality procedures and systems represented by BS 5750. Much development work remains to be done, however. The framework which follows may provide a basis.

Quality management involves the deployment of human and material resources so as to develop effective quality assurance systems for least cost. As with quality assurance itself it can be conceived as a dynamic system with potential for continuing improvement. It can be represented as a cycle, as shown in Figure 6.1.

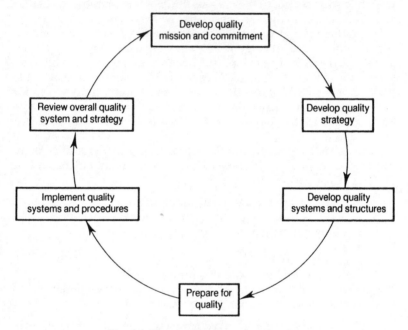

Fig. 6.1 The quality management cycle

Each stage of the cycle will now be briefly discussed.

Develop Quality Mission and Commitment

Industrial quality management developed from the work of Juran and Deming in post-war Japan. Both emphasised the significance of corporate commitment to quality and suggested that senior management were responsible for the development of a quality ethos throughout the company. More general commentaries on organisational development also stress the importance of corporate mission and values in determining successful innovation. If a proposed change is at odds with a company's existing value system it will be much more difficult to implement than one which is in harmony with it.

In health care, concern for quality of service and commitment to high standards is widespread but recognition that the establishment of quality assurance procedures and systems can help to improve quality is less so. The primary management task at this stage in the cycle is thus the articulation and dissemination of mission and policy statements which link the two in ways which are believable and acceptable. Credibility is improved if the statements reflect knowledge of a range of possible approaches and of ways they might be employed in the organisation concerned. It is also assisted by clear commitment of resources to setting up quality systems and procedures and to implementing such improvements as may eventually be proposed. Acceptability is improved if the mission statement recognises existing quality expertise, acknowledges the particular role of professional judgement in identifying and maintaining standards, and emphasises the organisation-wide benefits of improved quality.

Develop Quality Strategy

Quality mission statements are designed to answer the question *why* quality systems should be set up. Quality strategy should answer the question *how*. In other words, it is a broad plan setting out priorities, targets and schedules for the entire organisation. It is also the basis for subsequent review of the overall quality initiative. This stage in the cycle is thus analogous to the standard setting stage of the basic quality cycle.

The literature on prioritisation in quality assurance is limited. It can even be argued that the popularity of total quality approaches and of the 'quality is everybody's business' slogan have militated against systematic planning. Yet it is evident that without such planning quality development may be fragmentary and *ad hoc*, reflecting personal enthusiasms, easy options and superficial acquiescence rather than rational analysis and decision. As Dalley and Carr-Hill (1991) note, this was just the state of quality assurance in the NHS at the time of their survey. Almost all Regional Authorities had developed mission statements or policy documents and there were many diverse local initiatives (with a predominance of nursing standard setting and consumer satisfaction surveys). There was little evidence of co-ordination and overall management and the gap between mission and accomplishment was correspondingly large. Even in the longer established US quality systems fragmentation, overlap and lack of coordination are frequently noted.

Ovretveit (1992) suggests that one reason for the lack of strategic planning is failure to integrate quality management with other management systems. He argues that one way of doing so is to identify quality priorities and targets by reference to general business plans. This involves consideration of the overall business environment (including consumer preferences, labour markets, and purchaser and referrer characteristics) before development of a 'service quality brief'. The quality strategy is thus part of the general business strategy and the results of specific quality initiatives are fed back into the overall system of organisational review and development.

The most commonly cited technique for quality prioritisation in both health care and industry is cost benefit analysis. Priority areas are those where the maximum improvement can be obtained for the least expenditure of human and material resources. In industry improvement can generally be determined by reference to physical characteristics of products, degree of variation in processes and, ultimately, increased profitability. Detailed cost information is also likely to be available. In health care the estimation of both costs and benefits is less straightforward but the general principle holds good.

Motivational considerations can also contribute to prioritisation and strategic planning. Thus initial quality activities should be likely to achieve their objectives. If their success can be given a relatively high profile enthusiasm for future activities is likely to increase. At a more basic level consideration should be given to individual incentives for involvement in quality activities. Many quality strategies include prize schemes and opportunities for staff development, promotion and increased financial reward. In the first instance quality may have to be a loss leader if optimum participation is to be achieved.

As Zaltman and Duncan (1977) note, skilful management of innovation involves selection of strategies which take into account the past histories and predominant styles of the organisation concerned. The development of quality strategies could thus be informed by consideration of previous innovations. What has been successful in bringing about previous change? Where are the areas of greatest flexibility or rigidity and where are the champions of innovation who can be trusted to shepherd developments through formal and informal networks of influence?

Ovretveit (1992) emphasises the idea that quality activities should be phased in. They should 'start where the biggest improvements can be made for a low cost and go at a pace which staff can cope with' (Ovretveit, 1992, p. 130). Initially, he suggests, activities should be prioritised which tackle outstanding and generally recognised instances of poor quality. After this fire-fighting phase, quality problems should begin to emerge from locally established problem spotting systems (like quality circles or issue logs). Finally, all parts of the organisation should have systematic quality procedures designed to prevent rather than remedy quality problems. Ovretveit (1992) notes that it may take years before health care organisations can reach the prevention phase. He also observes that many NHS units are currently suffering 'quality over saturation'. This occurs when senior management or purchasers insist on detailed specifications for standards of service or for quality procedures before staff involved have had time to come to terms with either quality or the new purchaser provider relationships. Over saturation is also engendered where large numbers of off the shelf techniques are recommended with little consideration for local needs, or where actual standards and specifications are adopted from other units or settings. As Ovretveit comments this is 'frequently seen as a quick way of assuring others of the quality of the service, but it only ensures staff antagonism'.

However, priorities are established they should be enshrined in a clear and explicit strategy document. It should identify target areas, specify objectives and determine a schedule for their achievement. Since it will eventually be widely available it should be written with its readership in mind.

Develop Quality Systems and Structures

The process of strategic planning is likely to have generated ideas for project teams, individual responsibilities and communication channels. One issue which is regularly debated is the extent to which the quality management structure should be distinct from normal management structures and responsibilities. Separation can mean marginalisation and failure to take quality issues seriously but integration can mean that quality issues are regularly at the bottom of agendas and never given due attention. The problem is resolved in different ways (as the examples presented later in this chapter will show), but however it is done the structures must allow sufficient time and attention for quality to be regularly discussed. Responsibilities may be differently shared in different structures but it must be possible to identify people who are in the end both responsible and accountable.

Both BS 5750 and TQM assume that most organisations already have some elements of a quality system in place. A sensible beginning to development of the full system is thus the identification and documentation of these elements. In manufacturing industry these might include procedures for basic product inspection, process control, health and safety checks, and customer complaints procedures. In health care too there are likely to be existing procedures. Thus medical laboratories will have a quality control system, groups of consultants may have set up case review meetings, nurses are likely to have been involved in standard setting and there may have been a number of patient satisfaction surveys.

Alongside this identification and recognition of existing procedures both TQM and BS 5750 recommend a process of careful identification of the critical functions performed in the achievement of organisational objectives. This could include the development of process flow charts which make clear exactly who does what to whom and when. Quality standards will eventually be required for each of these functions or process flows. Standards will have to be documented and enshrined in a quality manual.

Harman (1992) notes that this emphasis on detailed documentation and control throughout the organisation may be most effective in manufacturing industry where the aim is to minimise product variation. In health care standards and procedures are required which allow for flexibility and variation to meet the individuality of patient needs. These may be more difficult to document.

Discussion of the strategic plan is also likely to have involved senior and middle management in considering broad approaches to be adopted in different parts of the organisation. These could (and arguably should) vary in light of local circumstances. Existing medical audit activities might be sustained and elaborated, new consumer relations initiatives might be established, quality control expertise in laboratory services might be shared with colleagues in other areas, and an Issue Logs system might be set up throughout the organisation. Some of these approaches may be deliberately top down (possibly in areas where the imperative is for rapid action to improve outstandingly poor quality) while others may be bottom up exercises designed to maximise participation and perceptions of quality ownership. Approaches would thus be selected to meet local need, to exploit local expertise and enthusiasm, and to attend to both short-term and long-term quality objectives. Committee structures and communication channels first proposed might have to be modified in light of such subsequent decisions.

At this stage, too, training needs are likely to be highlighted. Middle management at least must have had opportunities to increase quality knowledge and skills before structures are finally put in place and activities begun.

Prepare for Quality

Organisational change thrives on good communication. Zaltman and Duncan (1977) even suggest that if information about proposed changes and likely benefits are presented clearly enough commitment to change will emerge automatically. Peters and Waterman (1982) include commitment to good communication among the characteristic features of organisations which have a bias towards action. Quality innovations may stand or fall by the way they are communicated to staff and their initial launch may be critical in determining staff perception and response.

Discussing organisational culture change Ovretveit (1992, p. 134) suggests that 'there is a need to 'sell' service quality to staff before trying to convince external customers'. He comments on low morale in health care organisations where past changes have been perceived as cost cutting, and counter to the professional ethic of providing the best possible care for patients. In such contexts he suggests that quality initiatives must be presented as upholding professional and service standards and as increasing job satisfaction and pride in doing the job well. Tangible benefits such as improved job prospects and opportunities for development of new skills should also be stressed.

Bearing these considerations in mind preparatory activities should present the quality mission, and should detail the strategy and structures proposed. All staff should be involved in preparation and should have access to both face to face presentations and written documentation. There should be opportunities for comment and feedback and these should result in appropriate modifications to the proposals. At this stage too further training needs will be identified and all staff should have opportunities for the development of quality knowledge and skills.

Implement Quality Procedures

At this stage in the quality management cycle quality structures are in place and the system can finally operate. This is the point at which the basic quality cycle involving standard setting, appraisal and action for quality improvement is the relevant model. General approaches have already been determined in the strategic plan but choice of precise quality topic, identification or articulation of locally relevant standards, and selection of measurement techniques need not be finalised until this point.

It is assumed that by this stage most staff have some familiarity with the importance of quality initiatives and that some staff have specific knowledge and skills. As local activities progress, however, more detailed information and support may be needed. Many organisations set up a quality unit or identify a small group of quality facilitators whose job is provision of *ad hoc* guidance, information and support as well as more formal training activities.

At this stage for the first time procedures generate proposals for quality action. Some will be implemented at local level but others will involve inter-departmental or senior management discussion. Committee structures and communication channels must now facilitate effective transmission of information in relevant new directions. Wherever implementation takes place some record should be available for inclusion in overall quality statistics and for review of quality procedures and structures and of the overall system.

Review Quality System and Strategy

The quality strategy included target areas, objectives and schedules for their achievement. The final stage in the quality management cycle is review of the extent to which they have actually been achieved. It is thus quality assurance for quality assurance. Where there are opportunities for improvement each stage in the cycle is reviewed and modifications to structures and procedures can be proposed. New or modified priorities, target areas, approaches and training needs are then established. The review can be entirely internal or can involve external consultants or accreditation agencies. As in other reviews internal assessors have more detailed knowledge of local needs and possibilities but external assessors may have wider perspectives and more objectivity.

Once one cycle has been completed the next begins again with consideration of quality mission and commitment. These may not require particular modification but their reassertion in light of the recently completed quality review provides encouragement and reinforces the impression that the most senior managers are genuinely concerned to deliver the highest possible standard of care.

The cyclical framework presented here was developed from the literature and from the authors' knowledge of management practice in a number of health care and other quality assurance settings. The remainder of this chapter will present case studies of health care quality assurance management which can be found in more detail in published sources. They have been subdivided into hospital and community systems.

Case studies of Health Care Quality Assurance Management

Hospital Systems

The most comprehensive currently available account of the implementation and development of hospital-wide quality systems is Wilson's (1987) description of the systems developed in the member hospitals of the Ontario Hospitals Association in 1985 and 1986. Some quality assurance mechanisms already existed but they were somewhat patchwork in scope and state of development. The Canadian Council on Hospital Accreditation had just produced its standards for quality systems for acute care (CCHA, 1984) and the hospitals in which Wilson developed his ideas were therefore preparing for accreditation.

Wilson endorses the notion that quality is everyone's business and stresses participation in all departments and at all levels in the hospital. He describes a typical structure in which responsibilities are organised as set out in Fig. 6.2. In this system the quality assurance committee reports directly to the Chief Executive Officer (CEO) who is in turn responsible to the Board of Trustees or other top level committee. Wilson comments on alternative arrangements in which

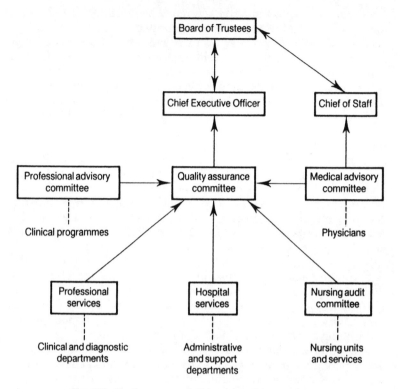

Fig. 6.2 Quality responsibilities (after Wilson, 1987)

final and exclusive responsibility for quality is in the hands of a designated quality co-ordinator, or in which responsibility for quality is integrated with other management functions and no one is particularly accountable. Finally responsible co-ordinators can become scapegoats for poor quality or can be seen as a management pawns. On the other hand, where no one takes responsibility quality issues never develop the high profile they need. Wilson's preferred solution is designation of a co-ordinator whose responsibilities are shared with other managers through a committee. Committee members are selected for seniority, expertise, representativeness, and enthusiasm. The committee's remit includes interpretation of its mandate from the CEO; developing programme objectives in the light of its mandate (and the accreditation requirements); organising and providing briefing, training and coaching for department heads and other relevant groups; evaluating quality assurance reports from the various centres and departments; giving supportive and challenging feedback on reports; stimulating action for quality improvement both

within departments and in the interfaces between them; and reporting back to the CEO and top-level committee.

One notable feature of Wilson's organisational approach is the
separate strand of medical audit responsibility. This he claims is
simply recognition of separate statutory obligations concerning
medical practice and resulting conventions in Canadian hospitals. In
the light of the somewhat hesitant response to quality assurance in
both the US and UK medical professions it is interesting to speculate
on whether this system is (a) what is likely to evolve elsewhere or (b)
necessarily the most effective approach.

Wilson identifies two approaches to the organisation and development of quality in the hospital. These he terms the logical approach
and the adult learning approach. The logical approach is defined as
the approach in which each department and function in the hospital
is expected to conform to general standards which are established by
reference to outside authorities (e.g. accreditation systems or professional bodies) and to move at once to the development of a
sophisticated and voluminous information base. The system is thus
both top down and time consuming. Wilson comments (1988, p. 28)
that quality assurance programmes in such a system 'take an
inordinately long time to organise and make productive' and that
they have a reputation for 'being a long, laborious, demanding and
unfulfilling excursion into detailed documentation'.

The adult learning model is designed to be both easier to
implement and more motivating for both staff and senior management. In this model the quality committee's relationship with each
department progresses through six stages as follows.

* Documentation of existing quality management.
* Improving recognition for quality activities.
* Incorporating all strategies for improving quality.
* Articulating standards.
* Planning criteria based audits for all functions.
* Endorsing the quality plan.

Each will now be described in more detail.

Documentation of existing quality management

It is recognised that concern for quality is in the nature of professional
activity and that many aspects of normal management and progress
chasing can in fact be defined as part of the incipient quality system
for the department. This is both motivating to staff and a short-cut to
setting up systems. The main functions of the department are
identified and a record is made of each relevant quality activity. At
this stage a mission statement is produced for the department and
passed on to the quality committee.

Improving recognition for quality activities

Existing quality activities are more carefully written up and presented to the quality committee as the first departmental quality reports. These are then available for dissemination round the hospital as instances of good practice.

Incorporating all strategies for assuring quality

Existing activities in the department and in other departments are carefully reviewed by department members and a draft departmental quality plan is drawn up.

Articulating standards

Standards which until this point have been fairly general are now made more explicit and more specific. Criteria by which the achievement of standards will be appraised are developed and documented by relevant groups of department members.

Planning criteria based audits for all functions

A quality manual is developed by the department. Each relevant aspect of the department's work now has a list of standards and criteria.

Endorsing the quality plan

The quality manual and confirmed plan are submitted to the quality committee and the first annual quality contract is drawn up between the department and the committee.

Wilson suggests that the model has the virtue of starting where people are and of giving them credit for what they are already doing. Novel elements are introduced step by step as a series of specific and reasonable demands.

Wilson also specifies a wider role for the quality committee as a quality change agent throughout the hospital. He suggests a gradual build up of activity through 10 steps as follows.

Structure

This involves setting up the various committees and designating individual responsibilities necessary for hospital wide quality activity.

Launch

This is a high profile event or series of events including the dissemination of information to relevant managers and the organisation of training sessions appropriate to their individual needs. Managers also prepare draft mission statements and give an account of the principal functions of their departments at this stage.

Coaching and feedback
The committee meets individually with managers to discuss and encourage the development of refined mission statements and the identification of existing quality activities.

Restructuring
The committee returns to the organisation structure it set up at the first stage and modifies it if necessary in the light of the mission statements and statements of function it now has.

Monthly reporting
The committee develops systems for receiving, storing and processing the information it is now receiving from managers on quality activities.

Negotiation
The committee calls on managers to produce departmental plans incorporating all functions.

Educational support
The committee supports and encourages the development of standards and criteria. This includes provision of training, time and documentation.

Evaluation
The committee provides feedback on departmental plans, standards and criteria and supports modifications where necessary.

Contract
Contracts are negotiated with all departments. Once collated these in turn become the contract between the quality committee and the top level board to which they are responsible.

Review
The committee is itself subject to annual review by the board.

While each department in the hospital goes through the same process of learning and negotiation the actual products of learning (i.e. the quality activities engaged in, the standards set and the improvements initiated) can vary considerably. Thus while responsibility for the overall system is centralised, responsibility for day-to-day activities is delegated to the lowest feasible level. It is suggested, however, that each department's annual quality plan and resulting contract should make reference to quality goals; quality promotion (staff development, investigation of new procedures, maintenance of high motivation for quality activities, etc.); activity monitoring (routine quality appraisal and action); and periodic overall review of departmental quality and quality assurance. Within that rubric departments are free to choose between externally set standards, locally developed standards, standards based on professional judgement or standards based on explicit specification of limits of variation – in other words to choose from the range of techniques and approaches set out in earlier chapters of this book.

While Wilson's adult learning approach to the initiation and management of hospital-wide quality assurance embodies many of the principles of both TQM and BS 5750 it does not make specific reference to either. Williams (1989) describes a system in action at the Norton and Kosair Children's Hospital in Louisville, Kentucky, which is explicitly based on TQM.

The Norton and Kosair system was initiated in 1987 and is described as still being in the process of achieving its goals. Its development was the result of a substantial period of consultation with experienced industrial quality managers and advisors from some of the largest companies in the US. The overall system embodies a philosophical framework, a management action plan and a model for quality review which applies to all hospital departments including medical staff groupings.

The philosophical framework is set out in written form and is essentially that of industrial TQM. It accepts the industrial definition of quality as being that which meets requirements, but notes that requirements may be established on the basis of meeting explicit standards or on the basis of customer perceptions. Error free work is the overall aim and management's task is taken to be management of the prevention of error. It is accepted that errors may occur, however, and action for improvement is therefore stressed. Performance measurement and appraisal are at the hub of the system and development of locally relevant models for quality review are said to be essential. Finally, the philosophical framework emphasises extending the sense of quality ownership throughout the organisation so as to induce feelings of responsibility, pride and involvement.

The action plan for quality management has the following sections:

- Statement of mission and policy.
- Management commitment and involvement.
- Organisational restructuring for quality.
- Education and training.
- Identifying customer requirements (external or internal).
- Employee involvement.
- Quality review.
- Recognition and reward.
- Appraisal and pay systems.

- Communication.
- Integrating TQM with other management systems.

The quality review model suggested for all departments requires performance to be appraised under six headings as follows:

- Competency and credentialling of staff.
- Appropriateness and accessibility of care.
- Resource utilisation.
- Effectiveness of care.
- Safety/risk management.
- Customer satisfaction.

Each department identifies and documents its main functions and processes and works on the development of quality indicators for each function or process under each of the six headings. Problems are then flagged and areas deserving review during a particular review cycle are identified. The basic indicators are routinely measured and problems are defined as undue variation from the predetermined standards. Each department thus establishes quality goals for each review cycle and reports on their achievement. This then contributes to the normal cycles of management reporting and planning.

As Donabedian (1991) notes fragmentation of both responsibility and influence is a particular feature of health care organisations which may militate against effective quality management. Neither Wilson's Canadian model nor the Norton and Kosair model, however, place particular stress on the tracking of problems and problem solutions from department to department or between professions. A number of so-called hospital-wide quality management systems are in fact systems for such tracking. They include the QIP system (Benson et al., 1986) and the Issue Logs system (Brown et al., 1984) both of which are described in Chapter 4 (p. 105).

Community Care Systems

The organisation of health care for entire communities or regions is by definition both more extensive and more complex than the organisation of care within the confines of a single hospital. In particular the types of facility offering care can vary from the large urban teaching hospital to the one practitioner rural clinic. The range of professional and non-professional staff involved is wider. The responsibility for care can last for years but individual episodes of care can be as short as half an hour. Record systems in different parts of the organisation may not be compatible. Finally, a variety of funding mechanisms may operate within the area. It follows that the management of health care in such contexts is also more difficult.

Quality may also be inherently more difficult to appraise in community settings. Palmer et al. (1984) note for example that the time elapsing between interventions of a preventive nature and the onset of adverse or beneficial outcomes may be substantial. Information about adverse outcomes cannot therefore be used to identify opportunities for improvement of current practice. Another problem is that many patients seen in community settings are suffering either from self-limiting disorders in which the same outcome would ensue with or without intervention, or from ill-defined or multiple disorders for which it is particularly difficult to track relationships between intervention and outcome. Finally, since treatment regimens are largely followed through at home, patient compliance and availability of suitable domiciliary support are major sources of uncertainty in determining the effectiveness of care.

Two community oriented systems will be considered here. They are the Johns Hopkins Health System Quality Review Process and the Park Nicollet Medical Centre system.

The Johns Hopkins Health System includes both hospital and community care, delivered in two major teaching hospitals, a community hospital, a group practice, and a multi-site health maintenance organisation, all operating in the city of Baltimore.

King and Jones (1989, p. 55) describe the Johns Hopkins Health System quality review process as a response to the following questions:

- Where does the commitment to high quality care begin?
- What organisational structures and linkages are required?
- Who must be involved in the development, management and monitoring of the programme?
- How can the programme be evaluated?

In the event commitment has been obtained from the highest levels in the organisation. The bylaws of each component care facility were altered (in 1986) to enshrine statements on the commitment to quality and the organisation of quality assurance procedures.

Organisational structures and linkages, however, were more difficult to establish. In the initial stages it was necessary to ensure simple compatibility between existing systems. Thus one area given immediate attention was differences in credentialling rules whereby medical practitioners were appointed and allowed to practise in the various specialisms. The same basic rules now operate across all facilities. Organisation of concurrent quality monitoring still varies between facilities but all have established a quality assurance committee which meets monthly and receives reports from the various departments. Systematic occurrence screening is carried out by nurses on records generated in each facility and criteria have been agreed for hospitals with respect to admission procedures, documentation, medical treatment, surgical treatment, drug usage, adverse occurrences (e.g. patient falls, nosocomial infection), discharge procedures, unexpected death, nursing care issues, and family or patient complaint. Existence of poor care in any of these areas can lead to intensive review by relevant physicians. A rather more limited list of occurrence screening criteria has been developed for the community parts of the system. These include unexpected returns to the operating room, unexpected readmissions, mortalities, and complaints from patients or other outside agencies. Again instances of poor care lead to intensive review.

A major feature of both the hospital and community parts of the system is the development of compatible data collection systems across the entire organisation. This permits problem tracking across the various facilities and also helps the total organisation to evaluate both care quality and its assurance.

The Park Nicollet Medical Centre is specifically designed for community care. Park Nicollet is the fifth largest multi-specialty centre in the US and provides care in seventeen locations in the suburbs of Minneapolis. Its 270 physicians are organised in 36 specialty departments and deal with about a million and a half patient visits per annum. About 60% of these are a function of membership in a managed care plan.

The Park Nicollet quality assurance system has been in existence for longer than the Johns Hopkins system, having been established in 1973. Batalden and O'Connor (1980) describe how it was set up as a four-step process of quality assessment and assurance. The four steps are as follows:

Problem seeking
This is carried out using chart reviews, staff and patient interviews and adverse incident monitoring.

Problem formulation
This relies on a group consensus approach and includes comparison with standards determined through a process akin to quality circles.

Problem resolution
At this stage the causes of problems are agreed and resolution plans are written with clear objectives and specified time scales.

Problem reassessment
After a specified time problem areas are reviewed to see whether improvements have been maintained.

Kind (1989) notes that while the Park Nicollet system is problem centred it has not just tried to improve poor care but has also tried to reward excellent care. Thus if review of a particular physician's practice identifies an absence of problems this is duly noted and the achievement is recognised in various positive ways.

Of particular interest in the Park Nicollet system are its inter-professionalism and its involvement of patients and third party purchasers. Thus medical practitioners are encouraged to become involved in the identification and solution of problems in the laboratory and other support systems available to them. They work in groups with relevant staff to develop standards and protocols for practice. They also work with non-medical staff on the development of guidelines for record audit and case review of their own practice.

Patient perspectives are examined through the system called the 'Art of Care' (Kind, 1987). This was developed subsequent to a survey of patients, physicians and other health care staff asking them what they thought the essential components of the interpersonal aspects of care were. The results of the survey provided a basis for protocols for a system of post care consultations with patients. These are carried out through telephone interviews focussing on recent visits and through mail surveys soliciting general views on the interpersonal skills of individual practitioners. Practitioners participate on a voluntary basis but seem to be generally enthusiastic about the feedback obtained. Finally, purchasers' perspectives are represented through involvement in epidemiologically informed decisions re-garding health promotion initiatives. They also help to organise health monitoring and surveillance exercises which are themselves part of the system's overall quality assurance programme.

The available accounts of these and other community oriented health care quality assurance systems offer less insight into the management philosophy and organisational model to which appeal is being made than do accounts of hospital wide systems. This may be a function of the relatively recent development of community care systems in the US. It may also be a function of the inherent diversity and diffuseness of community care and of the difficulty of all management in such settings.

Conclusion

This chapter has distinguished between health care quality assurance systems and their management. It has suggested that industrial approaches to organisational change and to quality assurance man-agement provide a useful framework but that further development work is required before they can be transferred to health care contexts. Despite that caution it can be concluded that health care quality assurance can only be successful if it is consciously managed and if its management is integrated with the more general pattern of health care management. Dialogue is therefore needed between quality assurance specialists, general managers, professionals and other health care staff. This chapter (and indeed this book) has been designed to encourage and assist the debate.

7

Future Developments in Quality Assurance in Health Care

Introduction

This book has reviewed the state of quality assurance in health care as it stands in early 1992. It has traced its historical origins and explored its relationship to analogous developments in manufacturing and service industry. It has also provided guidance on setting up and managing systems and procedures. Most significantly it has tried to provide as comprehensive a compendium as possible of the very many approaches and techniques which are currently available in published form.

Inevitably such review and would-be comprehensive coverage has highlighted both growth points and gaps in the current pattern of health care quality assurance. This brief chapter will identify these and will indicate directions in which health care quality assurance might profitably develop in future years.

Future Growth

Health care quality assurance has grown at an exponential rate over the past ten years. It is now a formal requirement in publicly funded health systems throughout the developed world and is regarded as both useful and marketable in the private sector. The economic, social, political and professional pressures which were identified in Chapter 1 as factors in this growth show no sign of losing their force. It can thus be predicted that future years will see growth continue. More people will be involved in health care quality assurance, more approaches and techniques will evolve, the literature will become more extensive, and public awareness and expectation will increase.

This book has demonstrated the plurality of possible approaches to health care quality assurance. While offering guidance on their selection it has rarely ventured into actual prescription. It has thus been an organising principle that there is no one 'right way' to 'do quality assurance'. Health care delivery and its organisation are inherently complex and variable and quality assurance for health care must necessarily reflect that. The optimum approach in a large high technology NHS trust hospital might be totally inappropriate in a small rural community service in a developing country. What this book has implicitly commended is careful, well-informed reflection and planning in selection of approach and design of procedures, followed by systematic monitoring of results and consequent modification of the implemented system. That is, of course, the very basis of quality assurance itself.

It seems likely, then, that quality assurance in some guise will continue to flourish in health care. How effective it will be in actually improving or even sustaining the quality of care may, however, depend on how systematically it is used and developed.

Desirable Developments

Systematic development of health care quality assurance implies more than simple growth. It implies identification of areas for improvement and selective attention to the development of new techniques in areas of greatest need. A number of these areas have been identified in previous chapters.

Standards

The fundamental problem in all quality assurance is the establishment of clear, appropriate and acceptable standards. In health care it involves not only the establishment of standards for the delivery and outcomes of care but the unpacking of causal relationships between process and outcome. Current standards are an uneasy mix of structure, process and outcome and relationships between them are the subject of some science, much professional judgement, and a fair degree of guesswork. There is a clear need for more research into the outcomes and effectiveness of specific treatments and procedures and for the systematic collation of results from medical audit and other outcome oriented quality activities.

Process standards have been more extensively developed in nursing than in any other professional area and almost all instruments for measuring process quality are designed for use in nursing. Other professions could profitably learn from the nursing experience.

Even in nursing the technical processes of care have received far more attention than the interpersonal. So far neither the growing literature on interpersonal communication in health care nor the better established literature on the analysis of teaching behaviour has been exploited in developing detailed standards for the interpersonal processes of care. Such exploitation would assist both standard setting and the development of related measurement and appraisal techniques.

Measurement

Measurement is of central importance in quality appraisal and this book described and reviewed many instruments for both process and outcome measurement. Regrettably very few were found to be satisfactorily reliable and valid. Better measurement tools are badly needed. Improved techniques for both outcome and process measurement and appraisal would in turn improve the prospects of detailed mapping of relationships between them.

Interprofessionalism

One feature of health care outcomes likely to be highlighted in any such detailed account is the extent to which they depend on a package of care delivered by a range of professionals. Health care is basically inter-professional yet its quality assurance is most frequently carried out by mono-professional groups. There is an obvious need for techniques and measures designed for inter-professional activities and for quality management systems which encourage their development and use. It would also be sensible to foster techniques which facilitate dialogue between professionals and other groups such as managers, support workers and indeed consumers. Health service organisation is itself relatively compartmentalised and there is a danger that current quality systems will consolidate divisions rather than break them down.

Consumerism

Quality assurance is often defined as 'meeting customer requirements' and consumer concern for maintenance of high standards is one of the factors creating current interest in health care quality. Despite this actual consumer involvement in health care quality assurance is very limited. Patient satisfaction measures could be much improved and a wider range of techniques for involving patients in the appraisal and improvement of quality could be considered.

Costs and Benefits

Relationships between costs and quality were discussed at several points in this book. In industry quality assurance is often said to pay for itself by cutting down waste and increasing profitability or market share. In health care relationships between quality costs and benefits are less certain. The costs of care are difficult to detail, relationships between supply and demand are complex, and quantification of the benefits of extended lifespan or improved health and quality of life remains elusive. More sophisticated economic analysis in each of these areas would be a highly desirable advance.

Management

Several approaches and systems for quality assurance management in health care were described and discussed in earlier chapters. It was noted, however, that most of them had been transferred directly from their industrial origins with little regard for the special conditions of health care organisations. There is need for careful monitoring of their implementation and modification in their new setting.

Review Systems

Systems for the review of quality assurance systems and procedures were also discussed and considerable reference was made to BS 5750 in the UK and to the accreditation procedures of the JCAHO and other bodies in the US. Neither seem entirely satisfactory. The US experience is of fragmented and overlapping review systems which are partly organisational reviews, partly reviews of actual care quality and almost incidentally reviews of quality assurance systems and management. BS 5750/ISO 9000 is designed specifically to review quality systems and it is in increasing use in UK health care. Unfortunately, it is perceived as having been designed for manufacturing industry and its use in the NHS to date has been restricted to non-clinical areas (Harman, 1992). Development of a review system which exploits the best features of BS 5750 but adapts it for the specific circumstances of health care quality assurance is badly overdue.

Education

None of the desirable developments identified above will occur without the commitment and enthusiasm of skilled and knowledgeable individuals. There is thus a prior need for systems of education and training in quality assurance and for recognition and accreditation of specialist expertise. Specifically, it would be desirable for all health care personnel at least to encounter quality assurance in their initial training and to have subsequent opportunities for more intensive study.

Dissemination

Finally, both the development of individuals and the development of quality assurance itself are assisted by the exchange of information and ideas. A great deal of health care quality assurance is carried out at local levels and is never reported. Better channels for the dissemination of knowledge and the sharing of experience would enhance both theory and practice.

Conclusion

This book is a handbook. It is designed to provide information, to stimulate interest and to provoke reflection. Primarily, however, it is designed to assist and encourage health care quality assurance activities and thus to maintain and improve standards of care. We hope that it has been fit for its purpose and that it has met consumer need.

References

Adair, M. *et al.* (1982). *Quality Circles in Nursing Service: a Step by Step Implementation process.* National League for Nursing, New York.

Allison, S. and Kinloch, K. (1981). Problem oriented recording. *The Canadian Nurse*, December, 39–40.

American Nurses' Association (1973a). *Standards of Nursing Practice.* American Nurses' Association, Kansas City.

American Nurses' Association (1973b). *Standards of Maternal/Child Nursing.* American Nurses' Association, Kansas City.

American Nurses' Association (1973c). *Standards of Psychiatric/Mental Health Nursing.* American Nurses' Association, Kansas City.

American Nurses' Association (1973d). *Standards of Community Health Nursing Practice.* American Nurses' Association, Kansas City.

American Nurses' Association (1974). *Standards of Medical/Surgical Nursing Practice.* American Nurses' Association, Kansas City.

American Nurses' Association (1976). *Standards of Gerontological Nursing Practice.* American Nurses' Association, Kansas City.

American Nurses' Association (1982). *Nursing Quality Assurance Management Learning System.* American Nurses' Association, Kansas City.

American Physical Therapy Association (1977). *Competencies in Physical Therapy: an Analysis of Practice.* APTA, Washington.

Anastasi, A. (1988). *Psychological Testing* (6th edn.). Collier Macmillan, New York.

Anderson, W.G. (1986). Definitions of quality. *American Medical News*, 12 December, 24.

Andrews, G. (1984). Treatment outlines for the management of schizophrenia. The quality assurance project. *Australia and New Zealand Journal of Psychiatry*, **18**, (1), 19–38.

Andrews, G. (1985). Treatment outlines for the management of anxiety states. The quality assurance project. *Australia and New Zealand Journal of Psychiatry*, **19**, (2), 138–151.

Aquinas, T. (1963). Summa theologica, question 77 'On fraud committed in buying and selling'. In *Summa Theologica*. Gilbey, T. (ed.), McGraw-Hill, Washington.

Argyle, M. (1963). *The Psychology of Interpersonal Behaviour*. Penguin, Harmondsworth.

Argyle, M. (1969). *Social Interaction*. Methuen, London.

Argyle, M. (1975). *Bodily Communication*. Methuen, London.

Ash, A.J. *et al.* (1990). The Self-Adapting Focused Review System. *Medical Care*, **28**, (11), 1025–1039.

Australian Council on Healthcare Standards (1990). *Quality Assurance for Speech Pathologists*. ACHS, Zetland.

Australian Council on Healthcare Standards (1991). *Quality Assurance for Occupational Therapists*. ACHS, Zetland.

Australian Council on Healthcare Standards (1991). *Quality Assurance for Physiotherapists*. ACHS, Zetland.

Axelsson, P. and Linde, J. (1978). Effect of controlled oral hygiene procedures on caries and periodontal disease in adults. *Journal of Clinical Periodontics*, **5**, 133.

Bair, J. and Joe, B. (1989). Viewpoints: occupational therapy. In *Quality Rehabilitation*. England, B. *et al.* (eds.), American Hospital Association, Chicago.

Balfe, B.E. *et al.* (1987). A health policy agenda for the American people. *Quality Progress*, May, 48–53.

Barnett, D. and Wainwright, P. (1987). Between two tools. *Senior Nurse*, **6**, (4), 40–42.

Barney, M. (1981). Measuring quality of patient care: a computerised approach. *Supervisor Nurse*, **12**, (5), 40–44.

Barter, J.T. (1988). Accreditation surveys: nit-picking or quality seeking? *Hospital and Community Psychiatry*, **39**, (7), 707.

Batalden, P.B. and O'Connor, J.P. (1980). *Quality Assurance in Ambulatory Care*. Aspen Systems Corporation, Germantown.

Belson, W. (1981). *The Design and Understanding of Survey Questions*. Gower, London.

Benedict, R. (1946). *The Chrysanthemum and the Sword*. New American Library, New York.

Benson, D. and Miller, J. (1989). *AMBUQUAL: an Ambulatory Quality Assurance and Quality Management System*. Methodist Hospital of Indiana Inc, Indianapolis.

Benson, D. *et al.* (1986). The QIP form: the one-page quality assurance tool. *Quality Review Bulletin*, **12**, (3), 87–89.

Bergner, M. (1985). Measurement of health status. *Medical Care*, **23**, 705–9.

Bergner, M. *et al.* (1981). The Sickness Impact Profile: development and final revision of a health status measure. *Medical Care*, **19**, 787–805.

Bersoff, D.N. and Kinports, K. (1988). Legal considerations in quality assurance. In *Handbook of Quality Assurance in Mental Health*. Stricker, G. and Rodriguez, A.R., (eds.), Plenum, New York.

Berwick, D.M. (1990). Peer review and quality management: are they compatible? *Quality Review Bulletin*, **16**, (7), 246–251.

Berwick, D.M. and Knapp, M.G. (1987). Theory and practice for measuring health care quality. *Health Care Financing Review*, Annual Supplement, 49–55.

Beyers, M. (1988). Quality: the banner of the 1980s. *Nursing Clinics of North America*, **23**, (3), 617–23.

Black, N.A. (1989). Annual reports on public health. *British Medical Journal*, **299**, 1059–1060.

Black, N.A. (1990). Quality assurance of medical care. *Journal of Public Health Medicine*, **12**, (2), 97–104.

Blumberg, H.H. *et al.* (1983). *Small Groups and Social Interaction*. Wiley, Chichester.

Blumberg, H.H. *et al.* (1986). Interacting in groups. In *A Handbook of Communication Skills*. Hargie, O. (ed.), Croom Helm, London.

Boyce, J. (1992) The role of the audit commission in the quality transformation. Paper delivered at the Annual Conference of the National Association of Quality Assurance in Health Care, Solihull.

Bradford, M. and Flynn, N. (1988). Ambulatory care infection control quality assurance monitoring system. *American Journal of Infection Control*, **16**, (1), 21A–28A.

Bradshaw, S. (1987). Phaneuf's nursing audit. In *Nursing Quality Measurement*. Pearson, A. (ed.), HM&M/John Wiley, Chichester.

Brenner, M. (1981). Skills in the research interview. In *Social Skills and Work*. Argyle, M. (ed.), Methuen, London.

Brenner, M. *et al.* (1985). *The Research Interview: Uses and Approaches*. Academic Press, London.

Brooks, T. and Pitt, C. (1990). *The Quality Question: Report on the 1st Year of the Organisational Audit Project*. King's Fund Centre, London.

Brown, D.E. *et al.* (1984). Patient-oriented quality assurance activities. *Quality Review Bulletin*, **10**, (1), 19–22.

Buchanan, B.G. and Shortliffe, E.H. (1984). *Rule-based Expert Systems: the MYCIN Experiments of the Stanford Heuristic Programming Project*. Addison-Wesley, Reading, Mass.

Buck, N. *et al.* (1987). *The Report of a Confidential Enquiry into Perioperative Deaths*. Nuffield Provincial Hospitals Trust and the King's Fund, London.

Buckland, A.E. (1989). In search of quality. *Journal of the American Medical Record Association*, **60**, (3), 27-31.

Bunn, D.W. (1984). *Applied Decision Analysis*. McGraw-Hill, Washington.

Burkholder, J.A. (1990). Practice parameters in medicine. *Pennsylvania Medicine*, **93**, (10), 32–33.

Cairns, J. *et. al.* (1991). *Developing QUALYs from Condition Specific Outcome Measures*. Health Economics Research Unit, University of Aberdeen, Aberdeen.

Calnan, M. (1989). Towards a conceptual framework of lay evaluation of health care. *Social Science and Medicine*, **27**, (9), 927–933.

Cameron-Jones, M. (1988). Looking for quality and competence in teaching. In *Professional Competence and Quality Assurance in the Caring Professions.* Ellis, R. (ed.), Chapman and Hall, London.

Campbell, A. (1981). *The Sense of Well-being in America.* McGraw-Hill, Washington.

Canadian Council on Hospital Accreditation (1984). *Standards for Accreditation of Canadian Health Care Facilities.* Canadian Council on Hospital Accreditation, Ottawa.

Carlzon, J. (1987). *Moments of Truth.* Bellinger Press, Cambridge, Mass.

Carnall, C.A. (1990). *Managing Change in Organisations.* Prentice-Hall, Hemel Hempstead.

Cartwright, A. (1986). *Health Surveys in Practice and Potential.* Oxford University Press, Oxford.

Casanova, J.E. (1990). Status of quality assurance programmes in American hospitals. *Medical Care,* **28**, (11), 1105–1109.

Chambers, L.N. *et al.* (1984). A self-monitoring method of resident care quality assurance in long-term care facilities. *Canadian Journal of Aging,* **2**, 137–51.

Chandler, A.D. (1977). *The Invisible Hand.* Harvard University Press, Cambridge, Mass.

Charlton, J.R.H. and Lakhani, A. (1986). *Avoidable Deaths Study.* Inter-Authority Comparisons, Birmingham.

Chartered Society of Physiotherapy (1990). *Standards of Physiotherapy Practice.* CSP, London.

Chassin, M.R. (1988). Standards of care in medicine. *Inquiry,* **25**, 437–453.

Clark, G. (1989). Managing the intangibles of service quality. *Total Quality Management,* February, 89–92.

Cleary, P.D. and McNeil, B.J. (1988). Patient satisfaction as an indicator of quality care. *Inquiry,* **25**, 25–36.

Coad, H. and Hyde, A. (1986). Hot on the quality assurance trail. *Health Services Journal,* 17 April, 518–519.

Codman, E.A. (1916). *A Study of Hospital Efficiency.* Thomas Todd, Boston.

Cohen, C. (1982) On the quality of life: some philosophical reflections. *Circulation,* **66**, 111–129.

College of Occupational Therapists (1989). *Standards, Policies and Procedures.* College of Occupational Therapists, London.

College of Speech and Language Therapists (1991). *Communicating Quality: Professional Standards for Speech and Language Therapists.* College of Speech and Language Therapists, London.

Cotton, R.E. *et al.* (1986). Results of Delayed Follow-up of Abnormal Cervical Smears. *British Medical Journal,* **292**, 799–800.

Craddick, J. (1987). *Medical Management Volume 2. Improving Quality and Resource Management Through Medical Management Analysis.* Medical Management Analysis International, Rockville.

Crombie, D.L. and Fleming, D.M. (1988). *Practice Activity Analysis.* Occasional Paper No. 41. Royal College of General Practitioners, London.

Cronbach, L. (1985). *Essentials of Psychological Testing (4th edn.)*. Harper & Row, New York.

Crosby, P.B. (1979). *Quality is Free*. McGraw-Hill, Washington, DC.

Crosby, P.B. (1984). *Quality Without Tears*. McGraw-Hill, Washington, DC.

Crosby, P.B. (1986). *Running Things*. McGraw-Hill, Washington, DC.

Dagher, D.O. and Lloyd, R.J. (1991). Managing negative outcome by reducing variances in the emergency department. *Quality Review Bulletin*, **17**, (1), 15–21.

Dalkey, N.C. and Helmer, O. (1963). An experimental application of the Delphi method to the use of experts. *Management Sciences*, **9**, (3), 458–467.

Dalley, G. and Carr-Hill, R. (1991). *Pathways to Quality, a Study of Quality Management Initatives in the NHS*. No. 2: a guide for managers. Centre for Health Economics, University of York, York.

Dalley, G. *et al.* (1991). *Quality Management initiatives in the NHS*. No. 3: Strategic approaches to improving quality. Centre for Health Economics, University of York, York.

Daugherty, J. and Mason, E. (1987). *Excelcare Nursing System*. Price Waterhouse, London.

David, J. and Pritchard, P. (1987). Using Monitor – quality measure for oncological nursing. *Senior Nurse*, **6**, (4), 42–45.

Davies, A.R. and Ware, J.E.Jr. (1981). *Measuring Health Perceptions in the Health Insurance Experiment*. Publication R1987/2 DHEW. Rand Corporation, Santa Monica.

Davies, P. and Van der Gaag, A. (1992). The Professional Competence of Speech Therapists I: Introduction and Methodology. *Clinical Rehabilitation* **6**, (3), 209–214.

Davis, J. and Restle, F. (1963). The analysis of problems and prediction of group problem solving. *Journal of Abnormal and Social Psychology*, **66**, 103–116.

Davis, K. D. (1989). Viewpoints: American physical therapy association. In *Quality Rehabilitation*. England, B. *et al.*, (eds.), American Hospital Publishing, Chicago.

Day, C. (1989). *Taking Action with Indicators*. Department of Health, HMSO, London.

Day, P. *et al.* (1988). *Inspecting for Quality: Services for the Elderly*. Bath Social Policy Paper, No. 12. University of Bath, Bath.

Delbecq, A.L. and Van de Ven, A.H. (1971). A group process model for problem identification and programme planning. *Journal of Applied Behavioural Science*, **7**, 466–492.

Demby, N.A. *et al.* (1985). A comprehensive quality assurance system for practising dentists. *Dental Clinics of North America*, **29**, (3), 545–556.

Deming, W.E. (1982). *Quality, Productivity and Competitive Position*. MIT Press, Cambridge, Mass.

Deming, W.E. (1986). *Out of the Crisis*. MIT Centre for Advanced Engineering Study, Cambridge, Mass.

Demlo, L.K. (1983). Assuring quality of health care. *Evaluation and the Health Professions*, **6**, (2), 161–196.

De Vaus, D.A. (1986). *Surveys in Social Research*. Allen and Unwin, London.

De Verdier, C.H. *et al.* (1986). Quality assurance in clinical chemistry. *Scandinavian Journal of Clinical Laboratory Investigation*, **46**, 393–396.

De Vos, G. (1985). Dimensions of the self in Japanese culture. In *Culture and Self: Asian and Western Perspectives*. Marsella, A.J. *et al.* (eds.), Tavistock, New York.

Dickson, D.A. *et al.* (1989). *Communication Skills for Health Professionals*. Chapman & Hall, London.

Dillman, D.A. (1978). *Mail and Telephone Surveys, the Total Design Method*. Wiley, New York.

Dillon, J.T. (1990). *The Practice of Questioning*. Routledge, London.

Di Primio, A. (1987). *Quality Assurance in Service Organisations*. Chilton, Radnor.

Dixon, P. and Carr-Hill, R. (1989). *The NHS and its Customers II: Customer Feedback Surveys - an Introduction to Survey Methods*. Centre for Health Economics, University of York, York.

Donabedian, A. (1966). Evaluating the quality of medical care. *Milbank Memorial Fund Quarterly*, **44**, 166–203.

Donabedian, A. (1985). Twenty years of research on the quality of medical care. *Evaluation and the Health Professions*, **8**, (3), 243–65.

Donabedian, A. (1986). Quality assurance: corporate responsibility for multi-hospital systems. *Quality Review Bulletin*, **12**, (1), 3–7.

Donabedian, A. (1980). *Explorations in Quality Assessment and Monitoring, Volume 1*. Ann Arbor, Health Administration Press.

Donabedian, A. (1987). Commentary on some studies of the quality of care. *Health Care Financing Review*, Supplement, 75–85.

Donabedian, A. (1989). The quest for quality health care: whose choice? Whose responsibility? *Mount Sinai Journal of Medicine*, **56**, (5), 406–422.

Donabedian, A. (1991). Reflections on the effectiveness of quality assurance. In *Striving for Quality in Health Care*. Palmer, R.H. *et al.* (ed.), Health Administration Press, Ann Arbor.

Donald, K.J. & Collie, J.P. (1981). The autopsy in quality assurance. *Australian Clinical Review*, **2**, 16-21.

Donegan, H.A. and Dodd, F.J. (1991). An analytical approach to consensus. *Applied Mathematics Letters*, **4**, (2), 21–4.

Douglass, P.S. and Batchelor, G.J. (1989). Clinical profiles as quality measurement tools. In *Innovations in Health Care Quality Management*. Spath, P., (ed.), American Hospital Publishing Inc.

Drummond, M.F. *et al.* (1988). Methods for the economic evaluation of health care programmes. *Community Health Studies*, **12**, (2), 224.

Duncan, A. (1980). Quality assurance: what now and where next? *British Medical Journal*, **280**, 300–302.

Dunnette, M.D. *et al.* (1963). The effects of group participation on brainstorming effectiveness for two industrial samples. *Journal of Applied Psychology,* **47**, 30–37.

Dupuy, H.J. (1978). Self representations of general psychological well-being of American adults. Paper presented at American Public Health Association Meeting, Los Angeles.

Dutkewych, J. and Buback, K. (1982). Quality circles – the Henry Ford hospital experience. *Dimensions,* **59**, (12), 20–22.

Eakin, P. (1989a). Assessments of activities of daily living: a critical review. *British Journal of Occupational Therapy,* **1**, 11–15.

Eakin, P. (1989b). Problems with assessment of activities of daily living. *British Journal of Occupational Therapy,* **2**, 50–54.

Eason, J. and Markowe, H.L.J. (1987). Controlled investigation of deaths from asthma in hospitals in the North East Thames region. *British Medical Journal,* **294**, 1255–258.

East Berkshire Health Authority (1990). *Heatherwood Hospital Physiotherapy Department Quality Assurance Programme.* East Berkshire Health Authority, Windsor.

Ekman, P. and Friesen, W. (1972). *Emotion in the Human Face.* Pergamon, New York.

Ellis, R. (1980). Simulated social skill training for interpersonal professions. In *The Analysis of Social Skill.* Singleton, W et al. (ed.), Plenum, New York.

Ellis, R. (1988). Quality assurance and care. In *Professional Competence and Quality Assurance in the Caring Professions.* Ellis, R. (ed.), Chapman and Hall, London.

Ellis, R. and Whittington, D. (1972). Contexts for microteaching. *APLET,* **2**, 37–46.

Ellis, R. and Whittington, D. (1981). *A Guide to Social Skill Training.* Croom Helm, Beckenham.

Ellis, R. and Whittington, D. (1988). Social Skills, Competence and Quality. In *Professional Competence and Quality Assurance in the Caring Professions.* Ellis, R. (ed.), Chapman and Hall, London.

Enderby, P. and Davies. P. (1989). Communication disorders: planning a service to meet the needs. *British Journal of Disorders of Communication,* **24**, 301–331.

England, B. *et al.* (1989). *Quality Rehabilitation.* American Hospital Publishing, Chicago.

Eppel, A. *et al.* (1991). A comprehensive and practical quality assurance program for community mental health services. *Canadian Journal of Psychiatry,* **36**, (2), 102–106.

Ervin, N.E. *et al.* (1989). Development of a public health nursing quality assessment measure. *Quality Review Bulletin,* **15**, (5), 138–143.

Evason, E. and Whittington, D. (1991). Patient Satisfaction Studies: Problems and Implications Explored in a Pilot Study in Northern Ireland. *Health Education Journal,* **50**, (2), 73–97.

Farrell, P. and Scherer, K. (1983). The delphi technique as a method for selecting criteria to evaluate nursing care. *Nursing Papers: Perspectives in Nursing*, **15**, (1), 51–60.

Feigenbaum, A.V. (1956). Total quality control. *Harvard Business Review*, 94–98.

Feigenbaum, A.V. (1983). *Total quality control (3rd edn.)*. McGraw-Hill, Washington.

Fernow, L.C. *et al.* (1981). Measuring the quality of clinical performance with hernia and myocardial infarction patients controlling for patient risks. *Medical Care*, **19**, (3), 273–280.

Ferrans, C.E. and Powers, M.J. (1985). Quality of life index: development and psychometric properties. *Advanced Nursing Science*, **8**, (1), 15–24.

Ferrell, B. *et al.* (1991). Pain management as a quality of care outcome. *Journal of Nursing Quality Assurance*, **5**, (2), 50–58.

Fine, R.B. (1986). Conceptual perspectives on the organization design task and the quality assurance function. *Nursing Health Care*, **7**, (2), 100–104.

Fisher, R. and Ury, W. (1981). *Getting to Yes*. Houghton Mifflin, Boston.

Flanagan, J.C. (1982). Measurement of quality of life: current state of the art. *Archives of Physical Medicine Rehabilitation*, **63**, 56–59.

Flanders, N. (1970). *Analysing Teaching Behaviour*. Addison Wesley, Reading, Mass.

Flexner, A. (1910). *Medical Education in the United States and Canada*. Carnegie Foundation, New York.

Flindall, J. *et al.* (1987). *PA/Royal National Orthopaedic Hospital Nursing Quality Measurement System*. PA/Royal National Orthopaedic Hospital, London.

Fowkes, F., Hall, R. and Jones, J. (1986). Trial of strategy for reducing the use of laboratory tests. *British Medical Journal*, **292**, 883–885.

Frangley, P.A. and Corkill, M.M. (1984). Physician variables in the treatment of myocardial infarction in a single metropolitan hospital. *Australian Clinical Review*, **5**, 119–26.

Freeborn, D.K. and Pope, C.R. (1981). Client satisfaction in a health maintenance organization. *Evaluation and the Health Professions*, **4**, (3), 275–294.

Freedman, J. (1978). *Happy People*. Harcourt, Brace and Jovanovich, New York.

Freeling, P. and Burton, R. (1986). Performance review in peer groups. In *In Pursuit of Quality*. Pendleton, D., *et al.* (ed.), Royal College of General Practitioners, London.

Friedman, B. I. (1986). Quality assurance and nuclear medicine: the challenge of change. *Journal of Nuclear Medicine*, **27**, (8), 1366–1372.

Furnham, A. (1988). Competence to practise medicine. In *Professional Competence and Quality Assurance in the Caring Professions*. Ellis, R. (ed.), Chapman and Hall, London.

Gafni, A. (1989). The quality of quality adjusted life years: do QALYS measure what they at least intend to measure. *J. Health Policy*, **13**, 81–83.

Gallup, G. (1947). The quintadimensional plan of question design. *Public Opinion Quarterly*, **11**, 385–393.

Garson, B. (1983). Quality circles: fad or management trend? *Journal of the American Health Care Association* **9** (3), 64–68.

Garvin, D. (1988). *Managing Quality*. Macmillan, New York.

Gatere, G. (1985). Quality assurance: a look at the concept. *Kenya Nursing Journal*, **13**, (2), 27–32.

Gilmore, H.L. (1974). Product conformance cost. *Quality Progress*. June, 16.

Gitlow, H. and Gitlow, S. (1987) *The Deming Guide to Quality and Competitive Position*. Prentice-Hall, Englewood Cliffs.

Glendinning, M. (1981). Quality assurance in physiotherapy. *Australian Clinical Review*, **3**, (11), 22.

Goldberg, D. (1978). *Manual of the General Health Questionnaire*. NFER Publishing, Windsor.

Goldstone, L.A. *et al.* (1983). *Monitor: an Index of the Quality of Nursing Care for Acute Medical and Surgical Wards*. Newcastle upon Tyne Polytechnic Products Ltd., Newcastle upon Tyne.

Gonnella, J.S. and Goran, M.J. (1975). Quality of patient care – a measurement of change: the staging concept. *Medical Care*, **13**, 467–473.

Gonnella, J.S. and Louis, D.Z. (1988). Severity of illness in the assessment of quality: disease staging. In *Perspectives on Quality in American Health Care*. Hughes, E. (ed.), McGraw-Hill, Washington.

Goodinson, S. and Singleton, J. (1989). Quality of life: a critical review of current concepts, measures and their clinical implications. *International Journal of Nursing Studies*, **26**, (4), 327–341.

Gordon, T.J. and Helmer, O. (1964). *Report on a Long-range Forecasting Study: P-2982*. Rand Corporation, Santa Monica.

Gould, E.J. (1985). Standardized home health nursing care plans: a quality assurance tool. *Quality Review Bulletin*, **11**, (11), 334–338.

Greenblatt, M. (1975). PSRO and peer review: problems and opportunities. *Hospital and Community Psychiatry*, **26**, 254–358.

Greenfield, S. *et al.* (1975). Peer review by criteria mapping: criteria for diabetes mellitus, the use of decision making in chart audit. *Annals of Internal Medicine*, **83**, 761–770.

Greenfield, S. *et al.* (1977). The clinical investigation and management of chest pain in an emergency department: quality assessment by criteria mapping. *Medical Care*, **15**, 898.

Greenfield, S. *et al.* (1978). Development of outcome criteria and standards to assess quality of care for patients with osteoarthritis. *Journal of Chronic Disorders*, **13**, 375.

Greenfield, S. *et al.* (1981). Comparison of a criteria map to a criteria list in quality of care assessment for patients with chest pain: the relation of each to outcome. *Medical Care*, **19**, (3), 255–272.

Gresham, G.C. and Labi, M.L.C. (1984). Functional assessment instruments currently available for documenting outcomes in rehabilitation medicine. In *Functional Assessment in Rehabilitation Medicine*. Granger, C.V. and Gresham, G. E. (eds.), Williams and Wilkins, Baltimore.

Grol, R. *et al.* (1988). The effects of peer review in general practice. *Journal of the Royal College of General Practitioners*, **38**, 10–13.

Gruer, R. *et al.* (1986). Audit of surgical audit. *Lancet*, **1**, 23–6.

Gummeson, E. (1989). Nine lessons on service quality. *Total Quality Management*, 83–7.

Gunn, L. (1988). Public management: a third approach? *Public Money and Management*, **8**, (1 and 2) (Spring/Summer), 21–5.

Gurel, L. *et al.* (1972). Physical and mental impairment of function evaluation in the aged: the PAMIE scale. *Journal of Gerontology*, **27**, 83–90.

Hackman, J.R. and Morris, C. (1983). Group tasks, group interaction and group performance effectiveness. In *Small Groups and Social Interaction*. Blumberg, H. *et al.* (ed.), Wiley, London.

Haggard, A. (1983). Quality Circles. *Nursing Management*, **14**, (2), 32–34.

Hall, J. and Dornan, M. (1989). What patients like about their medical care and how often they are asked: a meta-analysis of the satisfaction literature. *Social Science and Medicine*, **27**, 935–939.

Hall, J. *et al.* (1988). Meta-analysis of correlates of provider behaviour in medical encounters. *Journal of Medical Care*, **26**, 657–675.

Halpern, S. (1985). What the public thinks of the NHS. *Health and Social Services Journal*, **95**, 702–704.

Halpin, J.F. (1966). *Zero Defects*. McGraw-Hill, Washington.

Hanks, G.E. and Kramer, S. (1984). Consensus of best current management: the starting point for clinical quality assessment. *International Journal of Radiation Oncology and Biological Physics*, **10**, Supplement 1, 87–97.

Hannan, E. L. *et al.* (1989). A methodology for targeting hospital cases for quality of care record reviews. *American Journal of Public Health*, **79**, (4), 430–436.

Harman, D. (1992). Applying ISO 9000/BS 5750 to health care. Paper delivered at the Annual Conference of the National Association of Quality Assurance in Health Care, Solihull.

Harris, C.M. *et al.* (1985). Prescribing – a case for prolonged treatment. *Journal of the Royal College of General Practitioners*, **35**, 284–287.

Harris, J. (1987). QALY-fying the value of life. *Journal of Medical Ethics*, **11**, 142–145.

Hartmann, M.R. *et al.* (1990). Occurrence screening: a program for improving quality and appropriateness of care. *Journal of Nursing Quality Assurance*, **51**, 49–60.

Harvey, G. (1988a). The right tools for the job. *Nursing Times*, **84**, (26), 47–49.

Harvey, G. (1988b). More tools for the job. *Nursing Times*, **84**, (28), 33–34.

Harvey, G. (1991). An evaluation of approaches to assessing the quality of nursing care using pre-determined quality assurance tools. *Journal of Advanced Nursing*, **16**, 277–286.

Hastings, C.E. (1987). Measuring quality in ambulatory care nursing. *Journal of Nursing Administration*, **17**, (4), 12–21.

Hastings, G.E. (1980). Peer review checklist: reproducibility and validity of a method for evaluating the quality of ambulatory care. *American Journal of Public Health*, **70**, 222–228.

Hatfield, A.B. and Smith, H.B. (1988). The role of the consumer in quality assurance. In *Handbook of Quality Assurance in Mental Health*. Stricker, G. and Rodriguez, A. (eds.), Plenum, New York.

Haussman, R.K. and Hegyvary, S.L. (1977). *Monitoring Quality of Nursing Care Part 3*. DHEW HRA 77-70. Department of Health and Welfare, US Government Printing Office, Washington.

Haussman, R.K. *et al.* (1976). *Monitoring Quality of Nursing Care Part 2*. DHEW HRA 76–7. Department of Health and Welfare. US Government Printing Office, Washington.

Health Care Research Unit, Newcastle upon Tyne University (1990). *North of England study of Standards and Performance in General Practice*. HCRU, Newcastle upon Tyne University, Newcastle upon Tyne.

Hegyvary, S.T. and Haussman, R.K.D. (1975). Monitoring nursing care quality. *Journal of Nursing Administration*, **6**, 17–26.

Hegyvary, S.T. and Haussmann, R.K.D. (1976). Monitoring nursing care quality. *Journal of Nursing Administration*, **6**, 9.

Helmer, O. and Rescher, N. (1959). On the epistemology of the inexact sciences. *Management Sciences*, **6**, (1), 25–52.

HMSO (1956). *Committee of Enquiry into the Cost of the National Health Service: the Guillebaud Report*. Cmnd. 663, HMSO, London.

HMSO (1966). *Report of the Committee on Senior Nursing Staff Structure. Scottish Home and Health Department: the Salmon Report*. HMSO, Edinburgh.

HMSO (1975). *Committee of enquiry into the regulation of the medical profession (Merrison report)*. Cmnd. 6018, HMSO, London.

HMSO (1976). *Competence to practise: the Alment report*. HMSO, London.

HMSO (1979). *Report of the Royal Commission on the National Health Service*. Cmnd. 7615. HMSO, London.

HMSO (1982a). *Efficiency and Effectiveness in the Civil Service: the Financial Management Initiative*. HMSO, London.

HMSO (1982b). *Standards, Quality and International Competitiveness*. HMSO, London.

HMSO (1983). *National Health Service Management Enquiry: the Griffiths Report*. DHSS: NHS Management Enquiry Team, HMSO, London.

HMSO (1986). *DHSS Report on Confidential Enquiries into Maternal Deaths in England and Wales, 1979-1981*. HMSO, London.

HMSO (1989). *Working for Patients*. White Paper, Cmnd. 555, HMSO, London.

HMSO (1990a). *Medical Audit. Working for patients*. Working Paper No. 6, Department of Health, HMSO, London.

HMSO (1990b). *The Quality of Medical Care*. Report of the Standing Medical Advisory Committee. Department of Health, HMSO, London.

HMSO (1990c). *Family Practitioner Service Indicators 1988/89*. (Provisional Issue) FPCL 64/90. Department of Health, HMSO, London.

Hilton, I. and Dawson, J. (1988). Monitor Evaluated. *Senior Nurse*, **5**, 10–11.

Hinde, R. (1972). *Non-verbal communication*. Cambridge University Press, Cambridge.

Holmes, C.L. *et al.* (1978). Toward the measurement of primary care. *Milbank Memorial Fund Quarterly*, **56**, (2), 231–52.

Holmes, C.A. (1989). Health care and the quality of life: a review. *Journal of Advanced Nursing*, **14**, (10), 833–9.

Hooker, R.S. (1933). *Maternal mortality in New York City: a Study of all Puerperal Deaths 1930-32*. Oxford University Press, New York.

Horn, S.D. and Buckle, J.M. (1989). Severity-of-illness classification systems. In *Innovations in Health Care Quality Measurement*. Spath, P. (ed.), American Hospital Publishing, Chicago.

Hough, B.L. and Schmele, J.A. (1987). The Slater scale: a viable method for monitoring nursing care quality in home health. *Journal of Nursing Quality Assurance*, **1**, (3), 28–38.

Hounshell, D.A. (1984). *From the American System to Mass Production, 1800-1932*. Johns Hopkins Press, Baltimore.

Hughes, J. and Humphrey, C. (1990). *Medical Audit in General Practice*. King's Fund Centre, London.

Hughes, R.G. *et al.* (1987). Effects of surgeon volume and hospital volume on quality of care in hospitals. *Medical Care*, **25**, 489–503.

Hull, S.A. (1984). Why run a group? *British Medical Journal*, **288**, 1811–1812.

Hunt, S.M. *et al.* (1981). The Nottingham health profile: subjective health status and medical consultations. *Social Science and Medicine*, **15A**, 221–9.

Hutchins, D. (1990). *In Pursuit of Quality*. Pitman, London.

Hypertension Detection and Follow Up Programme (1979). Five year findings of the HDFP 1: reduction of mortality of persons with high blood pressure including mild hypertension. *Journal of American Medical Association*, **242**, 2562–2571.

Ingle, S. (1982). *Quality Circles Master Guide*. Prentice-Hall, Englewood Cliffs.

Institute of Medicine (1985). *Assessing Medical Technologies*. National Academy Press, Washington.

Inui, T. *et al.* (1979). Hospital screening for tuberculosis: a quality assurance trial. *Medical Care*, **17**, (4), 347–354.

Irvine, D.H. (1990a). *Managing for Quality in General Practice*. King's Fund Centre, London.

Irvine, D.H. (1990b). Standards in general practice: the quality intiative revisited. *British Journal of General Practice*, **40**, 75–77.

Isaac, D.N. (1983). Suggestions for organizing a quality assurance program. *Quality Review Bulletin*, **9**, (3), 68–72.

Ishikawa, K. (1982). *A Guide to Quality Control (2nd edn)*. Asian Productivity Organisation, Tokyo.

Ishikawa, K. (1985). *What is total quality control? – The Japanese way*. Lu, D.J. (trans.), Prentice-Hall, Englewood Cliffs.

James, K. (1992) The department of health's view of the quality transformation. Paper delivered at the Annual Conference of the National Association of Quality Assurance in Health Care, Solihull.

Janis, I. (1972). *Victims of Group Think*. Houghton Mifflin, Boston.

Janis, I. and Mann, L. (1977). *Decision Making: a Psychological Analysis of Conflict, Choice and Commitment*. Collier-Macmillan, London.

Jefferson, S. and Storm-Clark, C. (1989). Monitoring consumer satisfaction. *Family Practitioner Services*, **16**, (11), 18-24.

Jelinek, R.C. *et al.* (1974). *Methodology for Monitoring the Quality of Nursing Care*. US Department of Health and Welfare, DHEW Publication, HRA74, US Government Printing Office, Washington.

Jessee, W.F. (1981). Approaches to improving the quality of health care: organizational change. *Quality Review Bulletin*, **7**, (7), 13–18.

Joe, B. and Ostrow, P. (1987). *Quality Assurance Monitoring in Occupational Therapy*. American Occupational Therapy Association, Rockville.

Johnson, C. (1983). The 'Internationalisation' of the Japanese economy. *California Management Review*, **26**, 7–9.

Johnson, O.G. (1976). *Tests and Measurements in Child Development: Handbook 2*. Jossey-Bass, San Fransico.

Joint Commission on the Accreditation of Hospitals (1988). *Accreditation Manual for Hospitals*. JCAH, Chicago.

Juran, J.M. (1979). *Quality Control Handbook (3rd edn.)*. McGraw-Hill, Washington.

Juran, J.M. (1988). *Juran on Planning for Quality*. Free Press, New York.

Kagan, C. (1985). *Interpersonal Skills in Nursing: Research and Applications*. Croom Helm, London.

Kagan, R.H. (1984). Organizational change and quality assurance in a psychiatric setting. *Quality Review Bulletin*, **10**, (9), 269–277.

Kane, R.A. and Kane, R.L. (1981). *Long Term Care: Variations on a Quality Assurance Theme*.

Kanter, R.M. (1983). *The Change Masters*. Simon and Schuster, New York.

Kanter, R.M. and Stein, B.A. (1981). Productivity and QWL: pointers for managers. *Hospital Forum*, May/June, 21–27.

Kaplan, S. and Greenfield, S. (1978). Criteria mapping. Using logic in evaluation of processes of care. *Quality Review Bulletin*, **4** (1), 3–9.

Kaplan, R.M. and Bush, J.W. (1982). Health related quality of life measurement for evaluation research. *Health Psychology*, **1**, 61–80.

Keller, R.B. (1988). Enhancing quality through small area analysis: the Maine experience. In *Perspectives on Quality in American Health Care*. Hughes, E. (ed.), McGraw-Hill, Washington.

Kemp, N. and Richardson, E. (1990). *Quality assurance in nursing practice*. Butterworth-Heinemann, Oxford.

Kessner, D.M. *et al.* (1973). Assessing health quality – the case for tracers. *New England Journal of Medicine*, **288**, 189–94.

Keyser, W. (1989). Healthcare: is total quality management relevant? *Total Quality Management*, February, 110–115.

Kind, E.A. (1989). Quality assurance in the ambulatory setting. In *Innovations in Health Care Quality Measurement*. Spath, P. (ed.), American Hospital Publishing, Chicago.

Kind, E.A. *et al.* (1987). *An Art of Care Component of Quality Assurance: 1987 Group Health Proceedings*. Group Health Association of America, Seattle.

King, T. and Jones J.L. (1989). The Johns Hopkins health system quality review process. In *Innovations in Health Care Quality Measurement*. Spath, P. (ed.), American Hospital Publishing, Chicago.

Kitson, A. (1986). The methods of assuring quality. *Nursing Times*, 27 August, 32–34.

Kitson, A. and Kendall, H. (1986). Quality assurance. *Nursing Times*, **82**, (35), 28–31.

Kitson, A. (1990). Quality matters and standard setting. *Nursing Standard*, **4**, (44), 32–33.

Klein, R. (1980). *The politics of the National Health Service*. Longman, London.

Klein, R. and Carter, N. (1988). Performance measurement: a review of concepts and issues. In *Performance measurement: getting the concepts right*. Beeton, D. (ed.), Public Finance Foundation, London.

Knapp, M.R.J. (1976). Predicting the dimensions of life satisfaction. *Journal of Gerontology*, **31**, 595–604.

Koepke, J.A. (1974). The CAP proficiency programme in haematology. In *Haematology Laboratory Medicine*. Steine, E.A. (ed.), Symposia Specialists, Miami.

Kogure, M. and Akao, Y. (1983). Quality function deployment and CWQC in Japan. *Quality Progress*, October, 25.

Kohl, S.G. (1955). *Perinatal Mortality in New York City: Responsible Factors*. Harvard University Press, Cambridge.

Koska, M.T. (1990). Case study: quality improvement in a diversified health center. *Hospitals*, 5 December, 38–39.

Kroshus, M.G. and Abbott, J.A. (1988). Quality assurance review of a rheumatoid arthritis education programme. *Patient Education and Counselling*, **12**, 213–224.

Kuntavanish, A.A. (1987). *Occupational Therapy Documentation*. American Occupational Therapy Association, Rockville.

Laffel, G. and Blumenthal, D. (1989). The case for using industrial quality management science in health care organisations. *Journal of the American Medical Assocation*, **262** ,(30), 2869–2873.

Lakhani, A. (1985). *Application of Outcome Indicators in the NHS – a Conceptual Framework*. Seminar given at Guy's Hospital, London.

Lamki, L. *et al.* (1990). Quality assurance in a nuclear medicine department. *Radiology*, 177, (3), 609–614.

Lang, N.M. and Clinton, J.F. (1984). Quality assurance: the idea and its development in the United States. In *Measuring the Quality of Care*. Willis, L. and Linwood, M. (eds.), Churchill Livingstone, Edinburgh.

Law, M. *et al.* (1989). Criteria mapping: a method of quality assurance. *American Journal of Occupational Therapy*, **43**, (2), 104–109.

Lawton, M.P. (1975). The Philadelphia geriatric center morale scale: a reinterpretation. *Journal of Gerontology*, **30**, 85–89.

Lees, G.D. *et al.* (1987). Quality assurance: is it professional insurance? *Journal of Advanced Nursing,* **12**, 719–727.

Lesnik, M.J. and Anderson, B.E. (1955). *Nursing Practice and the Laboratory.* Lippincott, Philadelphia.

Lewin, K. (1947). Group decision and social change. In *Readings in Social Psychology.* Newcomb T. and Hartley, E. (eds.), Holt, Rinehart and Winston, New York.

Ley, P. (1988). *Communicating with Patients: Improving Communication, Satisfaction and Compliance.* Chapman and Hall, London.

Linstone, H. and Turoff, M. (1975). *The Delphi method, techniques and applications.* Addison-Wesley, Reading, Mass.

Locker, D. and Dunt, D. (1978). Theoretical and methodological issues in sociological studies of consumer satisfaction with health care. *Social Science and Medicine,* **12**, 283–292.

Lohr, K.N. (1988). Outcome measurement: concepts and questions. *Inquiry,* **25**, 37–50.

Lohr, K.N. and Harris-Wehling, J. (1991). Medicare: a strategy for quality assurance. *Quality Review Bulletin,* **17**, (1), 6–9.

Lohr, K.N. and Ware, J.E. Jr. (1987). Proceedings of the advances in health assessment conference. *Journal of Chronic Diseases,* **40**, Supplement No. 1.

London, B.J. and Harris, L.B. (1988). Quality health care in a cost-conscious environment: the intervention of third-party payers in determining medical necessity and the changing rights and liabilities of health care practitioners. In *Perspectives on Quality in American Health Care.* Hughes, E. (ed.), McGraw-Hill, New York.

Loughlin, K.G. and Moore, L.F. (1979). Using Delphi to achieve congruent objectives and activities in a paediatrics department. *Journal of Medical Education,* **54**, (2), 101–106.

Lower, M. and Burton, S. (1989). Measuring the impact of nursing interventions on patient outcomes – the challenge of the 1990s. *Journal of Nursing Quality Assurance,* **4** (1), 27–34.

Luft, J. (1984). *Group Processes (3rd edn.).* Palo Alto, Mayfield.

Luger, G. and Stubblefield, W. (1989). *Artificial Intelligence and the Design of Expert Systems.* Benjamin Cummings, Redwood City.

Lunn, J.N. and Mushin, W.W. (1982). *Mortality Associated with Anaesthesia.* Nuffield Provincial Hospitals Trust, London.

McAninch, M. (1988). Accrediting agencies and the search for quality in health care. In *Handbook of Quality Assurance in Mental Health.* Stricker, G. and Rodriguez, A.R. (eds.), Plenum, New York.

McCulloch, D. (1991). Can we measure output? Quality adjusted life years, health indices and occupational therapy. *British Journal of Occupational Therapy,* **54**, (6), 219–221.

McDowell, I. and Newell, C. (1987). *Measuring Health: a Guide to Rating Scales and Questionnaires.* Oxford University Press, New York.

McGuire, P. (1986). Social skills training for health professionals. In *Handbook of Social Skills Training.* Hollin, C. and Trower, P. (eds.), Pergamon, Oxford.

McIver, S. (1991). *Obtaining the Views (1–3)*. King's Fund Centre, London.

McIver, S. and Carr-Hill, R. (1989). *The NHS and its Customers 1. A Survey of the Current Practice of Customer Relations*. Centre for Health Economics, University of York, York.

Mahoney, F.I. and Barthel, D.W. (1965). Functional evaluation: the Barthel index. *Maryland State Medical Journal*, **14**, 61–65.

Maier, N.R.F. (1967). Assets and liabilities in group problem solving: the need for an integrative function. *Psychological Review*, **74**, 239–249.

Marquis, K.H. and Cannell, C.F. (1971). *Effect of Some Experimental Techniques on Reporting in the Health Interview Survey*. DHEW Publication. US Government Publishing Office, Washington.

Maxwell, R.J. (1984). Quality assessment in health. *British Medical Journal*, **228**, 1470–1477.

Mayers, M. *et al.* (1977). *Quality Assurance for Patient Care: Nursing Perspectives*. Appleton Century Crofts, New York.

Medley, D. and Mitzel, H. (1963). Measuring classroom behaviour by systematic observation. In *A Handbook of Research on Teaching*. Gage, N. (ed.), Rand McNally, Chicago.

Meenan, R.F. (1982). The AIMS approach to health status measurement. Conceptual Background and Measurement Properties. *Journal of Rheumatology*, **9**, 785–788.

Meenan, R.F. *et al.* (1982). The arthritis impact measurement scales: further investigations of a health status measure. *Arthritis and Rheumatism*, **25**, 1048–53.

Melzack, R. (1980). Psychologic aspects of pain. *Pain*, **8**, 143–154.

Merrall, A. *et al.* (1991). *Audit for the Therapy Professions*. Mercia Publications, Keele.

Millar, R. *et al.* (1991). *Professional Interviewing*. Routledge, London.

Miller, J. (1989). Evaluating structure, process and outcome indicators in ambulatory care; the AMBUQUAL approach. *Journal of Nursing Quality Assurance*, **4**, (1), 40–47.

Montemuro, M. (1988). CORE documentation: a complete system for charting nursing care. *Nursing Management*, **19**, (8), 28–32.

Morgan, G. (1986). *Images of Organisation*. Sage, Newbury Park.

Moritani, M. (1982). *Japanese Technology*. Simul Press, Tokyo.

Morley, I. (1986). Negotiating and bargaining. In *A Handbook of Communication Skills*. Hargie, O. (ed.), Croom Helm, London.

Morley, I. and Hosking, D.M. (1985). Decision making and negotiation: leadership and social skills. In *Social Psychology and Organisational Behaviour*. Gruneberg, M. and Wall, T.D. (eds.), Wiley, Chichester.

Morris, A. and Reid, A. (1989). *Directory of Expert System Tools*. Learned Information Europe, Oxford.

Mosberg, W.H. (1980). Trauma centers and truth in advertising. *Neurosurgery*, **7**, 191–194.

Moscovici, S. and Zavalloni, M. (1969). The group as a polariser of attitudes. *Journal of Personality and Social Psychology*, **12**, 125–135.

Moser, C.A. (1958). *Survey Methods in Social Investigation (1st edn.)*. Heinemann, London.

Moser, C. and Kalton, G. (1971). *Survey Methods in Social Investigation (2nd edn.)*. Heinemann, London.

Mulkay, M. *et al.* (1987). Measuring the quality of life: a sociological invention concerning the application of economics to health care. *Sociology*, **21**, (4), 541–564.

Mullen, K.D. and Gold, R. (1988). Wellness construct delineation: a Delphi study. *Health Education and Research*, **3**, (4), 353–366.

Mushlin, A.I. and Appel, F.A. (1980). Testing an outcome-based quality assurance strategy in primary care. *Medical care*, **18**, (5), Supplement.

Najman, J.M. and Levine, S. (1981). Evaluating the impact of medical care and technologies on the quality of life. *Social Science and Medicine*, **15F**, 107–115.

National Association of Theatre Nurses (1989). *National Association of Theatre Nurses Quality Assurance Tool*. NATN, London.

National Coalition for Recognition (NACOR) (1986). National standards and review criteria for diabetes patient education programs. *Diabetes Education*, **12** (3), 286–291.

Neufeld, V. and Chong, J.P. (1984). Problem-based professional education in medicine. In *Education for the Professions: Quis Custodiet...?* Goodlad, S. (ed.), Society for Research in Higher Education and NFER-Nelson, London.

Neugarten, B.L. *et al.* (1961). The measurement of life satisfaction. *Journal of Gerontology*, **16**, 134–143.

Neville, R.G. (1987). Notifying general practitioners about deaths in hospital – an audit. *Journal of the Royal College of General Practitioners*, **37**, 496–497.

Nightingale, F. (1859). *Notes on Nursing: What it is and What it is not*. Harrison & Sons, London.

Normand, C. *et al.* (1991). *Clinical Audit in Professions Allied to Medicine & Related Therapy Professions*. Report to Department of Health on a Pilot Study. Health and Health Care Research Unit, Queen's University of Belfast, Belfast.

Oakland, J.S. (1986). *Statistical Process Control*. Heinemann, London.

Oakland, J.S. (1989). *Total Quality Management*. Butterworth-Heinemann, Oxford.

Oakley, R.S. and Bradham, D.D. (1983). Review of quality assurance in hospital pharmacy. *American Journal of Hospital Pharmacy*, **40**, 53–63.

O'Leary, D.S. (1991). CQI – a step beyond QA. *Quality Review Bulletin*, **17**, (1), 4–5.

Openshaw, S. (1984). Literature review: measurement of adequate care. *International Journal of Nursing Studies*, **21**, (4), 295–304.

Oppenheim, A.N. (1992). *Questionnaire Design, Interviewing and Attitude Measurement*. (2nd revised edn.), Pinter, London.

Orem, D.E. (1971). *Nursing: Concepts of Practice*. McGraw-Hill, Washington.

Osborn, A.F. (1957). *Applied Imagination*. Scribner, New York.

Osborne, C.E. and Thompson, H.C. (1975). Criteria for evaluation of ambulatory child health care by chart audit: development and testing of a methodology. *Paediatrics*, **56**, (4), 625–692.

O'Sullivan, D.D. and Grujic, S.D. (1991). Implementing hospital-wide quality assurance. *Quality Progress*, **24**, (2), 28–32.

Ovretveit, J. (1992). Health Service Quality: an Introduction to Quality Methods for Health Services. Blackwell, Oxford.

Padilla, G.V. and Grant, M.M. (1982). Quality assurance programme for nursing. *Journal of Advanced Nursing*, **7**, 135–145.

Palmer, R.H., *et al.* (1984). Quality assurance in eight adult medicine group practices. *Medical Care*, **22** (7), 632–643.

Payne, S. (1951). *The Art of Asking Questions*. Princeton University Press, Princeton.

Pearson, A. (1987). *Nursing Quality Measurement*. Wiley, London.

Pelletier, L.R. and Poster, E.C. (1988). An overview of evaluation methodology for nursing quality assurance programmes (Part I) and quantitative and qualitative approaches to nursing quality assurance program evaluation (Part II). *Journal of Nursing Quality Assurance*, **2**, (4), 55-72.

Pendleton, D. (1983). Doctor patient communication: a review. In *Doctor–Patient Communication*. Pendleton, D. and Hasler, J. (eds.), Academic Press, London.

Pendleton, D.A. *et al.* (1986). *In Pursuit of Quality*. Royal College of General Practitioners, London.

Peters, T.J. and Waterman, R.H. Jr. (1982). *In Search of Excellence*. Harper & Row, New York.

Peterson, O.L. *et al.* (1956). An analytical study of North Carolina general practice, 1953-54. *Journal of Medical Education*, **31**, (2), 1–165.

Phaneuf, M.C. (1976). *The Nursing Audit – Self-regulation in Nursing Practice*. Appleton-Century Crofts, New York.

Phillips, L.R. *et al.* (1990). The QUALCARE scale: developing an instrument to measure quality of home care. *International Journal of Nursing Studies*, **27**, (1), 61–75.

Pike, J. (1991). *Total Quality Management*. Anglia Business School, Chelmsford.

Pollitt, C. (1987). The politics of performance assessment: some lessons for higher education. *Studies in Higher Education*, **12**, (1), 87–98.

Pollitt, C. (1988). Bringing consumers into performance measurement. *Policy and Politics*, **16**, (2), 77–87.

Pollitt, C. (1989). Consuming passions. *Health Service Journal*, **99**, 1436–1437.

Pollitt, C. (1990). Doing business in the temple? Managers and quality assurance in the public services. *Public Administration*, **68**, (4), 435–452.

Pollitt, C. (1991). The politics of medical quality: auditing doctors in the UK and the USA. Paper presented to the European Group for Public Administration Study Group on Quality and Productivity, The Hague.

Poulton, B. (1990). Evaluating health visiting practice. *Nursing Standard*, **5** (3), 36–39.

Povar, G.J. (1991). What does 'quality' mean? Critical ethical issues for quality assurance. In *Striving for Quality in Health Care: An Inquiry into Policy and*

Practice. Palmer, R.H. *et al.*, (eds.). Health Administration Press, Ann Arbor, Michigan.

Price, F. (1990). *Right Every Time*. Gower, Aldershot.

Price, S.B. and Greenwood, S.K. (1988). Using treatment plans for quality assurance monitoring in a residential center. *Quality Review Bulletin*, **14**, (9), 266–274.

Pridmore, B.R. and Gunthorpe, R. (1985). The use of antimicrobials in a maternity unit. *Australian Clinical Review*, June, 8–9.

Prothro, L. (1981). Quality circles redistribute decision making. *Hospital Forum*, May/June, 14.

Pullan, B. and Chittock, J. (1986). Putting proposals into practice: Monitor (Part 2). *Nursing Times*, **82**, (2), 47–48.

Rackham, N. and Morgan, T. (1977). *Behaviour Analysis in Training*. McGraw-Hill, Maidenhead.

Radford, G.S. (1922). *The Control of Quality in Manufacturing*. Ronald Press, New York.

Rajki, K.L. *et al*. (1985). Assessing the quality of nursing care in a dialysis unit. *American Nephrology Nurses Association Journal*, **12**, (1), 11–15 and 53.

Redfern, S. and Norman, I. (1990). Measuring the quality of nursing care: a consideration of different approaches. *Journal of Advanced Nursing*, **15**, 1260–1271.

Regional Pharmaceutical Officers Committee (1989). *Standards for Pharmaceutical Services in Health Authorities in England*. Regional Pharmaceutical Officers Committee, Manchester.

Reid, N. (1988). The Delphi technique: its contribution to the evaluation of professional practice. In *Professional Competence and Quality Assurance in the Caring Professions*. Ellis, R. (ed.), Chapman and Hall, London.

Richmond, V.P., *et al*. (1991). *Non-verbal Behaviour in Interpersonal Relations* (2nd edn.). Prentice-Hall, Englewood Cliffs.

Rickert, R.R. (1986). Quality assurance in anatomic pathology. *Clinical Laboratory Medicine*, **6**, (4), 697–706.

Roberts, J.S. (1987). Reviewing the quality of care: priorities for improvement. *Health Care Financing Review*, Supplement, 69–74.

Roberts, J.S. and Prévost, J.A. (1987). Using outcome indications to evaluate quality of care. *The Internist*, September, 10–15.

Robinson, A.L. (1980). Perilous times for US microcircuit makers. *Science*, 9 May, 582–586.

Robinson, E.J. and Whitfield, M.J. (1988). Contribution of patients to general practitioner consultations in relation to their understanding of doctors instructions and advice. *Social Science and Medicine*, **27A**, 895–900.

Robinson, J. and Shaver, P. (1973). *Measures of Social Psychological Attitudes*. Institute for Social Research, Ann Arbor.

Robson, M. (1984). Quality circles: the American experience. *Nursing Times*, 19 December, 32.

Rodriguez, A.R. (1988a). An introduction to quality assurance in mental health. In *Handbook of Quality Assurance in Mental Health*. Stricker, G. and Rodriguez, A.R. (eds.), Plenum, New York.

Rodriguez, A.R. (1988b). The effects of contemporary economic conditions on availability and quality of mental health services. In *Handbook of Quality Assurance in Mental Health*. Stricker, G. and Rodriguez, A.R. (eds.), Plenum, New York.

Romm, F.J. and Hulka, B.S. (1979). Developing criteria for quality of medical care assessment: effect of using the Delphi technique. *Health Services Research*, **14**, (4), 309–312.

Roos, L.L.(Jr.) (1986). Centralisation, certification and monitoring: readmission and complications after surgery. *Medical Care*, **24**, 1044–1066.

Rosenburg, K. *et al.* (1982). An audit of caesarian section in a maternity district. *British Journal of Obstetrics and Gynaecology*, **89**, 787–792.

Ross, P.J. (1988). *Taguchi Techniques for Quality Engineering*. McGraw-Hill, Washington.

Rost, K. *et al.* (1989). Introduction of information during the initial medical visit: consequences for patient follow through with physician recommendations for medication. *Social Science and Medicine*, **28**, (4), 315–321.

Royal College of General Practitioners (1983). The quality initiative. *Journal of the Royal College of General Practitioners*, **33**, 523–524.

Royal College of General Practitioners (1985a). *Assessing Quality of Care in General Practice*. Royal College of General Practitioners, London.

Royal College of General Practitioners (1985b). *What Sort of Doctor*? Report from General Practice, 23. Royal College of General Practitioners, London.

Royal College of Nursing (1990). *Dynamic standard setting system*. Royal College of Nursing, London.

Royal College of Physicians (1978). Medical services study report: Deaths Under 50. *British Medical Journal*, **286**, 1061–1062.

Rutherford, A.D. (1987). Blood usage and laminectomy. *Journal of the Royal College of Surgeons*, **32**, 72–73.

Rutstein, D.D. *et al.* (1976). Measuring the quality of medical care: a clinical method. *New England Journal of Medicine*, **294**, 582–588.

Saunders, C. and Caves, R. (1986). An empirical approach to the identification of communication skills with reference to speech therapy. *Journal of Further and Higher Education*, **10**, (2), 29–44.

Sbarbaro, J.A. (1990). The patient physician relationship: compliance revisited. *Annals of Allergy*, **64**, 325–331.

Schmele, J.A. (1985). A method for evaluating nursing practice in a community setting. *Quality Review Bulletin*, **11**, (4), 115–122.

Schmele, J.A. and Foss, S.J. (1989a). A process method for clinical practice evaluation in the home health setting. *Journal of Nursing Quality Assurance*, **3**, (3), 54–63.

Schmele, J.A. and Foss, S.J. (1989b). The quality management maturity grid. *Journal of Nursing Administration*, **19**, (9), 29–36.

Schön, D. (1991). *The reflective practitioner (2nd edn.)*. Avebury, Burgess Hill.

Secker-Walker, J. *et al.* (1989). Development of clinical audit. *British Journal of Hospital Medicine*, **42**, 169.

Selbmann, H.K. *et al.* (1982). Comparison of hospitals supporting quality assurance. *Methods of Information in Medicine*, **21**, 75–80.

Shackford, S.T. *et al.* (1987). Assuring quality in a trauma system – the medical audit committee: composition, costs and results. *Journal of Trauma*, **27**, (8), 866–875.

Shapiro, S. *et al.* (1958). Comparison of prematurity and perinatal mortality in a general population of a prepaid group practice medical care plan. *American Journal of Public Health*, 48, 170–187.

Shaw, C.D. (1990). *Medical Audit: a Hospital Handbook*. King's Fund Centre, London.

Shaw, M. (1932). A comparison of individuals and small groups in the rational solution of complex problems. *American Journal of Psychology*, **44**, 491–504.

Shewhart, W.A. (1931). *Economic Control of Quality of Manufactured Product*. Van Nostrand, New York.

Shortliffe, E.H. (1973). *MYCIN: Computer Based Medical Consultation*. Elsevier, New York.

Simon, A. and Bowyer, G. (1970). *Mirrors for Behaviour*. Research for Better Schools, Philadelphia.

Sisman, B. (1990). Quality assurance: a myth? *Quality Review Bulletin*, **16**, (8), 278.

Sketris, I. (1988). *Health service accreditation: an international overview*. King's Fund Centre, London.

Skillicorn, S.A. (1981a). A conversation with Dr Stanley A. Skillicorn, a leading proponent of integrated problem-oriented quality assurance. *Quality Review Bulletin*, **7**, (4), 20–23.

Skillicorn, S.A. (1981b). Improved quality controls in hospitals: a necessity. *Journal of Legal Medicine*, **2**, (4), 471–489.

Slack, W.P. (1985). Standards of care. *Nursing Times*, May, 28–32.

Slater, C.H. (1989). An analysis of ambulatory care quality assessment research. *Evaluation and the Health Professions*, **12** (4), 347–378.

Slater, D. (1975). *The Slater Nursing Competencies Rating Scale*. Wayne State University Press, Detroit.

Smeltzer, C.H. *et al.* (1983). Nursing quality assurance: a process, not a tool. *Journal of Nursing Administration*, **13**, (1), 5–9.

Smith, D.A. and Mukerjee, G. (1978). *Assuring Quality in Ambulatory Health Care*. Westview Press, Boulder, Colorado.

Society of Cardiac and Thoracic Surgeons of Great Britain and Ireland (1985). *Returns of the UK Cardiac Surgery Register*. SCTS, London.

Spath, P. (1989). Introduction. In *Innovations in Health Care Quality Measurement*. Spath, P. (ed.), American Hospital Publishing.

Spitzer, M. & Caper, P. (1989). Quality measurement through small-area analysis techniques. In *Innovations in Health Care Quality Measurement*. Spath, P. (ed.), American Hospital Publishing Inc., Chicago.

Spitzer, W.O. *et al.* (1981). Measuring the quality of life of cancer patients: a concise QL index for use by physicians. *Journal of Chronic Disease*, **34**, 585–599.

Stebbing, L. (1990). *Quality Management in the Service Industry*. Ellis Horwood, Chichester.

Stephenson, G. *et al.* (1984). Barium enema in the diagnosis of colonic carcinoma. *Australian Clinical Review*, June, 13–17.

Stewart, D.S. (1984). *The Stewart Evaluation of Nursing Scale*. Unpublished. Wayne State University, Detroit.

Stewart, M. J., Craig, D. (1987). Adaptation of the nursing audit to community health nursing. *Nursing Forum*, **23**, (4) 134–153.

Stoner, J. (1968). Risky and cautious shifts in group decisions: the influence of widely held values. *Journal of Experimental Social Psychology*, **4**, 442–459.

Strauss, J.H. and Ziegler, L.H. (1975). The Delphi technique and its uses in social science research. *Journal of Creative Behaviour*, **9**, (4), 253–259.

Tachakra, S.S. and Beckett, M.W. (1985). Why do casualty officers miss radiological abnormalities? *Journal of Royal College of Surgeons*, **30**, 311–313, Edinburgh.

Taylor, D.W. *et al.* (1958). Does group participation when using brainstorming facilitate or inhibit creative thinking? *Administrative Science Quarterly*, **3**, 23–47.

Taylor, F.W. (1919). *Shop Management*. Harper and Bros., New York.

Townsend, P.L. and Gebhardt, J.E. (1986). *Commit to Quality*. Wiley, New York.

Tuckman, B.W. (1965). Developmental sequence in small groups. *Psychological Bulletin*, **63**, 384–399.

Turoff, M. (1970). The design of a policy delphi. *Technological Forecasting and Social Change*, **2**, (2), 149–172.

United States Committee on Government Operations. (1989). *Quicker and Sicker: Substandard treatment of medicare patients, 7th report*. US Government Printing Office, Washington.

United States General Accounting Office (1990). *Quality assurance – a comprehensive national strategy for health care is needed*. Briefing report to the Chairman, United States Bipartisan Commission on Comprehensive Health Care, GAO/PEMD-90-14BR, GAO, Washington.

Van Cleave, E. (1989). Uses of risk-adjusted outcomes in quality assurance monitoring. In *Innovations in Health Care Quality Measurement*. Spath, P. (ed.), American Hospital Publishing, Chicago.

Van de Ven A.H. and Delbecq, A.L. (1972). The nominal group as a research instrument for exploratory health studies. *Journal of American Public Health Association*, March, 337–342.

Van de Ven A.H. and Delbecq, A.L. (1974). The effectiveness of nominal Delphi and interacting group decision making processes. *Academy of Management Journal*, **17**, (4), 605–621.

Van Maanen, H.M.T. (1979). Perspectives and problems on quality of nursing care. *Journal of Advanced Nursing*, **4**, 377–389.

Veatch, R. (1989). Contribution to symposium. In *The Quest for Quality Health Care: Whose Choice? Whose Responsibility?* Donabedian, A. (ed.), *Mount Sinai Journal of Medicine*, **56**, (5), 406–422.

Ventura, M.R. (1980). Correlation between the quality patient care scale and the Phaneuf audit. *International Journal of Nursing Studies*, **17**, 155–162.

Ventura, M.R. *et al.* (1982). Correlations of two quality of nursing care measures. *Research in Nursing and Health*, **5**, 37–43.

Wainwright, P. and Burnip, S. (1983a). Qualpacs at Burford. *Nursing Times*, **79**, (5), 36–8.

Wainwright, P. and Burnip, S. (1983b). Qualpacs – the second visit. *Nursing Times*, **79**, (33), 26–7.

Wandelt, M. and Ager, J. (1974). *Quality Patient Care Scale*. Wayne State University, Detroit.

Wandelt, M.A. and Stewart, D.S. (1975). *Slater Nursing Competencies Rating Scale*. Appleton Century Crofts, New York.

Ware, J.E. and Snyder, M.K. (1975). Dimensions of patient attitudes regarding doctors and medical services. *Medical Care*, **13**, 669–682.

Ware, J.E., *et al.* (1979). *Conceptualization and measurement of health for adults in the health insurance study: vol. 3, mental health*. Document R 1987/3 HEW, Rand Corporation, Santa Monica.

Webber, A. (1988). History and mission of quality assurance in the public sector. In *Perspectives on Quality in American Health Care*. Hughes, E. (ed.), McGraw-Hill, Washington.

Weed, L.L. (1968). Medical records that guide and teach (1 and 2). *New England Journal of Medicine*, **278**, 593–600 and 652–657.

Weiss, G. (1988). Patient satisfaction with primary health care. Evaluation of Sociodemographic and Predispositional Factors. *Medical Care*, **26**, 383–393.

Wells, K.B. and Brook, R.H. (1988). Historical trends in quality assurance in mental health. In *Handbook of Quality Assurance in Mental Health*. Stricker, G. and Rodriguez, A.R. (eds.), Plenum, New York.

Wennberg, J.E. (1987). Use of claims data systems to evaluate health care outcomes: mortality and reoperation following prostatectomy. *Journal of American Medical Association*, **257**, 933–936.

Wennberg, J.E. and Gittelsohn, A. (1973). Small area variations in health care delivery. *Science*, **182**, December, 1102–1108.

Wheeler, D. (1991). Introducing nursing quality. Paper delivered to Royal College of Nursing Society of Orthopaedic Nursing, 2nd International Conference, Warwick University.

Whelan, J. (1987). Using Monitor: observer bias. *Senior Nurse*, **7**, (6), 8–10.

Whittington, D. (1986). Chairmanship. In *A Handbook of Communication Skills*. Hargie, O. (ed.), Croom Helm, Beckenham.

Whittington, D. and Boore, J. (1988). Competence in nursing. In *Professional Competence and Quality Assurance in the Caring Professions*. Ellis, R. (ed.), Chapman and Hall, London.

Whittington, D. (1989). Performance indicators & quality assurance in the

NHS. Paper delivered to the European Group for Public Administration Study Group on Quality Assurance & Productivity, Chester.

Whittington, D. and Finlay, A. (1991). *Clinical Audit: a Literature Review with Special Reference to Physiotherapy, Occupational Therapy, Speech Therapy and Clinical Psychology.* Centre for Health and Social Research, University of Ulster, Occasional Paper No. 2. University of Ulster, Coleraine.

Wiles, A. (1987). *Quality of Patient Care Scale.* In *Nursing Quality Measurement.* Pearson, A. (ed.), Chichester, Wiley.

Wilkinson, R. (1990). *Quality Assurance in Managed Care Organisations.* Joint Commission for the Accreditation of Healthcare Organisations, Chicago.

Williams, A. (1985). Economics of coronary by-pass grafting. *British Medical Journal*, August, **291**, 326–329.

Williams, S.A. (1989). Total quality management. In *Innovations in Health Care Quality Measurement.* Spath, P. (ed.), American Hospital Publishing, Chicago.

Williamson, J.W. (1978). *Assessing and Improving Health Care Outcomes: the Health Accounting approach to quality assurance.* Ballinger, Cambridge, Mass.

Williamson, J.W. (1988). Future policy directions for quality assurance: lessons from the health accounting experience. *Inquiry*, **25**, 67–77.

Wilson, C.R.M. (1987). *Hospital-wide Quality Assurance: Models for Implementation and Development.* W.B. Saunders Company, Toronto.

Wine, J.A. and Baird, J.E.Jr. (1983). Improving nursing management and practice through quality circles. *Journal of Nursing Administration*, **13**, (5), 5–10.

Woods, P. (1990). Shopping for quality: the greater Cleveland health quality choice project. *Nursing Economics*, **8** (5), 319–321 and 332.

Woodward, C.D. (1972). *British Standards Institution: the Story of Standards.* British Standards Institution, Milton Keynes.

Woolhandler, S. and Himmelstein, D.V. (1988). Free care: a quantitative analysis of health and cost effects of a national health program for the United States. *International Journal of Health Services* **18**, (3), 393–399.

Wong, H. (1989). Quality measurement and customer service. In *Innovations in Health Care Quality Measurement.* Spath, P. (ed.) American Hospital Publishing, Chicago.

World Health Organisation (1958). *The First Ten Years of the World Health Organisation.* World Health Organisation, Geneva.

World Health Organisation (1985). *The Principles of Quality Assurance.* Report on working group meeting convened by Regional Office for Europe (Copenhagen) in Barcelona, 1983. European Reports and Studies, 94. World Health Organisation, Copenhagen.

Wragg, E. (1984). *Classroom Teaching Skills.* Croom Helm, London.

Wright, C. and Whittington, D. (1991). *Quality Assurance: a Workbook for Health Professionals.* Churchill Livingstone, Edinburgh.

Wright, S.M. and Riley, B. (1991). Quality assessment in support services: do practitioners concur with expert consensus? *Quality Review Bulletin*, **17**, (1), 10–14.

Wylie, M. (1989). *Quality Assurance Bulletin* No.14. Ulster Hospital Unit of Management, Eastern Health and Social Services Board, Belfast.

Youll, P. and Perring, C. (1991). Voice and choice: user participation in service development and evaluation. Paper presented to European Group for Public Administration Study Group on Quality and Productivity, The Hague.

Young, D. (1980). An aid to reducing unnecessary investigations. *British Medical Journal*, **281**, 1610–1611.

Yura, H. and Walsh, M. (1967). *The Nursing Process*. Catholic University of America Press.

Zaltman, G. and Duncan, R. (1977). *Strategies for Planned Change*. Wiley, New York.

Zastowny, T. *et al.* (1989). Patient satisfaction and the use of health services: explorations in causality. *Medical Care*, **27**, 705–721.

Zautra, A. and Goodhart, D. (1984). Quality of life indicators: a review of the literature. *Community Mental Health Review*, **4**, (1), 2–10.

Zimney, L., *et al.* (1980). Patient telephone interviews: a valuable technique for finding problems and assessing quality in ambulatory medical care. *Journal of Community Health*, **6**, (1), 35–42.

Glossary

Accreditation Process of subjecting individuals, products, services, facilities, or organisations to quality appraisal and recognising that standards have been met. Awarding those who meet standards a document which certifies their achievement. Possession of such awards can be made publicly known and may be associated with a licence to practice or provide products or services.

Ambulatory care North American term for care delivered in the community or in hospital outpatients departments. Does not normally include day surgery. Treatment given to UK ambulatory patients (outpatients) in hospitals is administered and resourced through the hospitals.

Audit Process of observing and recording events or scrutinising pre-existing records for subsequent comparison with standards. Standards may be for records, procedures or the events themselves. *Medical audit* is the common term for quality assurance procedures applied to the clinical activities of medical practitioners. *Clinical audit* is quality assurance applied to the clinical activities of any group of health care professionals. *Financial audit* is the scrutiny of financial records for comparison with accounting standards and conventions. In nursing audit is often taken to mean only scrutiny of pre-existing records for subsequent comparison with standards. Also see 'quality audit' below.

British Standard Standard set by the *British Standards Institution (BS1)*. Originally for physical dimensions of engineering components and products. Latterly for wide range of goods including consumer goods which commonly display *kitemark* which indicates that goods *conform* to relevant standard. Also award *BS 5750* which indicates that companies producing goods or delivering service operate quality systems which meet BSI standards. Analogous organisations include the *ISO* (International Organisation for Standardisation). The ISO equivalent of BS 5750 is *ISO 9000*.

Code of practice Broad indications of appropriate practice. Generally associated with level *below* which standards should not fall. Also *disciplinary code* produced by professional organisations which sets out sanctions for failure to conform to code of practice.

Company-wide quality control (CWQC) Japanese approach establishing quality control in all aspects of company activity including those only indirectly associated with production. Often involves *quality circles*.

Conformance Meeting standards; state of having met standards.

Consumer Recipient of product or service. In health care thought to have fewer connotations of subservience than analogous terms patient and client. Can be *external* (e.g. patient) or *internal* (e.g. referring professional). Also contrast 'customer' below.

Cost-benefit analysis Analysis of costs and benefits accruing from specified activities to establish the extent to which benefits outweigh costs (or vice versa). See 'health accounting' below.

Cost effectiveness Extent to which treatments, procedures or other activities are carried out for minimum cost while meeting appropriate standards (see 'cost-benefit analysis' above).

Criteria mapping System for selecting cases for review from hospital records. Screening personnel have maps or algorithms which outline sequence of decisions which should be taken and action which should be initiated during care of specified types of patient. Cases with more than a threshold number of wrong or absent decisions are selected for review.

Criterion Specification of expected or desirable quality of a product or service. Can be more or less specific than related term *standard*. Also *criteria lists* used in *occurrence screening* for selection of cases for subsequent review. Selection criteria in occurrence screening are usually instances of poor quality.

Customer Recipient of product or service who exchanges money for it. Can be *external* or *internal*. Contrast 'consumer' above.

Disease staging System for categorising patients and cases according to severity of illness.

Economy Minimum expenditure of resources.

Efficiency Producing maximum goods or delivering maximum services with minimum expenditure of resources.

Effectiveness The extent to which something achieves its aims. The extent to which goods are fit for their purpose or care is successful in improving patient health and well-being.

Equity Fairness. In health care the fair distribution of resources for care; ensuring fairness and lack of discrimination in access to care.

Feedback Provision of information on results of performance for use in modifying future performance.

Guideline Broad indication of appropriate practice or procedure. Less specific than *standards* or *criteria*. Often produced by professional organisations.

Health accounting System of cost benefit analysis in which quality is determined by balance of benefits of specified treatments or procedures over their costs. Involves *health currency* of psychosocial goods or utilities which are accounted alongside financial benefits.

Health care All services designed to improve health, well-being, and health related aspects of quality of life. Includes health education and promotion and in some delivery systems, personal social services. Irrespective of public or private sector funding and location.

Indicator Measurable entity taken to signify effectiveness of performance. Aspect of product or service selected for attention and possibly measurement during quality appraisal. *Performance Indicator* is related term which has currency in management analyses of health service delivery.

Inspection Process of scrutinising goods *after* production or at specified stages during production. Defective goods are scrapped or returned to the production line for modification. *Inspection engineering* is process of sampling goods for inspection to achieve cost effective inspection.

Joint Commission for the Accreditation of Hospitals (JCAH) Now known as the *Joint Commission for the Accreditation of Healthcare Organisations (JCAHO)*. US organisation which grants accreditation to hospitals and other health care facilities. Scrutinises many aspects of service including quality systems.

Kitemark Mark or logo which can be displayed by organisations which produce goods or deliver services which *conform* to standards specified by the British Standards Institution. Often displayed on products themselves.

Managed Health Care organisation North American organisation through which employers or other *third party purchasers* pay providers of care (individuals or organisations) to deliver packages of care to specified groups of individuals (e.g. employees) over specified periods of time. Packages include hospital and community care and health promotion programmes.

Manufacturing industry Industry in which the *production* of physical goods is the primary aim. Will have external and internal *service* functions (e.g. sales, finance).

Measurement The attribution of a value, expressed in numeric or literal form, to an entity which thus facilitates comparison with standards.

Medicaid US system of publicly funded health care provision for disadvantaged groups.

Medicare US system of publicly funded health care provision for the elderly.

Monitoring Observation and recording of events over time. Implies concurrent or subsequent comparison with standards.

Occurrence screening System for selecting cases from hospital records for subsequent review. Screening personnel have lists of *criteria* (often adverse occurrences) for selection.

Outcome The end result or effect of care as delivered. Its impact on patients. Related expression *outcome quality* is the quality of care outcomes.

Patient compliance Extent to which patients follow guidance and instruction provided during treatment or on discharge. Specifically, extent to which they take medicines or self-administer other prescribed treatment.

Patient satisfaction Extent to which patients express positive attitudes to specified treatments or to care in general. Often determined by administration of *patient satisfaction questionnaires*.

Peer review Technique for appraising quality of care in groups of individuals selected for their similar status and common interests. Can also involve determination of action for quality improvement.

Peer review organisation (PRO) US organisation which scrutinises care provided by individual practitioners and health care facilities who wish to treat publicly funded Medicare/Medicaid patients. *Professional Standards Review Organisation (PSRO)* was previous organisation with similar role.

Process Organised series of activities or events which comprise *production* of goods or *delivery* of service. In health care comprises all components of care delivery including diagnosis, treatment, aftercare and health promotion. Related expression health care *process quality* is the quality of service delivery.

Process control Systems and procedures for ensuring that production and service processes do not vary beyond predetermined limits. Most frequently employed in manufacturing industry and in areas of health care where material objects are processed or produced (e.g. medical laboratories).

Process control chart Chart displaying specified limits of variation with which actual variation (in products or services) can be compared. Excessive variation leads to modification of the processes of production or delivery.

Product Manufactured object.

Protocol Organised list of activities and events specified as necessary for execution of particular treatment so as to meet minimum or desirable standards of care. Often produced under aegis of professional organisation.

Provider Practitioner, group of practitioners or organisation which delivers care in UK National Health Service. Implies financial transaction with *sale* of care to *purchasers* in *internal market*. Terms current since 1990 Health Service Reform Act.

Purchaser Health Authority or other organisation in UK National Health Service which *buys* care from *providers*. Implies financial transaction in *internal market*. Terms current since 1990 Health Service Reform Act.

Quality The distinguishing attributes of an entity. The degree of excellence or fitness for purpose of a product or service.

Quality action Action taken to identify and implement procedures for *quality improvement* or *quality enhancement*. Usually follows *quality appraisal*. Second half of *quality cycle*.

Quality activity Any event or series of events designed to improve quality of goods or services.

Quality appraisal Series of activities including *standard setting, measurement,* and *interpretation* of measurements to determine extent to which products or services meet standards. Usually followed by *quality action*. First half of *quality cycle*. Related term is *quality assessment*.

Quality assurance Process whereby *customer, consumer* or *producer* is satisfied that appropriate *standards* will be met consistently for a product or service. Procedures and systems designed to maintain quality of goods or services. Emphasises attention to *processes* of production or delivery, *company wide* systems, and *prevention* of error and excessive variation from standards. Can be represented in *quality cycle* of *quality appraisal* and *quality action* which implies continuous *quality improvement* and *quality enhancement*.

Quality audit Scrutiny and review of *quality systems* to determine whether they meet standards. Alternatively, interchangeable term for *audit*.

Quality circle Group problem solving technique bearing on quality, and involving those close to production or service delivery.

Quality control Systems of *product inspection* and *process control* designed to minimise variation from standards.

Quality culture Organisation-wide ethos and value system which stresses importance of quality of products and services and effectiveness of quality assurance. Quality values are often formally articulated in statement of *mission* and reflected in *commitment* of time and material resources to quality activities.

Quality cycle Sequence of related activities comprising *quality appraisal* and *quality action* carried out iteratively in a process of continuous *quality improvement* and *quality enhancement*.

Quality documentation Records used in the process of *quality assurance*. Alternatively, records describing *quality systems and procedures*.

Quality enhancement Process of continuously setting and achieving higher standards. Implies quality is already high but can still be improved.

Quality improvement Process of continuously setting and achieving higher standards. Implies identification of areas of poor quality and solution of quality problems.

Quality initiative New quality activity or system.

Quality management Process of continuous planning, implementation and evaluation of quality assurance structures, systems, procedures and activities. Implies emphasis on human factors including motivation and development of *quality culture*.

Quality manual Compilation of *quality documentation*.

Quality mission Formal statement of quality ethos and values which underpin *quality culture*. Can include indication of *quality strategy*.

Quality plan Operationalisation of *quality strategy*. Includes specification of *quality structures*, *quality systems* and possibly *quality procedures*. Includes designation of quality responsibilities.

Quality procedure Sequence of events comprising *quality appraisal* and *quality action*. A particular way of executing the *quality cycle* at a relatively local level. See 'quality documentation' and 'quality plan' above.

Quality strategy Broad indication of organisation specific aims and intentions for quality assurance. Usually produced at a relatively high organisational level. Often includes indication of *quality structures* and designation of senior responsibilities.

Quality structures Organisation wide arrangement of designated individual duties, working groups, and committees for quality assurance. Reporting responsibilities and accountabilities for quality assurance. Designed to facilitate operation of *quality system*.

Quality system Arrangements for exchange of information and liaison between components of *quality structures*. The way structures are expected to *function*.

Reliability The extent to which a measuring instrument measures consistently. Contrast *validity* below.

Review Process of retrospective quality *appraisal*. Can also involve determination of *quality action*. Also reconsideration of appropriateness of any aspect of *quality assurance* or *quality management*.

Sentinel health events Instances of particularly poor quality or recurring quality problems which trigger subsequent investigation and *quality action*.

Service industry Industry in which the primary aim is the effective execution of a series of interactions between people, i.e. in which one group of people does things for, to or with other groups. Component activities can include production or processing of physical objects, e.g. food in catering services; documents in financial or legal services.

Standard Specification of expected or desirable measurable attributes of a product or service. Can be more or less specific than related term *criterion*.

Structure quality The quality of resources available for the delivery of health care and of the way their application is organised. Includes material and human resource quality.

Third party purchasers North American term for third parties such as insurance companies, employers or veterans' groups who purchase care on behalf of their subscribers, employees or members.

Total quality management An approach to quality management which stresses the establishment of *company-wide* structures, systems and procedures. Involves all personnel and encourages the development of a *quality culture*. Emphasises quality improvement as well as quality appraisal.

Validity The extent to which a measuring instrument measures what it claims to. Contrast *reliability* above.

Variation Deviation from a specified standard.

Zero defects An approach to quality control and quality management which stresses the prevention of error and variation. Related expression is the *right first time* approach.

Appendix

Techniques Included in the Compendium (Chapters 4 and 5)

This appendix has two main sections. The first contains an annotated list of all techniques included in the compendium in the order in which they appear in Chapters 4 and 5. It is subdivided in the same way as the chapters. Information on source, purpose, and main target setting and user group is given for each technique. Page numbers are indicated for each technique's location in the main text.

The second section contains an alphabetical listing of the techniques in the compendium with relevant page numbers.

Quality Specific Techniques

Professional Standards Systems

College of Occupational Therapists Standards
College of Occupational Therapists (1989).
Professional standards system.
Occupational Therapists. Hospital and community settings.
(p. 70)

Chartered Society of Physiotherapists Standards
Chartered Society of Physiotherapists (1990).
Professional standards system.
Physiotherapists. Hospital and community settings.
(p. 71)

College of Speech and Language Therapists Standards
College of Speech and Language Therapists (1991).
Professional standards system.
Speech and Language Therapists. Hospital and community settings.
(p. 73)

Regional Pharmaceutical Officers Committee Standards
Regional Pharmaceutical Officers Committee (1989)
Professional standards system.
Pharmacists. Hospital and community settings.
(p. 76)

Comprehensive Review Systems

Sunset Park/Lutheran Medical Centre Quality Assurance System for Practising Dentists
Demby et al. (1985).
Comprehensive review system including specified standards alongside procedures for appraisal and improvement.
Dentists. Community settings.
(p. 81)

Heatherwood Hospital Physiotherapy Department Quality Assurance System
East Berkshire Health Authority (1990).
Comprehensive review system including specified standards alongside procedures for appraisal and improvement.
Physiotherapists. Hospital settings.
(p. 83)

AMBUQUAL
Benson and Miller (1989).
Comprehensive review system including specified standards alongside procedures for appraisal and improvement.
Multi-professional. Ambulatory (community/outpatient) care.
(p. 85)

Davis Medical Centre Ambulatory Care Infection Control Quality Assurance Monitoring System
Bradford and Flynn (1988).
Comprehensive review system including specified standards alongside procedures for appraisal and improvement.
Multi-professional. Infection control in outpatient care.
(p. 87)

Dynamic Standard Setting System (DySSSy)
Royal College of Nursing (1990).
Comprehensive review system giving procedures for local standard setting, appraisal and improvement.
Nurses. Hospital and community settings.
(p. 89)

The American Occupational Therapy Association's Quality Assurance Monitoring System
Joe and Ostrow (1987).
Comprehensive review system giving procedures for local standard setting, appraisal and improvement.

Occupational therapists. Hospital settings.
(p. 92)

General Practice Group Peer Review
Hughes and Humphrey (1990), Irvine (1990a; b).
Comprehensive review system giving procedures for local review without preliminary standard setting.
General practitioners. Community settings.
(p. 95)

San Diego Medical Audit Committee (MAC)
Shackford et al. (1987).
Comprehensive review system giving procedures for local review without preliminary standard setting.
Multi-professional trauma care teams. Accident and Emergency Departments.
(p. 96)

Case Selection Techniques

Occurrence Screening
Rutstein et al. (1976); Hartmann et al. (1990).
Case selection technique identifying cases for in-depth review.
Multiprofessional. Hospital and community settings.
(p. 100)

Criteria Mapping
Greenfield et al. (1975; 1981), Demlo (1983), Law et al. (1989).
Case selection technique identifying cases for in depth review.
Multiprofessional. Hospital and community settings.
(p. 101)

Self-Adapting Focused Review System (SAFRS)
Ash et al. (1990)
Case selection technique identifying cases for in depth review.
Multiprofessional. Hospital and community settings.
(p. 103)

Local Problem Solving Techniques

Quality Circles
Hutchins (1990), Ingle (1982), Adair et al. (1982).
Local problem solving technique maximising staff participation.
Any group or setting in the health care system.
(p. 105)

Benson, Wilder and Gartner's Quality Improvement Plan (QIP)
Benson et al. (1986).
Local problem solving technique emphasising problem tracking.
Multi-professional. Community health centres.
(p. 107)

Issue Logs
Brown et al. (1984).
Local problem solving technique emphasising problem tracking.
Multiprofessional. Hospital settings.
(p. 108)

Process Measurement Techniques

The Phaneuf Audit
Phaneuf (1976).
Process measurement technique based on retrospective audit of records of care.
Nurses. Hospital and community settings.
(p. 111)

Barney's Nursing Care Plan System
Barney (1981).
Process measurement technique based on concurrent review of records of care.
Nurses. Hospital settings.
(p. 113)

The Craig Audit Instrument
Stewart and Craig (1987).
Process measurement technique based on retrospective audit of records of care.
Nurses. Community settings.
(p. 115)

The Ervin Quality Assessment Instrument (EQAM)
Ervin et al. (1989).
Process measurement technique based on retrospective audit of records of care.
Nurses. Community settings.
(p. 116)

Price and Greenwood's Treatment Plan System for Residential Child Care
Price and Greenwood (1988).
Process measurement technique based on concurrent audit of care plans.
Social workers and other residential child care staff. Residential care settings.
(p. 117)

The Slater Nursing Competencies Rating Scale
Slater (1975), Wandelt and Stewart (1975), Hough and Schmele (1987).
Process measurement technique based on direct observation of care. Focuses on individual nurse competence.
Nurses. Hospital and community settings.
(p. 119)

Qualpacs
Wandelt and Ager (1974).

Process measurement technique based on direct observation of care combined with review of relevant records of care.
Nurses. Hospital and community settings.
(p. 120)

The Rush Medicus Nursing Process Quality Monitoring Instrument
Jelinek et al. (1974), Hegyvary and Haussman (1975), Haussman et al. (1976), Haussman and Hegyvary (1977).
Process measurement technique based on direct observation of care combined with review of relevant records, and interviews with patients and nurses.
Nurses. Hospital settings. Special versions for medical, surgical, obstetrics, recovery room, accident and emergency, psychiatric, paediatric, and dialysis care.
(p. 122)

Monitor
Goldstone, et al. (1983).
Process measurement technique based on direct observation combined with review of relevant records and interviews with patients and nurses.
Nurses. Hospital and community settings. Special versions for medical and surgical, geriatric, district nursing, paediatric, neurological, nursing home, midwifery, health visiting, psychiatric, accident and emergency, and mental handicap settings.
(p. 123)

The National Association of Theatre Nurses Quality Assurance Tool
National Association of Theatre Nurses (1989).
Process measurement technique based on direct observation of care.
Nurses. Operating theatres.
(p. 127)

PA/Royal Orthopaedic Hospital Nursing Quality Measurement Scale
Flindall et al. (1987).
Process measurement technique based on direct observation of care combined with review of records and administration of questionnaires to patients or their representatives.
Nurses. Hospital settings.
(p. 128)

The Schmele Instrument to Measure the Process of Nursing Care (SIMP)
Schmele (1985).
Process measurement technique based on direct observation, review of records and patient satisfaction questionnaires.
Nurses. Community settings.
(p. 130)

Quality Control Techniques

Laffel and Blumenthal (1989), Dagher and Lloyd (1991), and other sources – see main text.

Statistical techniques designed to monitor conformance of products and processes to specified standards.

Any health care setting but chiefly applied in settings where material objects are processed or produced e.g. medical laboratories.

(p. 131)

Outcome Appraisal Techniques

General Health Indicators

Bergner (1985), Lohr and Ware (1987), McDowell and Newell (1987), Hunt et al. (1981), Bergner et al. (1981), Davies and Ware (1981), Dupuy (1978), Ware et al. (1979), Goldberg (1978), and other sources – see main text.

Scales measuring overall health and well-being.

Most scales are for use with general populations although some refer to particular conditions or diagnoses.

(p. 137)

Quality of Life Scales

McDowell and Newell (1987), Kaplan and Bush (1982), Williams (1985), and other sources – see main text.

Scales designed to measure quality of life. Also techniques designed to assess treatments and procedures for the extent to which they contribute to improved quality of life as well as extended lifespan.

All patients and settings.

(p. 139)

Disability Measures

McDowell and Newell (1987), Mahoney and Barthel (1965), and other sources – see main text.

Measures of disability in terms of restricted function. Includes scales measuring reduced ability to carry out activities of daily living.

All appropriate patients. All health care settings but particularly rehabilitation contexts and in care of older people.

(p. 143)

Pain Measures

McDowell and Newell (1987), Melzack (1980), and other sources – see main text.

Measures designed to assess the nature and intensity of the experience of pain.

All appropriate patients. All health care settings.

(p. 145)

Patient Satisfaction Measures

Several sources – see main text.

Scales assessing patient satisfaction with care. Some are standard instruments designed to assess a general construct of satisfaction. Others are designed to

provide feedback on specific services, identifying problems and potential improvements.
All patient groups. All health care settings.
(p. 146)

Severity of Illness Classifications
Horn and Buckle (1989), Gonnella and Louis (1988), and several other sources – see main text.
Systems for classifying groups of patients according to diagnosis and severity of illness. Used to moderate outcome measures.
All patient groups. All health care settings.
(p. 148)

Consumer Involvement Techniques
McIver (1991), Youll and Perring (1991), and several other sources – see main text.
Techniques for involving consumers in health care quality assurance which go beyond simple satisfaction measures.
All patient groups. All health care settings.
(p. 150)

Records Techniques
Weed (1968), and several other sources – see main text.
Techniques of health care recording which facilitate quality assurance procedures.
All patient groups. All health care settings.
(p. 153)

Generic Techniques

Consensus Development Techniques

Standard Committee Procedure
Several sources – see main text.
Consensus development through committees.
All health care groups. All health care settings.
(p. 159)

Brainstorming
Osborn (1957), and other sources – see main text.
Consensus development technique designed to maximise participation and creativity among members of face to face groups.
All health care groups. All health care settings.
(p. 159)

Nominal Group Technique
Delbecq and Van de Ven (1971), Van de Ven and Delbecq (1974).
Consensus development technique designed to maximise group participation and creativity in face to face groups.
All health care groups. All health care settings.
(p. 162)

Delphi
Helmer and Rescher (1959), Reid (1988), and several other sources – see main text.
Consensus development technique based on written information. Designed to avoid bias introduced by meeting in face to face groups.
All health care groups. All health care settings.
(p. 163)

Surveys
Several sources – see main text.
Techniques for gathering self-reports. Can be used to assess knowledge, understanding, attitudes, perceptions. Involves questionnaire design, data collection, sampling.
All health care groups (patients and staff). All health care settings.
(p. 166 (questionnaire design, p. 167; data collection, p. 170; sampling, p. 174)).

Psychometrics
Anastasi (1988), Cronbach (1985), McDowell and Newell (1987) and several other sources – see main text.
The scientific measurement of psychological variables. Several psychometric principles are relevant in quality measurement. The principles of validity and reliability are particularly important.
All health care groups. All health care settings.
(p. 176)

Interpersonal Skill Analysis
Ellis and Whittington (1981; 1988), Dickson et al. (1989) and several other sources – see main text.
Techniques for the observation and analysis of interpersonal interaction applicable in health care process appraisal.
All health care groups. All health care settings.
(p. 183)

Section 2: Alphabetical List of Techniques

AMBUQAL (p. 85)
The American Occupational Therapy Association's Quality Assurance Monitoring System (p. 92)
Barney's Nursing Care Plan System (p. 113)
Benson, Wilder and Gartner's Quality Improvement Plan (QIP) (p. 107)
Brainstorming (p. 159)
Chartered Society of Physiotherapists Standards (p. 71)
College of Occupational Therapists Standards (p. 70)
College of Speech and Language Therapists Standards (p. 73)
Consumer Involvement Techniques (p. 150)
The Craig Audit Instrument (p. 115)
Criteria Mapping (p. 101)
Davis Medical Centre Ambulatory Care Infection Control Quality Assurance Monitoring System (p. 87)

Delphi (p. 163)
Disability Measures (p. 143)
Dynamic Standard Setting System (DySSSy) (p. 89)
The Ervin Quality Assessment Instrument (EQAM) (p. 116)
General Health Indicators (p. 137)
General Practice Group Peer Review (p. 95)
Heatherwood Hospital Physiotherapy Department Quality Assurance
System (p. 83)
Interpersonal Skill Analysis (p. 183)
Issue Logs (p. 108)
Monitor (p. 123)
The National Association of Theatre Nurses Quality Assurance Tool (p. 127)
Nominal Group Technique (p. 162)
Occurrence Screening (p. 100)
Pain Measures (p. 145)
PA/Royal Orthopaedic Hospital Nursing Quality Measurement Scale
(p. 128)
Patient Satisfaction Measures (p. 146)
The Phaneuf Audit (p. 111)
Price and Greenwood's Treatment Plan System for Residential Child Care
(p. 117)
Psychometrics (p. 176)
Quality Circles (p. 105)
Quality Control Techniques (p. 131)
Quality of Life Scales (p. 139)
Qualpacs (p. 120)
Records Techniques (p. 153)
Regional Pharmaceutical Officers Committee Standards (p. 76)
The Rush Medicus Nursing Process Quality Monitoring Instrument (p. 122)
San Diego Medical Audit Committee (MAC) (p. 96)
The Schmele Instrument to Measure the Process of Nursing Care (SIMP)
(p. 130)
Self-adapting Focused Review System (SAFRS) (p. 103)
Severity of Illness Classifications (p. 148)
The Slater Nursing Competencies Rating Scale (p. 119)
Standard Committee Procedure (p. 159)
Sunset Park/Lutheran Medical Centre Quality Assurance System for Practis-
ing Dentists (p. 81)
Surveys (p. 166)

Author Index

Abbott, J.A. 151
Adair, M. 106
Ager, J. 111, 120, 121
Akao, Y. 45
Allison, S. 154
American Nurses' Association 23, 79, 90
American Physical Therapy Association 79
Anastasi, A. 177
Andersen, B.E. 111
Anderson, W.G. 20
Andrews, G. 80, 156
Appel, F.A. 15
Aquinas, T. 37
Argyle, M. 157, 185
Ash, A. 103, 104
Australian Council on Healthcare Standards 80
Axelsson, P. 81

Bair, J. 143
Baird, J.E. 106, 107
Balfe, B.E. 15
Barnett, D. 125, 126
Barney, M. 110, 113, 114
Barter, J.T. 30
Barthel, D.W. 144
Batalden, P.B. 212
Batchelor, G.J. 148
Beckett, M.W. 135
Belson, W. 170
Benedict, R. 43

Benson, D. 85, 105, 107, 210
Bergner, M. 137, 138
Bersoff, D.N. 28
Berwick, D.M. 22, 62, 109, 133, 151, 189
Beyers, M. 189
Black, N.A. 15, 17, 19
Blumberg, H.H. 157
Blumenthal, D. 132
Boore, J. 113
Bowyer, G. 187
Boyce, J. 17
Bradford, M. 87, 88
Bradham, D.D. 79
Bradshaw, S. 111, 112
Brenner, M. 167, 171
Brook, R.H. 14
Brooks, T. 14
Brown, D.E. 105, 108, 210
Buback, K. 106, 107
Buchanan, B.G. 103, 187
Buck, N. 12, 135
Buckland, A.E. 30
Buckle, J.M. 149
Bunn, D.W. 103
Burkholder, J.A. 79
Burnip, S. 121
Burton, R. 96
Bush, J.W. 140

Cairns, J. 32
Calnan, M. 148
Cameron-Jones, M. 188

Campbell, A. 141
Canadian Council on Hospital Accreditation 204
Cannell, C.F. 172
Caper, P. 15, 136
Carlzon, J. 54
Carnall, C.A. 195
Carr-Hill, R. 18, 29, 64, 106, 146, 166, 167, 168, 171, 172, 174, 199
Carter, N. 17
Cartwright, A. 167
Casanova, J.E. 13
Caves, R. 187, 188
Chambers, L.N. 102
Chandler, A.D. 37
Charlton, J.R.H. 135
Chartered Society of Physiotherapy 13, 71
Chassin, M.R. 159
Chittock, J. 125
Chong, J.P. 157
Clark, G. 53, 54
Cleary, P.D. 136, 146, 148
Clinton, J.F. 90
Coad, H. 189
Codman, E.A. 11
Cohen, C. 140
College of Occupational Therapists 13, 70
College of Speech and Language Therapists 13, 73
Collie, J.P. 98
Corkill, M.M. 135
Cotton, R.E. 135
Craddick, J. 100
Craig, D. 111, 114, 115, 116
Crombie, D.L. 95
Cronbach, L. 177
Crosby, P.B. 45–46

Dagher, D.O. 30, 132, 133, 161
Dalkey, N.C. 163
Dalley, G. 13, 18, 29, 64, 146, 147, 166, 199
Daugherty, J. 135
David, J. 123, 125
Davies, P. 137, 138, 157, 162
Davis, J. 157
Davis, K.D. 79
Dawson, J. 125

Day, P. 17
De Vaus, D.A. 167, 172
De Verdier, C.H. 41
De Vos, G. 43
Delbecq, A.L. 91, 162, 163, 165
Demby, N.A. 80, 81, 82
Deming, W.E. 33, 42, 48, 61, 198
Demlo, L.K. 102, 148
Di Primio, A. 53
Dickson, D.A. 184
Dillman, D.A. 172
Dillon, J.T. 167, 169, 170
Dixon, P. 167, 168, 174
Dodd, F.J. 164
Donabedian, A. 15, 20, 21, 22, 25, 32, 93, 103, 109, 134, 195, 196, 210
Donald, K.J. 98
Donegan, H.A. 164
Dornan, M. 29, 146, 148, 184
Douglass, P.S. 148
Drummond, M.F. 31
Duncan, A. 11, 30, 191, 192, 200, 202
Dunnette, M.D. 162
Dunt, D. 147
Dupuy, H.J. 138
Dutkewych, J. 106, 107

Eakin, P. 144, 145
Eason, J. 135
East Berkshire Health Authority 80, 83
Ekman, P. 185
Ellis, R. 22, 54, 109, 157, 183, 184, 185, 186, 194, 195
Enderby, P. 157
England, B. 29, 113, 135, 154
Eppel, A. 29
Ervin, N.E. 111, 116, 117, 164
Evason, E. 29, 146, 148

Farrell, P. 164, 166
Feigenbaum, A.V. 43, 44, 45
Fernow, L.C. 150
Ferrans, C.E. 141
Ferrell, B. 146
Fine, R.B. 30
Finlay, A. 29
Fisher, R. 157
Flanagan, J.C. 142
Flanders, N. 186, 187

Fleming, D.M. 95
Flindall, J. 111, 128
Flynn, N. 80, 87, 88
Foss, S.J. 130, 131, 189
Fowkes, F. 12
Frangley, P.A. 135
Freeborn, D.K. 29
Freedman, J. 142
Freeling, P. 96
Friedman, B.I. 132
Friesen, W. 185
Furnham, A. 184

Gafni, A. 142
Gallup, G. 168
Garson, B. 106, 107
Gartner, C. 107
Garvin, D. 43, 45, 46, 47, 58, 61
Gatere, G. 154
Gebhardt, J.E. 53
Gilbey, T. 37
Gilmore, H.L. 58
Gitlow, H. 42
Gitlow, S. 42
Gittelsohn, A. 15, 136
Glendinning, M. 80
Gold, R. 164
Goldberg, D. 138
Goldstone, L.A. 111, 123
Gonnella, J.S. 148, 149
Goodhart, D. 139
Goodinson, S. 142
Goran, M.J. 149
Gordon, T.J. 163
Gould, E.J. 113
Grant, M.M. 103
Greenblatt, M. 14
Greenfield, S. 27, 102, 103, 148
Greenwood, S.K. 111, 117, 118, 119
Gresham, G.E. 144
Grol, R. 96
Gruer, R. 135
Grujic, S.D. 189
Gummeson, E. 53, 54
Gunn, L. 63
Gunthorpe, R. 135
Gurel, L. 137

Hackman, J.R. 157
Haggard, A. 104, 106

Hall, J. 29, 146, 148, 184, 187
Halpern, S. 147
Halpin, J. 45–46
Hanks, G.E. 134
Hannan, E.L. 101
Harman, D. 197, 202, 218
Harris, C.M. 28, 96, 142
Harris-Wehling, J. 22, 23
Hartmann, M.R. 100
Harvey, G. 121, 125
Hastings, G.E. 164
Hatfield, A.B. 150, 151
Haussman, R.K. 112, 122, 123
Health Care Research Unit
    (Newcastle upon Tyne
    University) 13, 26
Hegyvary, S.L. 112, 122, 123
Helmer, O. 163
Hilton, I. 125
Himmelstein, D.V. 32, 136
Hinde, R. 185
HMSO
    1976 Alment Report 17
    1986 DHSS Report on
        Confidential Enquiries into
        Maternal Deaths in England
        and Wales, 1979–81 12, 135
    1982 *Efficiency and Effectiveness
        in the Civil Service: the
        Financial Management
        Initiative* 17
    1990 *Family Practitioner Service
        Indicators 1988/89* 95
    1983 *Griffiths Report* 17, 30
    1956 *Guillebaud Committee* 16
    1990 *Medical Audit* Working for
        Patients Working Paper
        No. 6 13, 96
    1975 *Merrison Report* 11, 17
    1966 *Salmon Report* 30
    1982 *Standards Quality and
        International Competitiveness*
        47
    1990 *The Quality of Medical Care*
        17, 96, 136
    1989 *Working for Patients* (White
        Paper) 17
Holmes, C.A. 139, 141, 142, 164
Hooker, R.S. 12, 135
Horn, S.D. 149

Hosking, D.M. 157
Hough, B.L. 119, 120
Hounshell, D.A. 38
Hughes, R.G. 95, 135
Hulka, B.S. 164
Hull, S.A. 96
Humphrey, C. 95
Hunt, S.M. 138
Hutchins, D. 61, 160, 162
Hyde, A. 189
Hypertension Detection and
  Follow-up Program (1979),
  *Journal of American Medical
  Association* 134

Ingle, S. 41
Institute of Medicine 133
Irvine, D.H. 13, 95, 96, 153
Ishikawa, K. 44, 45, 105, 160
Issac, D.N. 189

James, K. 197
Janis, I. 157
Jefferson, S. 147
Jelinek, R.C. 111, 122
Jessee, W.F. 30, 61, 189
Joe, B. 89, 92, 143
Johnson, O.G. 43, 137
Joint Commission on the
  Accreditation of Hospitals 14
Jones, J.L. 211
Juran, J.M. 43, 44, 48, 61, 198

Kagan, R.H. 184, 189
Kalton, G. 167
Kane, R.A. 137
Kane, R.L. 137
Kanter, R.M. 106, 192
Kaplan, R.M. 140
Kaplan, S. 103, 148
Keller, R.B. 15, 136
Kemp, N. 91, 112, 113, 121, 122, 123,
  126, 129, 135, 153, 154
Kendall, H. 89
Kessner, D.M. 26
Keyser, W. 30
Kind, E.A. 29, 151, 212, 213
King, T. 211
Kinloch, K. 154
Kinports, K. 28

Kitson, A. 13, 89, 135
Klein, R. 17, 25
Knapp, M.R.J. 22, 62, 109, 133, 142,
  151, 189
Koepke, J.A. 132
Kogure, M. 45
Kohl, S.G. 135
Koska, M.T. 189
Kramer, S. 134
Kroshus, M.G. 151
Kuntavanish, A.A. 113

Labi, M.L.C. 144
Laffel, G. 132
Lakhani, A. 135, 136
Lamki, L. 132–33
Lang, N.M. 90
Law, M. 102, 103
Lawton, M.P. 139
Lees, G.D. 195
Lesnik, M.J. 111
Levine, S. 141, 142
Lewin, K. 157
Ley, P. 29, 146, 184
Linde, J. 81
Linstone, H. 164
Lloyd, R.J. 30, 132, 133, 161
Locker, D. 147
Lohr, K.N. 22, 23, 135, 136, 137, 138,
  144
London, B.J. 28
Loughlin, K.G. 164
Louis, D.Z. 148, 149
Luft, J. 157
Luger, G. 103, 187
Lunn, J.N. 12, 135

McAninch, M. 14
McCulloch, D. 32
McDowell, I. 137, 138, 139, 141, 142,
  143, 144, 145, 146, 177, 180, 183
McGuire, P. 184
McIver, S. 29, 146, 150, 166, 171, 172
McNeil, B.J. 136, 146, 148
Mahoney, F.I. 144
Maier, N.R.F. 162
Mann, L. 157
Markowe, H.L.J. 135
Marquis, K.H. 172
Mason, E. 135

Maxwell, R.J. 12, 16, 18, 22
Mayers, M. 112, 113, 119, 135, 153,
  154
Medley, D. 185
Meenan, R.F. 137
Melzack, R. 146
Merrall, A. 113, 154
Millar, R. 167
Miller, J. 15, 29, 80, 85, 87
Mitzel, H. 185
Montemuro, M. 113
Moore, L.F. 164
Morgan, G. 190
Morgan, T. 54
Moritani, M. 43
Morley, I. 157
Morris, A. 103, 157
Mosberg, W.H. 98
Moscovici, S. 157
Moser, C.A. 167, 172
Mukerjee, G. 29
Mulkay, M. 141, 142
Mullen, K.D. 164
Mushin, W.W. 12, 135
Mushlin, A.I. 15

Najman, J.M. 141, 142
National Association of Theatre
  Nurses 111, 127
National Coalition for Recognition
  152
Neufeld, V. 157
Neugarten, B.L. 141
Neville, R.G. 135
Newcastle upon Tyne University
  (Health Care Research Unit) 13,
  26
Newell, C. 137, 138, 139, 141, 142,
  143, 144, 145, 146, 177, 180, 183
Normand, C. 29

Oakland, J.S. 41, 48, 52, 54, 131–32,
  197
Oakley, R.S. 79
O'Connor, J.P. 212
O'Leary, D.S. 15, 29, 30, 189
Openshaw, S. 112, 121, 123
Oppenheim, A.N. 167
Orem, D.E. 103
Osborn, A.F. 45, 91, 159

Osborne, C.E. 164
Ostrow, P. 89, 92
O'Sullivan, D.D. 189
Ovreteit, J. 199, 200, 202

Padilla, G.V. 103
Palmer, R.H. 211
Payne, S. 167, 170
Pearson, A. 121, 135
Pelletier, L.R. 166
Pendleton, D. 95, 184
Perring, C. 62, 150
Peters, T.J. 61, 192, 202
Peterson, O.L. 94
Phaneuf, M.C. 110, 111, 112, 113
Phillips, L.R. 121
Pitt, C. 14
Pollitt, C. 13, 17, 19, 148, 150, 195
Pope, C.R. 29
Poster, E.C. 166
Poulton, B. 91
Powers, M.J. 141
Prevost, J.A. 20
Price, F. 47, 53, 61
Price, S.B. 111, 117, 118, 119
Pridmore, B.R. 135
Pritchard, P. 123, 125
Prothro, L. 106
Pullan, B. 125

Rackham, N. 54
Radford, G.S. 39
Rajki, K.L. 122
Regional Pharmaceutical Officers'
  Committee 76–7
Reid, N. 103, 163, 164, 165
Rescher, N. 163
Restle, F. 157
Richardson, E. 91, 112, 113, 121,
  122, 123, 126, 129, 135, 153, 154
Richmond, V.P. 185
Rickert, R.R. 132
Riley, B. 164
Roberts, J.S. 20, 25, 26, 27, 30
Robinson, A.L. 47
Robinson, E.J. 187
Robinson, J. 142
Robson, M. 106
Rodriguez, A.R. 20, 32
Romm, F.J. 164

Roos, L.L. 136
Rosenburg, K. 12
Ross, P.J. 41, 59, 132
Rost, K. 187
Royal College of General
    Practitioners 12, 94, 95
Royal College of Nursing 13, 89
Royal College of Physicians 12, 135
Rutherford, A.D. 135
Rutstein, D.D. 100

Saunders, C. 187, 188
Sbarbaro, J.A. 146
Scherer, K. 164, 166
Schmele, J.A. 111, 119, 120, 129, 130,
    131, 189
Schon, D. 109
Secker-Walker, J. 153
Selbmann, H.K. 150
Shackford, S.T. 95, 96, 98
Shapiro, S. 135
Shaver, P. 142
Shaw, C.D. 13, 41, 96, 134, 148, 153
Shaw, M. 157
Shewhart, W.A. 40, 46, 59
Shortliffe, E.H. 103, 187
Simon, A. 187
Singleton, J. 142
Sisman, B. 29
Sketris, I. 14
Skillicorn, S.A. 104, 105
Slack, W.P. 125
Slater, C.H. 96, 134
Slater, D. 111, 119
Smeltzer, C.H. 123
Smith, D.A. 29, 150, 151
Snyder, M.K. 147
Society of Cardiac and Thoracic
    Surgeons of Great Britain and
    Ireland 12
Spath, P. 15
Spitzer, M. 15, 136
Spitzer, W.O. 139
Stebbing, L. 33, 54
Stein, B.A. 106
Stephenson, G. 134
Stewart, D.S. 111, 119, 120, 131
Stewart, M.J. 114, 115, 116
Stoner, J. 157
Storm-Clark, C. 147

Strauss, J.H. 164
Stubblefield, W. 103, 187

Tachakra, S.S. 135
Taylor, D.W. 162
Taylor, F. 38
Thompson, H.C. 164
Townsend, P.L. 53
Tuckman, B.W. 157
Turoff, M. 164

Ury, W. 157
US Committee on Government
    Operations 15
US General Accounting Office 15,
    29

Van Cleave, E. 148, 150
Van de Ven, A.H. 91, 162, 163, 165
Van der Gaag, A. 157, 162
Van Maanen, H.M.T. 112, 123
Veatch, R. 31
Ventura, M.R. 121

Wainwright, P. 121, 125, 126
Walsh, M. 113, 115, 116, 122, 124,
    129, 182
Wandelt, M. 111, 120, 121
Wandelt, M.A. 111, 119, 120, 121,
    131
Ware, J.E. 137, 138, 147
Waterman, R.H. Jr. 61, 192, 202
Webber, A. 15
Weed, L.L. 79, 113, 153
Weiss, G. 147
Wells, K.B. 14
Wennberg, J.E. 15, 136
Wheeler, D. 128, 129
Whelan, J. 126
Whitfield, M.J. 187
Whittington, D. 17, 25, 29, 54, 109,
    112, 113, 146, 148, 154, 157, 159,
    183, 184, 185, 186
Wilder, B. 107
Wiles, A. 120, 121
Wilkinson, R. 14, 15, 22
Williams, A. 32, 140, 141
Williams, S.A. 30, 62, 189, 209
Williamson, J.W. 26, 33, 93, 194
Wilson, C.R.M. 28, 204–6

Wine, J.A. 106, 107
Wong, H. 30, 33, 64
Woods, P. 152
Woodward, C.D. 37, 38, 39, 46
Woolhandler, S. 32, 136
World Health Organisation 6, 12, 23, 24, 30, 137, 189
Wragg, E. 186
Wright, C. 112, 113, 154
Wright, S.M. 164
Wylie, M. 129

Youll, P. 62, 150
Young, D. 12
Yura, H. 113, 115, 116, 122, 124, 129, 182

Zaltman, G. 191, 192, 200, 202
Zastowny, T. 147
Zautra, A. 139
Zavalloni, M. 157
Zeigler, L.H. 164
Zimney, L. 29, 151

Subject Index

ABNA 33
Accreditation
  agencies 28
  surveys 30
  systems 13–14, 18, 99
Action for improvement 29
ADL scales (activities of daily
    living) 143–44, 145
  Barthel Index 144, 145
Administrative waste 32
AIM (acuity index measure) 149
Alment Committee (1976) 17
AMA parameters 79
Ambulatory care
  AMBUQUAL system 85–87
  Davis Medical Centre QA
    monitoring system 85–87
AMBUQUAL 85–87
American Association of
    Occupational Therapy 143
American Civil War 38
American College of Surgeons
  Hospital Standardisation
    Programme 13
American Institute of Medicine 22–23
American Medical Association 11
  AMA parameters 79
American National Standards
    Institute 39
American Native Peoples Health
    Service (Shawnee, Oklahoma)
    129
American Nurses' Association 23

home health care standards 129,
    130
  QA model 34, 90
  standards 79
American Occupational Therapy
    Association
  QA monitoring system 92–93
American Physical Therapy
    Association
  standards 79
American Society of Hospital
    Pharmacists
  standards 79
"American" system of
    manufacturing 38
ANA standards 79
AOTA quality assurance
    monitoring system 92–93
APACHE II classification system
    149
Appraisal 25 See also Outcome
    appraisal techniques; Process
    measurement techniques
APTA standards 79
Assurance
  definition 3
Audit 5 See also Craig audit
    instrument; Phaneuf audit
Audit Commission 17
Australia
  professional standards systems 80
Avoidable morbidity data 136
Awareness programmes 48

Baptist Medical Centre
(Birmingham, Alabama) 122
Barney's nursing care plan system
113–14
Barthel Index 144, 145
Bell Telephone Company 40
Benson, Wilder and Gartner's
Quality improvement plan
107–8, 210
Bespoke tailoring 36–37
Bevan, Aneurin 16
Blue Cross 14
Brainstorming 45, 91, 159–62
British Standards Institution 37
"kitemark" scheme 46
origins of 38–39
quality assurance council 46
quality assurance standard *See* BS
5750
BS449 41
BS600 41
BS5750 5–6, 53, 54, 56, 60, 69, 197,
201, 218
requirements 51–52
BS90/97100 (ISO DIS 9004–2) 54–57

Canadian Council on Hospital
Accreditation 204
Canadian Society of Hospital
Pharmacists 77
CAP quality control scheme 132
Carnegie Foundation 11
Case selection techniques 68, 99–104
criteria mapping 101–3
occurrence screening 100–101, 103
SAFRS (self-adapting focus
review systems) 103–4
Category scaling 179–80
CDC system (clinical data capture)
148
Chartered Society of Physiotherapy
standards 13, 71–72, 85
Charters 6
Child care
Price and Greenwood's treatment
plan system 117–19
Civil Communications Section 42
Cleveland project 152
Codman, Ernest Avery 11, 12
College of American Pathologists

quality control scheme 132
College of Occupational Therapists
standards 13, 70–71
College of Speech and Language
Therapists
standards 13, 73–76
Commitment 35, 48
Communications 52, 184
Community care quality systems
210–11
Johns Hopkins Health system
211–12
Park Nicollet Medical Centre
system 211, 212–13
Community Health Councils 17
Company-wide quality control
(CWQC) 45, 105
Comprehensive review systems 68,
80–99
AMBUQUAL 85–87
AOTA quality assurance
monitoring system 92–93
Davis Medical Centre ambulatory
care system 85–87
DySSy (RCN) 89–91
explicit review 94, 96
General Practice Group Peer
Review 95–96
Heatherwood Hospital
Physiotherapy Department
system 83–85
implicit review 94, 96
MAC (San Diego Medical Audit
Committee system) 96–99
Sunset Park/Lutheran system
81–82
Concurrent case review 25
Consensus development techniques
155, 156–66
brainstorming 159–62
Delphi 163–66
group processes 157
nominal group technique 162–63
standard committee procedure
159
standard setting 156–57
Consumer involvement techniques
68, 150–52
Cleveland project 152
mutual self-help groups 151–52

patient satisfaction instruments
151
Consumer movement 7, 217
Consumer participation 29, 61, 62
Consumer protection 46
Consumer satisfaction 4, 5; *See further* Patient satisfaction
Consumer surveys 29
Consumers of health care 4–5
Cost-benefit analysis 31–32, 33, 194, 218
Cost-effectiveness 33
Costs and quality 30–34, 63–64, 194
  ABNA (achievable benefit not presently achieved) 33
  administrative waste 32
  expenditure and quality 32
  failure costs 33, 64
  industrial context 62–63
  measurement of costs 49
  QALY (quality adjusted life year) 32, 140, 141, 142
COT standards 70–71
Craft guilds 37
Craig audit instrument 114–16
Criteria mapping 27, 101–3, 148
CSI (computerised severity index) 149
CSLT standards 73–76
CSP standards 71–72
Customer satisfaction *See* Patient satisfaction
Customers of health care *See* Consumers
CWQC *See* Company-wide quality control
Cyclical model 34, 66

Data collection techniques
  interviews 170–72
  postal surveys 172, 173
  telephone surveys 172–73
  unassisted questionnaires 173
Davis Medical Centre ambulatory care system 85–87
Defensive medicine 32
Definitions 2–6, 20–24
  industrial context 57–59
Delphi 163–66, 167
Demand for health care 6–7, 31

Deming, W. Edwards 42
Deming cycle 42
Dentists
  Sunset Park/Lutheran Medical Centre review system 81–82
Design for quality 50
Development Team for the Mentally Handicapped 16
Disability measures *See* Disease and disability measures
Disease and disability measures 142–45 *See also* Severity of illness classifications
  ADL scales (activities of daily living) 143–44, 145
  Barthel Index 144, 145
  IADL measures (instrumental activities of daily living) 144
Disease staging 148, 149
Dissemination of knowledge 219
DRG classification system 148, 149
Dynamic standard setting system (DySSY) 89–91

East Berkshire Health Authority Heatherwood Hospital quality assurance system 83–85
Education and training 52, 218–19
  awareness programmes 48
Embryonic health care quality assurance 10
Engineering industry manufacturing standards 38–39
EQAM (Ervin quality assessment instrument) 116–17
Ervin quality assessment instrument (EQAM) 116–17
Excellence 34
Explicit review 27, 94, 96

Failure costs 33, 64
Feedback loop 5
Feigenbaum, Armand 43, 44, 45
Financial efficiency 194
Financial Management Initiative 17
Fitness for purpose 41
Flexner Report (1910) 11
Funding *See also* Costs and quality
  resource allocation 31
  US/UK comparisons 19

Future developments 215
　desirable developments 216–19
　future growth 215–16

Genba-To-QC 44
General health indicators 137–38
General practice group peer review
　95–96
Generic techniques 155–88
　consensus development 155,
　　156–66, 258–59
　interpersonal skill analysis 156,
　　183–88, 259
　psychometrics 155, 176–83, 259
　surveys 155, 166–76, 259
Greater Southeast Community
　Hospital (Washington DC) 108
Griffiths Report (1983) 17
Group consensus techniques *See*
　Consensus development
　techniques; Quality circles
Group Peer Review
　general practitioners 95–96
Guillebaud Committee 16

Hammurabi (King) 10
Harvard Care Plan 151
Health accounting 33–34, 194 *See*
　also Costs and quality
Health Advisory Service 16–17
Health care organisations *See also*
　Organisational change
　financial efficiency 194
　innovation for quality 193–96
Health care outcomes *See* Outcomes
Health care quality
　costs and *See* Costs and quality
　definitions 20–23
　dimensions 21–22
Health care quality assurance
　aim of 23–24
　current emphasis 6–8
　definition 23–24
　desirable developments 216–19
　embryonic stage 10
　emergent stage 10–14
　essential characteristics 34–35
　future growth 215–16
　historical development 2–18
　industrial experience, lessons

　from 62, 64–65
　management of *See* Quality
　　management
　mandatory 14–18
　National Health Service 16–18, 19
　techniques *See* Generic
　　techniques; Quality specific
　　techniques
　themes in literature 20–34
　United Kingdom 16–18, 18–20
　United States 14–15, 18, 19
　"Working for Patients" White
　　Paper (1989) 17
Health care quality circles 105–7
Health currency 194
Health economics 31, 63–64 *See also*
　Costs and quality
Health professionals *See*
　Professionals
Health Service Reform Bill 17
Heatherwood Hospital
　Physiotherapy Department
　quality assurance system 83–85,
　166
Hewlett-Packard 47
Hippocratic oath 10, 33
Historical development 2–18
Home health care
　SIMP (Schmele instrument)
　　129–31
Hospital accreditation *See*
　Accreditation
Hospital-wide quality systems 28
　Norton and Kosair system 209–10
　Ontario Hospitals Association
　　case study 204–9

IADL (instrumental activities of
　daily living) 144
Implicit review 27, 94, 96
Industrial quality assurance
　brainstorming 160
　costs and 62–64
　definitions of "quality" 57–58
　historical development 36–48
　inspection 38, 39, 41
　Japanese development 42–44, 53
　"kitemark" scheme 46
　measurement and methodology
　　59–60

organisational contexts 60–62
process control charts 41
quality circles 44–45
quality control 39–42
scope 59
service industries 53–57
themes in literature 57–64
total quality management (TQM)
    48–53
UK development 46–47
Industrial Revolution 37–38
Industrial standards 37–39
Innovation for quality
  health care organisations 192–96
  health professions 193–96
Institution of Civil Engineers 38
Interpersonal skill analysis 156,
    183–88
  category systems 185–86
  observation 185–86
  practitioner–patient
    communication 183–84
  sign systems 186
  teaching behaviour 185–86
Interpersonal skill training 184
Interprofessionalism 28–29, 217
Interval scales 178–79
Interviews 170–72
Ishikawa, Kaoru 44
ISO 9000 5, 51–52, 54, 60
ISO DIS 9004–2 54–57
Issue logs 108–9, 210

Japanese Federation of Economic
    Organisations 43
Japanese quality assurance 46–47,
    53
  development 42–45
  Z8101–1981 45
Japanese Union of Scientists and
    Engineers 43
JCAH 14, 92
JCAHO 14, 28, 30, 85, 87, 92, 218
  characteristics of health care
    quality 22
John of God, Saint 10
Johns Hopkins Health System
  quality review process 211–12
Joint Commission on the
    Accreditation of Healthcare

Organisations *See* JCAHO
Joint Commission on the
    Accreditation of Hospitals *See*
    JCAH
Juran, Joseph 43, 44

Kendall's Index of Concordance 180
King's Fund 12
"Kitemark" scheme 6, 46

Life Satisfaction Index 141
Local problem solving techniques
    68, 104–9
  issue logging 108–9
  QIP (Quality improvement plan)
    107–8
  quality circles 105–7
Lothian audit 135
Lutheran Medical Centre
  comprehensive review system
    81–82

MAC (San Diego Medical Audit
    Committee system) 96–99
McCormick harvester company 38
McGill pain questionnaire (MPQ)
    146
Malpractice suits 7, 15, 17
Managed care organisations 15
Management of quality *See* Quality
    management
Mandatory health care quality
    assurance 14–18
Marks and Spencer 63
Measurement 25–27 *See also* Process
    measurement techniques;
    Psychometrics
  desirable developments 217
  industrial context 59–60
  tracer methodology 26
  treatment outcomes, of 25
Medicaid 14
Medical audit 13, 94–95, 134–35, 195
  General Practice Group Peer
    Review 95–96
  San Diego Medical Audit
    Committee (MAC) 96–99
Medical profession 195
  quality assurance and 195–96
  specialisation 196

Medical record systems 152–54 *See also* Records techniques
Medicare 14, 19, 22
 DRG classification system 148
Medicus Systems Corporation of Chicago 121
MEDISGROUPS classification system 149
Merrison Committee (1975) 17
Methodist Hospital of Indiana AMBUQUAL 85–87
Mission statements 199
Monitor 123–27
Mortality data 135–36
MPQ (McGill pain questionnaire) 146

NACOR (National Coalition for Recognition) 151–52
National Aeronautics and Space Administration 162
National Association of Theatre Nurses
 QA tool 127–28
National Coalition for Recognition (NACOR) 151–52
National External Quality Assessment Scheme (NEQAS) 16, 41, 132
National Health Service 16
 medical audit in community care 96
 quality assurance in 16–18, 19
 reforms 33, 69, 96
National Highway Traffic Safety Commission (USA) 46
NATN quality assurance tool 127–28
NEQAS *See* National External Quality Assessment Scheme
New Zealand
 professional standards systems 80
NGT (Nominal group technique) 91, 162–63, 165
NHS *See* National Health Service
Nightingale, Florence 11
 Notes on Nursing (1859) 11
Nippon Telephone and Telegraph Company 44

Nominal group technique (NGT) 91, 162–63, 165
North West Regional Health Authority 123
Norton and Kosair Children's Hospital (Louisville, Kentucky)
 hospital-wide quality system 209–10
NQMS 128–29
Nursing 13, 28
 Barney's nursing care plan system 113–14
 Craig audit instrument 114–16
 dynamic standard setting system (DySSy) 89–91
 EQAM (Ervin quality assessment instrument) 116–17
 Monitor measurement instrument 123–27
 NATN quality assurance tool 127–28
 NQMS (PA/RNOH scale) 128–29
 outcome appraisal 135
 Phaneuf audit 111–13
 QA initiatives 13
 QUALPACS scale 120–21
 Rush Medicus monitoring instrument 121–23, 126
 SIMP (Schmele instrument) 129–31
 Slater nursing competencies rating scale 119–20

Occupational therapy 13
 AOTA quality assurance monitoring system 92–93
 COT standards 70–71
Occurrence screening 100–101, 103
Office of Population Censuses and Statistics 12, 136
Ontario Hospitals Association
 hospital-wide quality systems 204–9
Ordinal scales 178, 179
Organisation for quality 49
Organisational change 29–30, 189, 190–93
 Peters and Waterman's model 192–93
 preparation for quality 202–3

Zaltman and Duncan's model 191–92
Organisational culture 47–48, 53, 61
Organisational development 47
Outcome appraisal techniques 68, 133–50
  avoidable morbidity data 136
  disease and disability measures 142–45
  general health indicators 137–38
  medical audit procedures 134–35
  mortality data 135–36
  nursing, in 135
  pain measures 145–46
  patient death 135–36
  patient satisfaction measures 146–48
  process measures and 134
  quality of life measures 139–42
  regional comparisons 136
  severity of illness classifications 148–50
Outcomes of care 21, 25, 133 *See also* Outcome appraisal techniques
  studies 12
Oversaturation 200–201
Oxfordshire Health Authority 121

PA/RNOH scale (NQMS) 128–29
Pain measures 145–46
  MPQ (McGill pain questionnaire) 146
Park Nicollet Medical Centre QA system 211, 212–13
Participation in quality assurance 27–29
Patient death 135–36
Patient records 152–54; *See also* Records techniques
Patient satisfaction 29, 136
  measures 146–48, 151
  surveys 136, 166
Patient's charter 6
Pearson, E.S. 41
Peer review 95
Peer review groups
  General Practice Group Peer Review 95–96
Peer Review Organisation programme 15

Performance indicators 17
Phaneuf Audit 111–13
Pharmacists
  RPOC standards 76–79
Physiotherapy 13
  CSP standards 71–72
  Heatherwood Hospital QA system 83–85
Planning for quality 49–50, 199–201
PMCs (patient management categories) 149
Policy development 48
Policy statements 199
POMR (Problem oriented medical record) 153–54
Postal surveys 172, 173
Practitioner-patient communication 183–84
Prevention costs 31, 64
Preventive medicine 31
Price and Greenwood's treatment plan system 117–19
Prioritisation 33, 199–201
Problem solving 52 *See also* Brainstorming; Local problem solving techniques
Process 21
Process control charts 41
Process measurement techniques 68, 109–31
  Barney's nursing care plan system 113–14
  Craig audit instrument 114–16
  EQAM (Ervin quality assessment instrument) 116–17
  Monitor 123–27
  NATN quality assurance tool 127–28
  NQMS (PA/RNOH nursing quality measurement scale) 128–29
  outcome measures 134
  Phaneuf Audit 111–13
  Price and Greenwood's system 117–19
  QUALPACS scale 120–21
  Rush Medicus instrument 121–23, 126
  SIMP (Schmele instrument) 129–31

Slater nursing competencies
rating scale 119–20
Process standards 110, 216–17
Professional education 12
Professional groups 28–29
Professional Standards Review
Organisation 14–15
Professional standards systems 13,
68, 69–80
Australia and New Zealand 80
Chartered Society of
Physiotherapy 71–72, 85
College of Occupational
Therapists 70–71
College of Speech and Language
Therapists 73–76
Regional Pharmaceutical Officers
Committee 76–79
United States 79
Professionals
interprofessionalism 28–29, 217
management for change 194–96
quality assurance and 7–8
Professions *See also* Medical
profession
participation in QA 28–29
PSRO *See* Professional Standards
Review Organisation
Psychometrics 155, 176–83
basic characteristics of scaling
178–79
category scaling 179–80
definition 176
health care application 177
scale reliability 180–81
scale validity 181–83
standards of measurement 177
Public accountability 24, 33

QALY (quality adjusted life year)
32, 140, 141, 142
QIP (Quality improvement plan)
107–8, 210
Quality *See also* Health care
quality
costs and *See* Costs and quality
customer satisfaction 4, 5
definitions 2–3, 20–23, 57–58
Quality adjusted life year (QALY)
32, 140, 141, 142

Quality appraisal 25 *See also*
Outcome appraisal techniques;
Process measurement
techniques
Quality assurance
definition 23
health care *See* Health care quality
assurance
industrial standard *See* BS5750
meaning of 3
Quality audit 5
Quality circles 61
development of 44–45
health care applications 105–7
Quality control 131
CAP scheme 132
company-wide 45
control chart 132
health applications 131, 132
industry, in 39–42
meaning of 3–4
NEQAS 132
statistical techniques 41, 131–32
techniques 131–33
Quality Control for Foremen
(Japanese magazine) 44
Quality costs *See* Costs and quality
Quality council 61
Quality culture 53, 191, 197
Quality cycle 34, 66
Quality documentation and control
50–52
Quality improvement plan (QIP)
107–8
Quality inspection 38, 39, 41
Quality management 5, 189–90
case studies 204–13
community care systems (case
studies) 210–13
desirable developments 218
health care framework 196–98
Hospital systems (case studies)
204–10
innovation for quality 192–96
mission and commitment 198–99
organisational change 189, 190–93
preparation for quality 202–3
prioritisation 199–201
quality procedures 203
quality strategy 199–201

quality systems and structures
201–2
review quality system and
strategy 203–4
Quality of life measures 139–42
Life Satisfaction Index 141
QALY technique 140, 141, 142
QWB scale 140–41, 142
Quality oversaturation 200–201
Quality plan 49–50, 199–201
Quality procedures 203
Quality revolution 47
Quality specific techniques
case selection techniques 68,
99–104, 254
comprehensive review systems
68, 80–99, 253
consumer involvement 68,
150–52, 258
local problem solving techniques
68, 104–9, 254
outcome appraisal 68, 133–50, 257
process measurement 68, 109–31,
255–56
professional standards systems
68, 69–80, 252–53
quality control techniques 131–33,
257
records techniques 68, 152–54, 258
Quality strategy 199–201
Quality system 5, 201
QUALPACS scale 120–21
QUAN network 90, 91
Questionnaire design 167–70
piloting 170
QWB scale (quality of well-being)
140–41, 142

Rand Corporation 163
Random sampling 175
Ratio scales 179
Records techniques 68, 152–54, 196
POMR (Problem oriented medical
record) 153–54
Reflective practitioners 109
Regional Pharmaceutical Officers
Committee
standards 76–79
Report of the Royal Commission on
the Health Service (1979) 17

Report of the Standing Medical
Advisory Committee (1990)
17–18
Residential child care
Price and Greenwood's treatment
plan system 117–19
Resource allocation 31
Retrospective case review 25, 99,
104
Review *See also* Comprehensive
review systems
case selection *See* Case selection
techniques
concurrent 25
desirable developments 218
explicit and implicit systems 27
retrospective 25, 99, 104
Royal Australian and New Zealand
College of Psychiatrists 156
Royal College of General
Practitioners
quality initiative 12, 95
"What Sort of Doctor?" initiative
94
Royal College of Nursing
dynamic standard setting system
(DySSy) 89–91
Standards of Care project 13
Royal College of Physicians
Charter (1518) 10
Royal Colleges 11
RPOC standards 76–79
Rush Medicus instrument 121–23,
126
Rush Presbyterian–St. Luke's
Medical Centre (Chicago)
121–22

SAFRS (self-adapting focus review
systems) 103–4
St Joseph Hospital (Denver,
Colorado) 113
Sampling 99, 174–76
San Diego Medical Audit
Committee (MAC) 96–99
Scaling
basic characteristics 178–79
category scaling 179–80
interval scales 178–79
ordinal scales 178

ratio scales 179
scale reliability 180–81
scale validity 181–83
Selection techniques *See* Case
    selection techniques
Self-adapting focus review systems
    (SAFRS) 103–4
Service industry quality assurance
    53–57
  BS 90/97100 (ISO DIS 9004–2)
    54–57
  communication with customers 56
Severity of illness classifications
    148–50
  AIM (acuity index measure) 149
  APACHE II 149
  CDC system (clinical data
    capture) 148
  CSI (computerised severity index)
    149
  disease staging 148, 149
  DRG system (diagnosis related
    groups) 148, 149
  MEDISGROUPS 149
  PMCs (patient management
    categories) 149
Shewhart, W.A. 40, 42
SIMP (Schmele instrument) 129–31,
    166
Singer sewing machine company 38
Slater scale 119–20
Small area studies 136
Social skill training 54, 184
Specificity 34
Speech and language therapy
  CSLT standards 73–76
Standard Committee procedures
    159
Standard setting 69, 156–57
  committee procedures 159
  RCN dynamic standard setting
    system (DySSy) 89–91
Standards 1–2, 3, 6, 34, 216–17 *See
    also* BS5750; Professional
    standards systems
Standing Medical Advisory
    Committee 136
Statistical control 40, 41, 50
Statistical techniques 131
Strategic planning 199–201

Stratified sampling 175
Structure 21
Sunset Park/Lutheran Medical
    Centre review system 81–82,
    166
Survey techniques 155, 166–76
  data collection 170–73
  interviews 170–72
  postal surveys 172, 173
  questionnaire design 167–70
  sampling 174–76
  telephone surveys 172–73
  unassisted questionnaires 173
  uses of surveys 166

Taylor, Frederick W. 38
Teamwork and involvement 52
Techniques *See* Generic techniques;
    Quality specific techniques
Telephone surveys 172–73
Test validity 181–83
Total quality management (TQM)
    5, 48, 197, 201
  awareness programmes 48
  commitment and policy
    development 48–49
  communications 52
  definition 48
  design for quality 50
  education and training 48, 52
  features of 48–57
  health care 62
  measurement of quality costs 49
  organisation for quality 49
  planning for quality 49–50
  quality systems documentation
    and control 50–52
  statistical process control 50
  teamwork, involvement and
    problem solving 52–53
Trauma care
  MAC (San Diego Medical Audit
    Committee system) 96–99
Treatment outcomes
  measurement *See* Outcome
    appraisal techniques

UHDDS (uniform hospital
    discharge data) 149
United Kingdom

industrial quality assurance 46–47
United States
  criteria mapping 101
  health care QA 14–15, 18, 19
  hospital-wide QA and
    accreditation system 99
  mandatory health care QA 14–15
  occurrence screening 100, 101
  professional standards systems 79
United States Ordnance
  Department 38
University of California Medical
  Centre
  Davis Medical Centre ambulatory
    care QA system 85–87
US Bipartisan Commission on Com-
  prehensive Health Care 15, 29
US Institute of Medicine 133
US National League for Nursing 106
Utilisation review 14

Utility analysis 31–32

Wayne State University (Detroit)
  119
West Berkshire Health Authority 89
White Paper on Standards, Quality
  and International
  Competitiveness (1982) 47
Whitworth, Sir Joseph 38
"Working for Patients" White
  Paper (1989) 17
World Health Organisation 6
  aim of quality assurance 23–24
  aims of care 137
  European working group 12
  organisational change 189
  QA working group 23–24

Z8101–1981 (Japanese Industrial
  Standard) 45